LIFE HISTORIES
FROM THE REVOLUTION

LIFE HISTORIES
FROM THE REVOLUTION

Three militants from the
KENYA LAND AND FREEDOM ARMY
Karigo Muchai, Ngugi Kabiro
& Mohamed Mathu
tell their stories

Taped and edited by Donald Barnett

Illustrated by Selma Waldman

Daraja Press

Published by Daraja Press
https://darajapress.com

In association with

Zand Graphics Ltd, Kenya

The essays contained here were first published by
the Liberation Support Movement Information Centre (LSM)
to whom we acknowledge our thanks for permission to reproduce them.

Cover design: Kate McDonnell
Illustrations: Selma Waldman

Library and Archives Canada Cataloguing in Publication

Title: Life histories from the revolution : three militants from the Kenya land and
    Freedom Army / Karigo Muchai, Ngugi Kabiro, & Mohamed Mathu tell their
    stories ; taped and edited by Donald Barnett ; illustrated by Selma Waldman.
Names: Barnett, Don, 1930-1975, editor. | Container of (work): Muchai, Karigo,
    1914- Hardcore. | Container of (work): Kabiro, Ngugi, 1929- Man in the middle.
    | Container of (work): Mathu, Mohamed. Urban guerrilla.
Description: All three works were published separately in the 1970s by LSM
    Information Center.
Identifiers: Canadiana 2021032354X | ISBN 9781990263132 (softcover)
Subjects: LCSH: Muchai, Karigo, 1914- | LCSH: Kabiro, Ngugi, 1929- | LCSH: Mathu,
    Mohamed. | LCSH: Mau Mau. | LCSH: Kenya—History—Mau Mau Emergency,
    1952-1960. | LCGFT: Autobiographies.
Classification: LCC DT433.576.A2 L54 2022 | DDC 322.4/20922—dc23

To all Kenyans who fought for freedom
and to all those who are engaged in that struggle today.

The Hardcore: The Story of Karigo Muchai

Man in the Middle: The Story of Ngugi Kabiro

The Urban Guerrilla: The Story of Mohamed Mathu

Introduction to
Life Histories from the Revolution

History is as much about the future as it is about the past. Without an appreciation of history, it is not possible to conceptualize what the future could be, informed by the past, but not imprisoned by it. To contribute to reflections about what has been, is now and what could be tomorrow, Daraja Press wishes to make available books such as this one.

In 1960, Don Barnett went to Kenya with his family. There he conducted a number of interviews with militants of the Kenya Land and Freedom Army (the so-called Mau Mau), including an extensive interview with Karari Njama that was subsequently published in 1966 by Monthly Review as *Mau Mau From Within: An Analysis of Kenya's Peasant Revolt* and republished in 2021 by Daraja Press as *Mau Mau: The Story of the Kenya Land and Freedom Army from Within*. In 1968, Don founded the Liberation Support Movement Information Centre (LSM), aimed at enabling freedom fighters to speak about their experiences. The LSM subsequently published a series of pamphlets entitled *Life Histories from the Revolution* based on recordings made by Don that include interviews with cadres from MPLA in Angola, SWAPO in Namibia, and ANC from South Africa.

LSM published interviews that Don had conducted in Kenya with three militants from the Kenya Land and Freedom Army: Karigo Muchai, Ngugi Kabiro and Mohamed Mathu (the latter had in fact introduced Don to Karari Njama). Members of LSM maintained an archive of many of these publications and recordings. Daraja Press was fortunate to have made contact with them (thanks to Ole Gjerstad) and was provided with copies of the the pamphlets from the Kenyan militants.

Daraja Press has brought together here the complete text (and illustrations) of the stories of the three militants from the Kenya Land and Freedom Army as means of enabling a new generation of activists in Kenya – and beyond – to get a sense of the struggles, sacrifices and achievements of those who contributed to the struggle for national freedom and for human emancipation against the brutality of British colonial rule. These are moving stories, devoid of romance and modest in recounting their heroism.

Just as *Mau Mau: The Story of the Kenya Land and Freedom Army from Within* enables a young generation of Kenyans to understand the heroic struggles for freedom, so this collection will, as Kamoji Wachiira put it in his introduction to that book, "serve a new generation of militants to gain not only a deeper understanding of Kenya's revolutionary history but also to reflect on what lessons may be drawn for our continuing struggle to achieve true independence and freedom."

Firoze Manji
Publisher, Daraja Press
January 2022

FOREWORD

The vast majority of peasants and workers in the super-exploited hinterland of the imperialist system are illiterate. It is part of their oppression. They comprise almost half of the world's population, some 75% of the population in the "free world", and the emiserated broad base from which all contemporary anti-imperialist revolutions draw their essential moral and material strength. These are the masses who, under the leadership of revolutionary vanguards, are making modern history. Yet, due largely to the chains of their enforced illiteracy, these makers of history rarely have the opportunity to document their own experiences within it. Their "backwardness" condemns them to literary silence as well as to poverty, disease and a short life.

One of our objectives in launching this series of Life Histories from the Revolution is to provide a medium through which individual members of these classes-in-motion within the revolution can speak. We also believe it important that they *be heard* by those of us who comprise imperialism's privileged and literate metropolitan minority. Their recounted lives throw our own into sharp relief, while at the same time they offer us fresh perspectives on the processes of repression and revolution from a unique vantage point: *from below*. Their life stories provide us with a window into the qualitative – as distinct from the merely statistical and quantitative – aspects of class conflict, thus enabling us to better understand and weigh the various factors at work in transforming oppressed masses into revolutionary classes. Again, their remembered life experiences can provide us with significant insights into the dialectical relationships between material and subjective conditions which shape the revolutionary situation, embrace the revolutionary transformation of individuals and classes alike, and move humanity forward toward a new international social formation.

Not all of the individuals whose life histories are included in this series are illiterate peasants or workers. Some are educated defectors from petty bourgeois classes who have joined the revolution and identified their interests with those of the oppressed masses in a very concrete way. They constitute a very important part of the revolutionary vanguard – i.e., the middle cadres who articulate the relationship between leadership and base, who carry forward the military and civilian programs in day-to-day contact with the armed militants and popular masses. The selfless dedication, integrity, comportment and skill of the middle cadres is an essential ingredient within any successful revolutionary process.

The life histories in this series have been recorded and prepared as historical documents from the revolutionary struggles of our time. The techniques and methods employed at each stage of the process, from initial contact to final editing, have therefore been chosen or fashioned with the purpose of guaranteeing the authenticity and integrity of the life history concerned. These stories, then, to the best of our ability to make them so, constitute a body of data and testimony as revealed by a few of those history-makers normally condemned to silence while others speak on their behalf.

Don Barnett
January 3, 1973
Vancouver, Canada

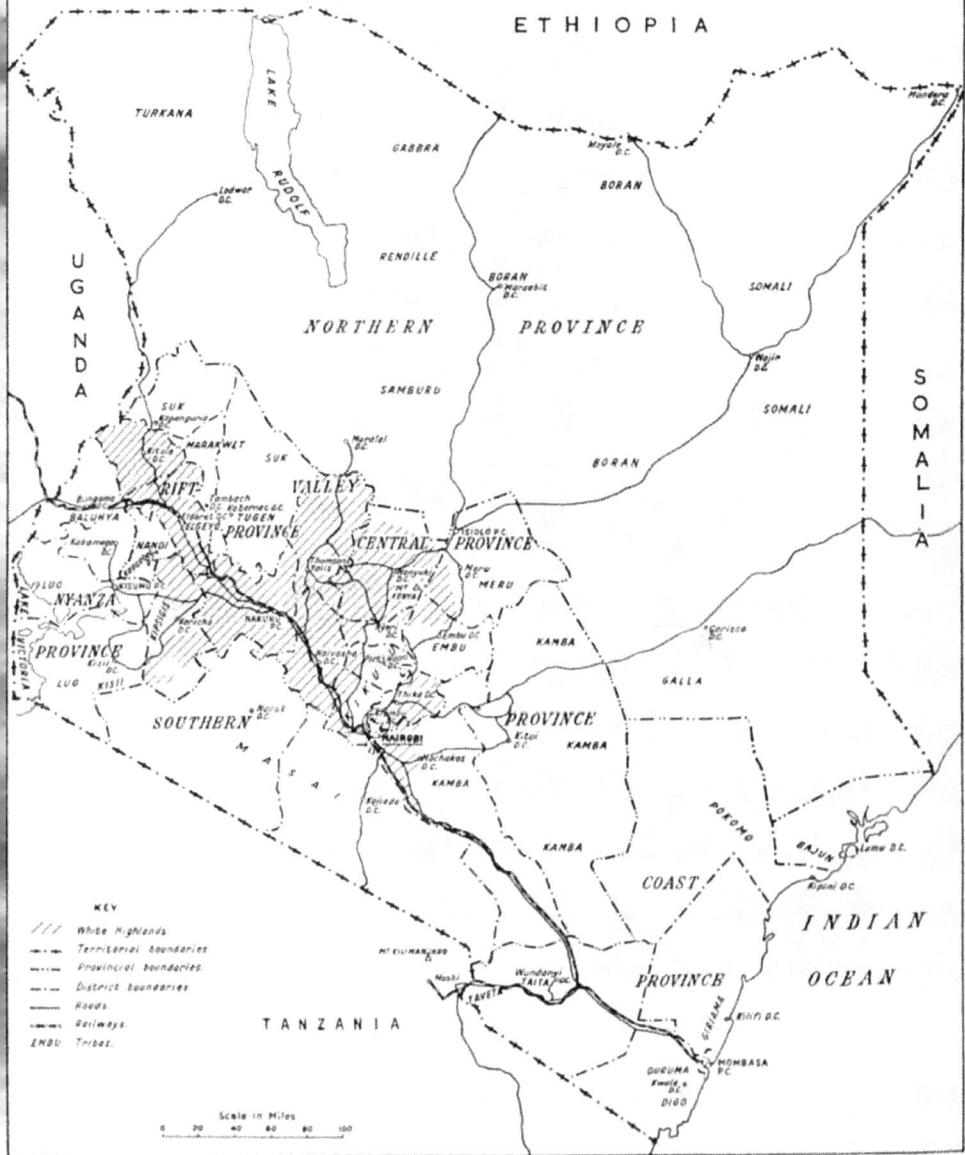

KENYA

ETHIOPIA

UGANDA

TURKANA

LAKE RUDOLF

GABBRA

Lodwar D.C.

Moyale D.C.

BORAN

RENDILLE

BORAN
Marsabit D.C.

SOMALI

NORTHERN PROVINCE

SAMBURU

Wajir D.C.

SOMALI

SUK
Kapenguria D.C.

MARAKWET

SUK

Maralal

BORAN

SOMALIA

Bungoma D.C.
BALUHYA
Eldoret D.C. TUGEN
Tambach D.C. *Kabarnet D.C.*
ELGEYO

RIFT

VALLEY PROVINCE

CENTRAL PROVINCE

Isiolo D.C.

MERU

Meru D.C.
Nyeri D.C. KENYA
Thomson's Falls

Kakamega D.C.
NANDI

Kericho

LUO
NYANZA PROVINCE

Kisii D.C.
KISII

LAKE VICTORIA

Kisumu D.C.

Nakuru D.C.
NAKURU

Naivasha D.C.

EMBU
Embu D.C.

KAMBA

Garissa D.C.

GALLA

SOUTHERN

Narok D.C.

MASAI

NAIROBI

Thika D.C.
Kiambu

PROVINCE

Machakos D.C.
KAMBA

Kitui D.C.

KAMBA

Kajiado D.C.

KAMBA

POKOMO

BAJUN
Lamu D.C.

Kipini D.C.

COAST

INDIAN OCEAN

MT KILIMANJARO

Moshi

Wundanyi
TAITA D.C.

PROVINCE

Kilifi D.C.

TAVETA

GIRYAMA

TANZANIA

DURUMA
Kwale D.C.
DIGO

MOMBASA
D.C.

KEY
/// White Highlands.
Territorial boundaries.
Provincial boundaries.
District boundaries.
Roads.
Railways.
EMBU Tribes.

Scale in Miles
0   20   40   60   80   100

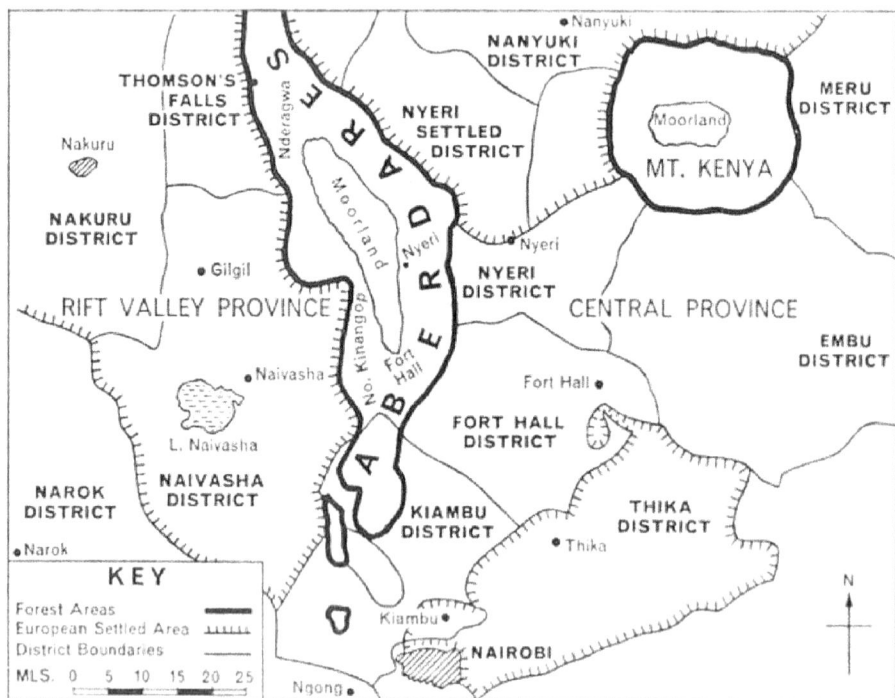

THE HARDCORE
The Story of Karigo Muchai

INTRODUCTION
Kenya: Two Paths Ahead

As part of a collective effort by several Kenyans and myself, the following article was written, mimeographed and distributed at the Kenya African National Union (KANU) Conference held in Nairobi, Kenya in December 1961.

◊   ◊   ◊

The struggle for Kenya's future is being waged today on three distinct though interrelated levels – political, racial and economic. It seems to us that we Africans are being allowed to "win" in the first two spheres as long as we don't contest the battle being waged on the third, all-important economic level.

Since the end of the Second World War, Great Britain, knowing it could not contain the wave of nationalist revolutions spreading throughout the colonial world, has embarked on a course of "guiding" these nationalist movements down a path most conducive to the perpetuation of British and multi-national capitalist economic domination. The old colonialism involving direct political control is fast dying and a quick transition to the new colonialism – for which the United States had framed such an admirable model in Central and South America – is felt necessary to avert a *genuine* social revolution, which would result in economic as well as political independence and thus stop the flow of Kenya's surplus capital into the banks of the western capitalist world. The British Master Plan is thus quite simple in outline: "Carefully relinquish political control to a properly indoctrinated group of the "right kind" of Africans, i.e., those whose interests are similar to and compatible with our own, so that we retain economic control." In short, the British Government wants to leave in political *form* so that its capitalist "sponsors" might remain in economic *content*. Put into slogan form, this plan would be: LEAVE IN ORDER TO STAY.

What are the techniques being employed by the British to facilitate our transition from colonial to neo-colonial status? Though they are many, we shall here mention two of the most important. First is a technique which might be called *Racial Harmony: A Disguise for the Recruitment of African Stooges and Frontmen.*

Realizing that their old policies of economic protection and privilege for European settlers and non-African businessmen had resulted in the almost complete absence of Africans within the middle class, the British Government undertook hurried plans to recruit Africans to economic positions which would allow them to become the spokesmen for this class. It was necessary, in brief, to sufficiently break down the colour barriers so as to allow the formation of a "multiracial" economic front whose spokesmen would have black faces even while its planners and largest profit makers remained European and Asian. They proceeded to allow us freehold titles to our land and the right to grow certain cash crops, such as Arabica coffee, so that an African landholding group might emerge which, employing cheap African labour just as their European counterparts, would find its interests identified with the capitalists of the dominant economic group.

Today, in addition to the resettlement scheme, we are bombarded with talk of mergers between the Kenya National Farmers' Union (KNFU) and the African Farmers and Traders Association; between the African, Asian and European Chambers of Commerce, and even between African and European Medical Associations. These intended mergers are clear evidence of a calculated plan (revealed most boldly by Blundell and Delamere during a recent meeting of the KNFU) on the part of the economic elite to partially dissolve racial barriers in order to consolidate its position along class lines and to use Africans as frontmen and spokesmen for its interests.

"Africanization" is the term used for the process by which selected Africans are being recruited to executive or bureaucratic posts and thus acquiring a vested interest in the status quo – an interest it shares with a growing number of businessmen, professionals and prosperous farmers and which manifests itself in a desire for "economic stability" and the rule of "law and order". All these moves parade themselves, of course, as signs of the coming racial harmony, as humanitarian gestures reflecting a genuine change of heart among the avowed European racists.

Interestingly enough, we hear our African colleagues shouting that they want to "stabilize" an economy of poverty and wage-slavery for the masses and to perpetuate a body of "law and order" which acts as the moral and militant protector of those who currently control this economy. Aren't they aware that this economy they wish to "stabilize" is at the root of Kenya's present backward economic condition, shipping abroad or spending on lavish consumption the surplus capital generated yearly by our labour? Don't they know that in times of crisis, when their economic interests are threatened by the imminence of sweeping social changes, the reactionary elements of countries throughout history have taken refuge and attempted to consolidate their forces under the banners of "law and order" and the need for "stability"? Don't they know from their own experiences in Kenya's recent revolutionary effort and the British repression that some of the gravest crimes of man against man are committed under the banner of "law and order"?

Let us investigate this body of law and decide whether we want the system of economic inequality which it protects through the maintenance of order. At present we are merely echoing the slogans put forward by those who stand to lose by our gains, who are now profiting by a system which exploits us; who, in fact, drafted and imposed that very body of law which our people are daily forced to follow in unbearable degradation and humiliating poverty. Let us instead struggle against a "stability" which is in fact stagnation; let us struggle to liberate that vast reservoir of creative ability which now lies dormant amongst our people; let us, in short, create a new society which allows to each man the right to eat, the right to the products of his labour, the right to clothe, house and educate his children, the right, in short, to live in dignity amongst equals. It is a socialist society we should be struggling to build, a system which, unlike capitalism, concerns itself with the welfare of the masses rather than with the profits and privileges of a few.

A second technique being utilized so that our rulers might "leave in order to stay" can be called *Nationalism: A Colonialist Substitute for Ideology*. Nationalism is essentially a negative philosophy based on strong popular feelings, demanding freedom from foreign political domination. It is no substitute for a positive ideology. The British, along with many other colonial powers, have attempted to utilize this negative political slogan (which, by the way, they themselves have popularized) to forestall or hinder the emergence of a revolutionary ideology, which they feared might mean the end of their economic domination. A set of ideas, carefully articulating the Kenya peoples' present condition and needs and putting forward in bold terms a rational program for Kenya's future economic development, could not but frighten Kenya's present and potential capitalist investors. This is so because planning and rationality regarding the economic and social development of a people are not the virtues of an exploitative capitalist system. We see this wherever we find an economically backward country fathered by western capitalism. Whether we look at Kenya, British Honduras or economic dependencies of the United States such as Liberia or Chile, we see the same thing: mass poverty and illiteracy combined with highly profitable foreign-owned extractive industries in agriculture or minerals.

Nevertheless, our political leaders and other spokesmen plead for more foreign investment, promising to honour existing contracts, protect land rights and maintain the stability we've talked of earlier. They seem willing, in fact, to do almost anything so long as their nationalist's dream of "political" independence is given them. They seem willing to sell everything so that we might inherit a political power stripped of the ability to make far-reaching economic decisions. Political power is essentially a means, an instrument in the hands of a people which entitles them to make decisions regarding their future development. If we are to inherit a Government unable to make the vital decisions necessary for our economic development, then political independence will be a shallow victory indeed; the victory of a man who, spotting a great feast ahead, is satisfied with a dry bone thrown by the wayside. Our political leaders who shout nothing but *"Uhuru sasa"* will be proud and arrogant in their fine clothes and cars on the day our cherished independence arrives; but those who have thrown us this bone will chuckle to themselves, knowing that the real victory was theirs, while our people will face perhaps another decade or more of poverty and deprivation.

Without an ideology for vast social and economic change our politicians are easy game, regardless of their high motives and intentions, for the international corporations. It is difficult to fight something you do not see clearly, and the eyes of our leaders appear blurred by the din and wail of press and radio concerning the coming *Uhuru*, by the unquestioning enthusiasm displayed at the utterance of wilting slogans by the throngs of poor peasants which comprise their following, and by their growing international "status" and the continued invitations by "important" people to cocktails at the New Stanley Hotel. Their lack of sound ideology based on firmly held principles of human worth and dignity will make them easy prey for the foreign industrialist and financier, always ready with an envelope of money in return for political favours. In this kind of atmosphere opportunism rules the day: every man for himself and each with a price, willing to sell his political influence to the highest bidder.

The unity which can be achieved by nationalism alone is weak and thinly covers the many severe antagonisms in our society. Thus in Kenya today, with the goal of *Uhuru* seen clearly on the road ahead, individuals, tribes and vested interest groups are starting to vie for positions of strength and privilege; with the coming of independence the veneer of unity is smashed and all the latent antagonisms come to the fore. Real unity, you see, cannot be based on a slogan or on an illustrious personality; it can only be achieved by an ideology which unifies people in a common struggle and program. Let us then fashion an ideology which will unify the vast majority of our people by articulating their needs and by advancing a program of socialist development in agriculture and industry which promises to eradicate poverty, disease and illiteracy, a program which will draw out the creative talents and energies of our people, giving them that personal dignity and pride which comes from socially constructive and productive activity. Let us, in short, provide our people with the ideological and organizational tools necessary for the achievement of genuine independence and development. Let us not sell them cheaply down the glittering path of neo-colonialism and social, economic and cultural stagnation.

◊   ◊   ◊

Unfortunately, since the above was written, Kenya has unmistakably entered the path of neocolonial accommodation. The Kenyatta regime, even before the flag-waving independence ceremony of 12 December 1963, had embarked on a course of self-aggrandizing opportunism and blatant disregard for the peasant and worker masses of Kenya. Virtually every warning contained in this article, every "pitfall of national consciousness" Fanon cautioned against in his *Wretched of the Earth*, has been succumbed to in a Kenya which today is the very antithesis of that creative and developing socialist nation hoped for by radical Kenyans in 1961. Leaders of integrity and dedicated to serving the interests of the

6

masses, men such as Pio Gama Pinto, Bildad Kaggia and Oginga Odinga, have been assassinated, deported, imprisoned or harassed and intimidated into silence and accommodation. Kenya is today a police state run by a mafia-like clique of self-serving politicians-cum-businessmen. Jomo Kenyatta, two-time betrayer of the Kenya masses (in 1953-4 at Kapenguria and 1962-3), largest African landowner in Kenya, leader of the new Black bourgeoisie and of the corrupt bureaucratic bourgeoisie which comprises the government, was described to me in 1962 by Pio Pinto – then editor of *Sauti ya Mwafrica* and a top Kenyatta advisor – as simply an "amoral man". Pinto was assassinated by the regime on 24 February 1965 and Kenya has yet to replace him.

Toward those like Karigo Muchai, whose life history you are about to read, and the thousands of others who fought in the forests, reserves and towns during Kenya's unsuccessful "Mau Mau" revolt, the Kenyatta regime has shown nothing but scorn and contempt. This became clear in a speech by Kenyatta shortly after his release in 1962. At Githunguri, an African-run Teacher Training School turned into a butchery during the revolt, where over one thousand Kikuyu were hung by the British forces of law and order, Kenyatta referred to Mau Mau as "...a disease which has been eradicated and must never be remembered again".[1] For those who remembered the promises of the revolution, to which the detained "leaders" paid lip service on the eve of "independence", the repression was swift and severe.

Karari Njama, co-author of *Mau Mau from Within*,[2] described the situation to me in a letter dated 12 July 1965.

> The Kenya revolution is now a mere history covered by a sweeping statement that everyone fought for freedom until we grabbed it from the Colonial Imperialists – and that no forest fighter should call himself a freedom fighter. This being strongly advocated by the Government shows that the forest fighters' past service is not appreciated. I am filled with great regret on realization of the fact that the forest fighters' survivors, the widows and orphans of those who volunteered to sacrifice their lives in order to liberate the Kenya nation from colonial rule, have no place to enjoy the fruits of their fallen parents' and husbands' labour. Indeed, many of them are still jobless, landless and as hungry as before. And worse, they are covered

---

1 *East African Standard*, 10 September 1962, Nairobi, Kenya
2 *Mau Mau From Within*, Barnett & Njama. Monthly Review Press, New York, 1967
  [new edition with commentary, Daraja Press, 2021]

by shame because of their participation in our unrecognized fight for freedom. The realization that nobody now admits to having promised them that they could occupy the stolen land if they could get rid of the white settler is a shocking one. The Government has ruled that there is no "free land" and that anyone who wants to occupy land would have either to buy it direct from the settler or from the Government – which will buy it from the settlers and then sell it to peasant farmers. The peasant who succeeds in getting land would then get a loan from the Government to develop his farm.

Please note that last year a number of Mount Kenya forest fighters, who had remained in their hideouts for the last eleven years before independence, returned to the forest and stated that they wouldn't come out again until they were given free land which they were promised and which they had fought for for eleven years. The Government sent its forces to Mount Kenya with authority to shoot them as "enemies of peace". Their leader and three others were shot dead; the rest surrendered. Government threatened all the other forest fighters, warning them that if they wanted anything free they had better go back to the forests and be prepared to fight against the Government – which was quite strong enough to combat them. One Member of Parliament criticised the Government for this and he was dismissed from his position as Parliamentary Secretary to the Ministry of Education. He was rebuked as being anti-Party, anti-Government, anti-President and an advocate of imported Communism.

Karigo Muchai was trying desperately to scratch out a living for himself and his family when I met him in Nairobi in February 1962. Without land, without a job, he was making charcoal in the forest and selling it as a mini-trader on the streets of the city. His life history was taped in Kikuyu then translated into English by Ngugi Solomon Kabiro, another Kenyan whose life history you will read in this series. I am responsible for editing the final draft of this English version.

The story of Karigo Muchai reveals in simple unreflective terms the experiences, struggles and sacrifices of a Kikuyu peasant, son of a squatter on a white settler farm, who joins the peasant-based revolt for Land and Freedom, fights for these objectives until captured, then spends six cruel years as a hardcore in over a dozen detention (i.e. concentration) camps. It is the unrecognized and unrewarded sacrifices of men like Karigo which Karari Njama refers to above. In 1962 Karigo could still hope for "... a decent job or a piece of land to cultivate" in order to provide for his family after independence. "These are the things we Kikuyu fought and died for," he said. "I only pray that after independence our children will not be forced to fight again."

The story of "Mau Mau", Kenya's peasant revolt of 1952-56, as well as its aftermath in the years leading up to and following the "granting" of independence to this British colony, should be studied carefully for the lessons that can be learned from such bitter failures.[3] Political independence without genuine decolonization and socialism yields continued misery and oppression for the peasant-worker masses. Karigo's prayer, as with those of other peasants and workers caught up in the web of neocolonial accommodation after long years of struggle, will not be answered. His children and theirs *will* be forced to fight again.

Don Barnett
Vancouver, B. C.
11 September 1972

---

3 See *Not Yet Uhuru*, Oginga Odinga, Heinemann, London 1967.

Karigo wa Muchai

I was born in the Limuru area of Kiambu during the year 1914. My father was living on a piece of land left him by my grandfather. When his *shamba* was included in the large Limuru section of Kiambu grabbed by the British Government for settlement by Europeans in 1918, my father was forced to move. He decided to go to Elementeita, which is located in the Rift Valley Province some 120 miles from our former home. There he got a job on a large European farm as a labourer. In those early days African squatters like my father were allowed to cultivate a plot of land for their own use and keep animals on the settlers farm. In return they gave their labour and that of their wives and children to the settler for most of the year. Salaries, where they existed at all, were barely enough to meet the Government poll tax.

As a small child, I used to look after my father's many sheep and goats with my younger brothers. In 1926, however, we were forced to get rid of most of our animals, and I was left with little work to do. I approached my father's European employer for a job and he hired me as a kitchen boy on a salary of one and a half shillings per month. After four years, at the age of 16, I was advanced to a junior cook with a salary of 6s. After a few years, thinking the money I was earning in domestic employment too little, I decided to leave the farm and go to Nairobi in search of another job.

In the city I found work as an apprentice driver and mechanic for a European firm. I went through a long training program and for the next two years I remained as an apprentice mechanic. In 1935, preferring driving to mechanical work, I took a job with a commercial firm as driver for 45s. a month.

All this time, as I was trying to make my own way in the world, my father remained as a squatter on the farms of the White Highlands. Conditions there for African labourers were becoming worse as a result of increasing restrictive measures. In 1936 squatters were allowed to keep only 20 animals. My father decided a short time later to give up his job in the Rift Valley and return to Kiambu. He had no land of his own and had to settle as a tenant or *muhoi* on a small *shamba* belonging to a friend.

In 1939 I went to live with my parents in Kiambu. The Second World War had just broken out and Africans were volunteering or being called to serve in the army. At first I had no desire to fight for the British. I remained in the reserves dodging the chief's *askari* who were sent around to register the able-bodied men for the army. By July 1942 I had grown tired of this game and decided to enlist. I trained for three months as an army driver and was then attached to a transport unit heading north with arms and ammunition for the army units fighting the Italians and their supporters in Somaliland.

I spent four years in the army, moving from Ethiopia to Madagascar, Ceylon, India and finally to Burma where I was made a corporal and placed in charge of a small transport unit. In the jungles of Burma we had to abandon our motor vehicles and each of the 55 men in my unit was given two mules loaded with provisions for the front-line troops. Our forces suffered heavy losses as the Japanese were very strong and much more skilled in the kind of fighting required by the tropical terrain. Many of our men were killed and many more died of diseases.

I remained in Burma from July 1944 until January 1946 when, with the war over, I was returned to Kenya and discharged in June. While serving in the army we Africans were told over and over again that we were fighting for our country and for democracy, and that when the war was over we would be rewarded for the sacrifices we were making. We would be given priority in trade and employment and could look forward to a much better life than the one we had left. For my part I was only hoping to be given a small piece of land somewhere and to be treated a little more decently by the Kenya Government and white settlers.

It didn't seem too much to hope that the democracy we were supposed to be fighting for would be extended to cover the Africans of Kenya.

These hopes and dreams of mine were quickly crushed on my return home. The army talk was false propaganda intended only to get Africans like me to risk our lives for Britain and the white settlers of Kenya. The life I returned to was exactly the same as the one I left four years earlier: no land, no job, no representation and no dignity.

After remaining at home for some time and getting married, I finally got a job as a driver for a film company in Nairobi.

It was 1930 when as a young boy of 16 I first heard of the Kikuyu Central Association. Though I did not become a member, I made contributions and agreed with the KCA demands for return of our land, representation for Africans in the Kenya Government, higher wages and better education for African children. In these early years KCA was an open and legal society. It recruited only trusted elders who swore an oath of allegiance to the association over a Bible.

I heard nothing about KCA after it was banned in 1940 for so-called collaboration with the Italians. When discharged from the army, however, I discovered that the association still existed underground and continued to hold meetings secretly in the homes of its members.

I joined KCA in February 1949. By this time the oath had been changed and strengthened in order to prevent the leaking of information to Government, which suspected our banned association was still in existence. The organization now used a more traditional "blood oath" which served to bind all those who took it to secrecy concerning the existence and activities of KCA. The membership at this time was still rather small and a new person would be brought in only if he was a trusted friend of one of the members.

It was toward the middle of the next year, when KCA was beginning to increase its membership rapidly, that I first heard the term "Mau Mau". Several Africans had been brought to court in Naivasha for illegal oathing and one man, when asked about the proceedings, replied that the oath was administered in a dark hut at night and all he could make out was the murmer of voices. Now in Kikuyu when referring to whispers or voices that cannot quite be understood, one uses the expression "mumumumu". This apparently was heard by a journalist in the court as "Mau Mau", and the following day the newspapers reported that the men had taken a Mau Mau oath.

Through this mistake the name "Mau Mau" came to be applied to our association by people all over the world. To those of us who were members of KCA the name "Mau Mau" was seen as the name given to our movement by the Europeans. And since Mau Mau as such was not banned until August 1950, some of our people caught oathing during this period admitted to having taken a "Mau Mau" oath in order to keep secret the existence of KCA. Among ourselves we didn't use the word "Mau Mau". In our own language the movement was often referred to as *Muingi*, meaning "the Community", *Gikuyu na Mumbi* or simply *Gikuyu*, referring to the male and female founders of our Kikuyu tribe …. but never as "Mau Mau".

In late 1950 I joined the Kenya African Union. KAU had been started in 1945. It was a registered association attempting, under the leadership of Jomo Kenyatta, to unite all Kenya Africans and get the British Government to yield to African demands in the fields of education, wages, racial discrimination and, most importantly, land and political representation. Since all Kikuyu supported these aims, most of us in the underground KCA also joined and supported KAU. There were, of course, thousands of people who were members of KAU – including many Kikuyu – who knew nothing at all about the existence of our secret organization.

In the two years before the Emergency both organizations grew in numbers and gained strength. In the underground association our policy had changed since the time I joined. Now we were attempting to unify all Kikuyu by bringing them into the movement. All would be bound to one another through the Oath of Unity and could then act as a single, unified muingi or community. We had no plan during this period to use violence in achieving our objectives. Rather than preparing a military fight to get rid of the European settlers and British Government as some people have suggested, we wanted only to unify our people within a single organization in order to gain greater strength in pushing forward our political demands.

By the time Government declared its "State of Emergency" on 20 October 1952 and arrested the top leadership of KAU, our underground movement had gained the support of the vast majority of Kikuyu people. Every member attempted to bring in as many friends and acquaintances as possible. I would estimate that over a two year period I introduced about 600 men and women into the association of Gikuyu na Mumbi. This, and my participation in many oathing ceremonies, gave me great satisfaction. I felt that I was doing something good and important for my people and country. As our strength grew, so grew the chances for achieving our political objectives.

During this early period I was a member of the council of elders formed in my sub-location. Along with the other sub-locations in Kiambaa, we sent three men to represent us on the location committee. There were three locations in Githunguri Division and each sent representatives to the divisional committee. The other two divisions within the district, Chura and Gatundu, also had their committees. Each division committee sent two men to the Kiambu District Community. Kiambu almost surrounds Nairobi and, as there were many Kiambu Kikuyu living in the city, they also sent two men to represent them on the eight-man Kiambu District Committee. It had three officers, a chairman, secretary and treasurer, and met in Nairobi. To the Central Province Committee (CPC), which also had its headquarters in Nairobi, the Kiambu and other district committees each sent three representatives.

With the declaration of the Emergency in October 1952, certain changes were made, at least so far as Kiambu was concerned. Government stepped up its activities in Nairobi and travel to and from the city became more difficult. Our district committee broke down. Each division representative returned to his home area in Kiambu and for a time we had no active district committee. Up to June 1953 contact with the CPC in Nairobi was maintained through the division committees. The district committee members representing the three Kiambu divisions who had served on the CPC continued to represent their divisions directly to the latter committee. They by-passed the now defunct Kiambu District Committee. The Kiambu Kikuyu living in Nairobi who had earlier elected two members to the district committee also sent their representatives directly to the CPC.

I had changed jobs a few times and when the Emergency was declared I was working as a driver for the Kenya Cooperative Creameries. I was going to Naivasha at night, loading my truck with milk, and driving back to Nairobi in time for the early morning delivery. Driving at night was becoming more dangerous and in December, as I was returning to Nairobi, I ran into an ambush by the security forces. Instead of signalling us to stop they just opened fire on my truck. By the time they saw their mistake my lorry attendant had been shot in the leg and the milk was splattered all over the road, the containers riddled with bullets.

When I finally reached Nairobi I told my employers I wanted to resign and at the end of December I left the firm and returned to Kiambaa Location. In the reserves life was made very difficult by the repressive measures of Government. Sweeps by the security forces, beatings, arrests and torture to gain confessions were common daily happenings.

In January 1953 I was elected to the Kiambaa Location Committee. My tasks were to investigate Government brutalities, collect funds, and make arrangements to assist women who had lost their husbands and men who were arrested and taken to court on Mau Mau charges. As I made my rounds of the 16 sub-locations in Kiambaa, I would collect dues, gather information on the activities of the security forces and keep notes on the number of young men available as recruits for our fighters in the Narok, Longonot or southern Aberdare forests.

In February I was arrested during a sweep of my sub-location. I was taken to the Karura Police Station near my home. What I had heard from others I was now to experience myself. Once inside the station I was brought before the Government interrogators. They asked me a series of questions and demanded a confession. When I refused, claiming to know nothing of Mau Mau, I was beaten unconscious by the Special Branch men and their *askari* and thrown into a pit six feet deep and filled with muddy water. Regaining consciousness, I was given a little rest and then brought back before the interrogators, where the process began all over again. Almost every day for two weeks I was beaten with clubs, whips, rifle butts, feet and fists and then thrown into the pit of dirty water. Thinking that if I was guilty I would have confessed rather than continue suffering their torture they finally released me. I was warned to stay clear of Mau Mau if I valued my life and wanted to avoid even worse treatment than I'd just received.

The Batuni Oath

Shortly after my release, being more convinced than ever that our movement had to succeed, I took the second or Batuni Oath. A friend of mine led me to a place about four miles from my village. It was around 4 o'clock in the afternoon when we reached the hut. My friend went in leaving me to wait outside. A few minutes later I was called in. Just inside the doorway I received a blow from someone standing in the darkness and was pushed into the hut. As I moved forward I was hit once more and ordered to remove all my clothing and sit down on the banana leaf which had been placed on the floor in the center of the room. I was beginning to get used to the dark. I could see that the man giving me instructions held a pistol while three other men, two armed with *simis* or Kikuyu swords, stood close by.

As I sat completely naked on the banana leaves facing the oath administrator a long strip of goat's meat was placed around my neck. One ene lay across my chest and the other dropped down my back, around my waist several times and then up between my legs. I was ordered to hold this end up against my penis. Near me, on the floor, was a cooking pot placed upside down. By my right hand were seven pieces of a vine called *mukengeria*, each about four or five inches long. A three-foot stake was stuck in the ground in front of me and on it hung the *ngata* or neck bone of a goat. While repeating each of the seven vows I was to pick up one of the thin pieces of vine and rub it slowly into each of the seven holes of the *ngata*.

Under the *ngata*, lying on a banana leaf, were the two eyes of an uncastrated he-goat, called a *kihei*. This word means "uncircumcised youth" or simply "son", but during the revolution it was used to refer to a man who had taken the Batuni Oath. Seven thorns were placed near the eyes and after each vow I picked one up and stuck it into one of the eyes. They were removed by the administrator after each initiate had completed his vows.

Finally, after repeating each of the following vows spoken first by the oath administrator, I took a small bite of the meat which lay across my chest near my right hand:

1 I speak the truth and swear before Ngai and before everyone
present here
And by this *Batuni* Oath of *Muingi*
That if called upon to fight for our land,
To shed my blood for it,
I shall obey and never surrender.
And if I fail to do so:

May this oath kill me
May this *thenge* kill me
May this seven kill me
May this meat kill me

2 I speak the truth and swear before *Ngai* and before everyone
present here
And before the children of *Gikuyu* and *Mumbi*
That I shall never betray our country
That I shall never betray a member of *muingi* to our enemies
Whether they be European, Asian or African,
And that if I do this:

May this oath kill me, etc.

3 I speak the truth and swear...
That if I am called upon at night or during a storm
To destroy the house or store of a European or other enemy
I shall do so without fear and never surrender.
And if I fail to do this:

May this oath kill me, etc.

4 I speak the truth and swear....
That if I am called to fight
Or to kill the enemy, I shall go
Even if that enemy be my father or mother, my brother or sister.

And if I refuse:

May this oath kill me, etc.

5 I speak the truth and swear....
That if the people of *muingi* come by day or by night
And ask me to hide them
I shall do so and I shall help them.
And if I fail to do this:

May this oath kill me, etc.

6 I speak the truth and swear....
That I shall never seduce the woman of another man
That I shall never take up with prostitutes
That I shall never steal anything belonging to a member
of *muingi*
Nor shall I ever hate or speak badly of another member
And if I fail to do these things:

May this oath kill me, etc.

7 I speak the truth and swear....
That I shall never sell my country for money or other wealth
That I shall keep until death all the vows I have made here today
That I shall never disclose our secrets to the enemy
Nor shall I reveal them to anyone not a member of *muingi*
And if I break any of the vows I have taken today
I will agree to any punishment that this society decides to
give me
And if I fail to do these things:

May this oath kill me
May this *thenge* kill me
May this seven kill me
May this meat kill me

When the six of us who were being initiated had finished taking these vows we were brought together by the administrator who pricked a finger of each of us with a pin. We then smeared some of our blood on a small piece of goat's meat which was cut into pieces. Each of us was then given a portion of the meat to eat. This, we were told, made us blood-brothers and by creating a blood-tie between all *ihei* [pl. of *kihei*] guaranteed cooperation and brotherhood among *Gikuyu* and *Mumbi*'s fighters. We should now help and assist one another in any way possible and never think of doing harm to our own brothers. Finally the oath administrator told us to disperse and return to our homes.

Shortly after taking the *Batuni* or "Platoon" Oath I was made location head of the fighters in Kiambaa. In addition to the men fighting in the forests a number of fighters remained in their locations. These men carried out their normal activities during the day while at night they became fighters. Besides raiding home guard or police posts and assisting the forest fighters as scouts and spies, these men did much work in gathering information for the elders of the district committee. They were sometimes given the task of killing traitors selected by the elders and of providing accommodation for forest fighters entering the reserve for a raid or passing through on their way to the forest. It was from these reserve units that most fighters were recruited to go into the forest.

One of my main duties at this time was to arrange meals and accommodation for fighters, often from distant places, who were passing through Kiambaa on their way to the forest. They usually came at night and I would take them two or three at a time to the huts of my fighters who would provide them with meals and a place to sleep. The following night I directed them to the next station, where they received similar treatment. They would thus be able to make their way into the forests unnoticed by the security forces. Almost all of the fighters recruited from Nairobi made their way into the Aberdares through Kiambu and spent a night in Kiambaa Location.

I continued during this period to gather information for the district committee on Government brutalities and atrocities. One day in March 1953 as I was walking through Karura Sub-Location I heard a woman screaming. I ran over to see what was happening and saw Kamithi, the headman, beating a woman just outside her hut. I waited to see what would happen and shortly a group of home guards came along and carried the unconscious woman to their post. I continued on my way to see the man I had intended to meet and later reported the incident to the location committee. A lawyer was arranged for and he asked to visit the detained woman. Kamithi, knowing he couldn't prove his charge that the woman was Mau Mau, was obliged through the pressure applied by our lawyer to release her.

Kamithi was very well known in the location for the way he tortured and beat people into confessing their Mau Mau activities. It was decided that he should be killed. One night our men raided his house and killed three of his home guards. Kamithi was not at home during the raid and thus escaped with his life. In fact, he is still alive today though we made several attempts to kill him. He now leads a very lonely existence in his village. No one will speak to or even look at him because of the crimes he committed against his own people.

As a result of killing the three home guards the security forces came to the sub-location the following day and badly beat all the people. In addition they rounded-up all the livestock and took them to the Karura police post where they were either eaten or sold. The money went to the D.C.

During this same week as I was passing the fenced trading center containing the police post I saw Kamithi drive up in a Land-Rover and dump out three bodies. I went over as he called all the people around to come see what happened to those who were Mau Mau. The three dead men were all from Kamithi's sub-location. I learned later that he had killed them himself. His charge that they were Mau Mau was never proven, but in those days details didn't matter. Being accused by a "loyalist" was enough "evidence" for the taking of a man's life.

Everyone in the location knew that the actions carried out by Kamithi were intended to revenge the three dead home guards. In order to prevent this kind of incident we passed a resolution at our next location committee meeting that no fighter was to take the life of a home guard or other loyalist without the consent of the committee. If anyone violated this rule he was to be severely punished. Killings were always followed by harsh repressive measures by the security forces. We felt they were only justified in cases where the person was found by the committee of elders to have committed grave crimes against the people.

Lari Massacre

It was very early on the morning of 26 March 1953 when I heard some *askari* talking about a massacre that had taken place that night at Lari Location. Thinking I should investigate, I took the first bus I could catch for Lari. Arriving at about 8:30 a.m., I found the whole area swarming with security forces. To avoid arrest, or perhaps worse, I made my way to the forest edge on a hill overlooking the area and together with a group of local people observed the events taking place below. Hundreds of people were being beaten and herded into the nearby Uplands Police Post. Many huts were burned to the ground, still smoldering. Others were still aflame and looked like they had been set on fire quite recently. Repeated bursts of gunfire from the security forces could be heard and I saw several people fall to the ground injured or killed under the rain of Government bullets.

I remained on the hill throughout the morning and into the afternoon, often having to shift to a new position in order to avoid the security forces who were searching the location and surrounding bush. I watched as over 10,000 people, arrested as far away as ten miles from the location, were beaten and dragged or pushed into an open area in the field below. As the day wore on and the security forces began to leave the area I decided to take a chance and go down for a look around. What I observed was not a pleasant sight. Many people lay dead on the ground or in the ashes of their burned huts. Some had been killed by *pangas*

21

[a single-edged garden tool], others by the fire in their huts, and still others by the bullets of the security forces. After a time, and thinking I'd seen enough of death, I returned home to report on what I'd seen at Lari.

Sometime later, after speaking to many people who had seen or participated in the affair, I learned what happened during that night and early morning at Lari. Late at night some of our fighters attacked the village of Chief Luka, killing the chief, one headman and a certain home guard and burning down their huts. Some of the family of these men may have been trapped inside their huts and died in the flames. Later, in the very early hours of the morning, the security forces arrived and began to take their revenge on the peasants in and around Chief Luka's village. They entered the location in large numbers, setting huts on fire, slaughtering many innocent people – men, women and children – and shooting suspects and anyone who tried to flee into the bush. In Lari there was a massacre on 26 March 1953, but most of the blood was on Government hands.

For weeks after this incident as many as 50 people a day out of the 10,000 who had been rounded up and detained at Uplands were taken into the bush, shot and left for the hyenas. Many skeletons still remain scattered over the area, though Government has attempted to remove this evidence of its inhumanity. In addition to those shot in the bush 92 Kikuyu were tried, found guilty and hung at Githunguri, in the buildings that once housed the Githunguri Teacher's Training College. The British had earlier closed this college, converting its buildings into a prison and butchery and replacing our teachers with hangmen and education with death.

On the day following the Lari massacre I was passing near the Tigoni Police Post and heard the screams of a man. Turning toward the noise I saw someone being mercilessly beaten with clubs by some *askari*. He lay unconscious by the roadside and after the *askari* left I went over. The man was dead.

Later this same day, 27 March, there was a sweep by security forces in a large area of Kiambu. Homes were broken into late at night and searched. People were manhandled and beaten. Dozens of men were dragged out of their huts, loaded onto lorries, driven to the edge of the forest and shot. It was part of my job to investigate these brutalities and I know the names of many men who met their fate this way.

I recall one case in Limuru when 30 men were taken from their homes at night and driven into the bush. Here they were bound together and tied between two trees. The group of security force men who brought them to the place then moved a short distance away and, using their live prisoners as targets, had a little rifle practice. Of the 30 men, only one survived to tell the story. He had miraculously escaped being hit. The European leader of the security force group, thinking perhaps that the man had a charmed life, took him back to the home guard post. I know this man, Daudi Kariuki, very well and remember the incident clearly. A report reached our location committee. I was sent out to investigate and found the 29 dead men in just the condition described. I later visited Daudi at the post and got his first-hand story.

In addition to the daily fears of death faced by people in the reserves we were made to work long hours in what Government called "communal labour". Every able-bodied person – man, woman and youngster alike – was awakened early in the morning and taken into the field. He was assigned enough work to keep him busy the whole day. In this communal labour we were forced to dig roads and bench terraces and to construct home guard and police posts surrounded by barbed wire and a deep staked trench. At night there was the worry and fear which denies a man sleep. During the day there was only the thankless labour forced on us by Government. For a Kikuyu in the reserves there was no rest.

In the Forest

The repressive measures of Government increased. Sweeps of the villages became more frequent and beatings, arrest, theft of property and rape of our women became the order of the day. Many of our fighters left to join their comrades in the forests. Three camps had been set up in Narok, two in the Longonot area and three others in the southern regions of the Aberdares. Apart from the investigations I was carrying out I made several trips into these areas acting as messenger, delivering guns and ammunition and escorting new fighters from the reserves and Nairobi into the forests.

In June 1953 a new Kiambu District Committee was formed. It consisted of 24 members who stayed in the Limuru European-settled area. I was elected with another man from my location to represent Kiambaa. Two members were elected from each of the three division committees and from each of Kiambu's nine locations, making a total of 24 elders on the district committee. Our people in Nairobi also sent two members to attend important meetings.

At this time travel became very difficult and meetings in the locations were harder and more dangerous to hold. All of the lower committees in Kiambu were disbanded. The location representatives on the district committee acted on behalf of their people in the various locations and maintained communications with them through messengers. Most of the members of the district committee were housed by our fighters in the Limuru area.

Soon after this reorganization when a man was needed to represent our fighters in Kiambu I was selected for this post by the district committee and given the rank of Field Marshall. Our fighters were organized on the sub-location, location and district level. Representatives from each lower group were sent to the next highest committee. Our district committee of fighters consisted of 19 members, two from each

SUDAN
ETHIOPIA

Lokitaung
Lodwar
LAKE RUDOLF
North Horr
Moyale
Marsabit
Wajir
UGANDA
MT. ELGON
Kapenguria
Maralal
Archer's Post
Kitale
Eldoret
Kabarnet
Baringo
Isiolo
Kakamega
Kapsabet
Thomson's Falls
Rumuruti
Naro Moru
Meru
Kisumu
Eldama Ravine
Nakuru
ABERDARE RANGE
MT. KENYA
Chuka
Garissa
Kissi
Sotik
Gilgil
Nyeri
Embu
Fort Hall
LAKE VICTORIA
Naivasha
Githugu
Tana River
Narok
Kiambu
Thika
TANGANYIKA
NAIROBI
Kitui
Magadi
Kajiado
Machakos
Sultan Hamud
Garsan
Lamu
Makindu
Kibwezi
Mtito Andei
Tsavo
Galana River
Kidini
MT. KILIMANJARO
Voi River
Malindi

KENYA
SCALE
MLS 0 20 40 60 80 100

White Highland:
Kikuyu Reserve:
Gen. Area of Revolt:

MOMBASA
INDIAN OCEAN

location fighting unit and myself as chairman. My main job was to represent our fighters on the district committee of elders. I put forward the requests, suggestions and grievances of the fighting units and passed on to them the directives of the elders. I was, in effect, the link between the district committee of elders and the fighters of the district as well as the link between the forest fighters and our people in the reserves.

A man named Waruingi, later killed by security forces, was one of our most successful and daring leaders in the Kiambu bush. It was my responsibility to maintain contact with him and to supply him with arms, food and men. The Kiambu people in Nairobi were our main source of arms, medicine, clothing and other necessary supplies. These would be delivered to me and I would take them directly to Waruingi or to one of our other leaders in Narok, Longonot, Ngong or the southern Aberdares.

In July the Government, apparently getting some information from informers, sent a group of tribal police to arrest me. I was in my house late one night when I heard footsteps outside. Quickly I grabbed a few of my belongings and went out through a window, disappearing unnoticed into the darkness of a cornfield. My wife and aged parents were interrogated for some time as to my whereabouts. But all had sworn an oath of secrecy and they just kept repeating that they didn't know where I was.

From this time on I remained in hiding with the district committee of 24. Here I had the protection of 36 fighters and could more easily carry out my work for the movement. With Government repressive measures mounting and our fighters operating more and more out of the forests, the Kiambu District Committee concerned itself increasingly with the welfare of relatives of killed or detained members. Collections of money were made for their care and assistance. Money was also collected to pay the legal fees of men accused on capital charges such as possessing arms or ammunition. It was a favorite game of some European Special Branch men to place a bullet or two in the pocket of a man they were searching during a sweep. They would then "discover" the bullets in the presence of witnesses and charge the man. Several men were tried and hung as a result of tricks like this.

I also continued helping the committee investigate Government atrocities. The findings were sent to the Central Province Committee in Nairobi where attempts were made to bring these facts before the eyes of the world through the press or a few sympathetic Europeans. New and more horrible methods of extracting confessions were constantly being invented by the Special Branch officers. Some suspects were dragged by a rope tied to a Land-Rover. Others were taken into the bush, forced to dig a deep hole and stand in front of it, and then shot if they failed to cooperate. Many of our people were killed by these two techniques.

The innocent as well as the "guilty" suffered under the heavy hand of Government. I know of a case where a man named Dedan Mugo was sentenced to seven years hard labour. He left his two wives and children at home. These two women had nothing to do with Mau Mau. Nevertheless one was shot and killed by a European Police Reserve officer named Dr. Wood who was known to have killed hundreds of Kikuyu around the Limuru area. And the other died as a result of beatings she received at the hands of home guards. These are just some of many such incidents I could mention. In my work with the committee hardly a day passed without at least one verified report of Government brutality.

Our Kiambu warriors were not at this time integrated with the Aberdare forest fighters from Fort Hall and Nyeri. When news reached our district committee that units of our men had twice been attacked and disarmed by Fort Hall men under General Kago it was decided by the elders, and agreed upon by the Central Province Committee in Nairobi, that Kago should be contacted and an attempt made to set matters straight. In August 1953 I was sent with three elders and an escort of four fighters into the southern Aberdares to meet with Kago. He was operating in the forests around the Fort Hall/Kiambu boundary. When we met I told him our grievances and handed him a letter from the district committee setting out in detail the two incidents in which his men were involved. I explained to him that it was stupid for us to fight one another in order to gain firearms. We were all engaged in a war against the European and should act in unity whether from Fort Hall, Nyeri, Kiambu, Embu or Meru. Kago replied that he had already learned of the incidents and that they had been carried out by some of his men without his knowledge. He said he had already punished the men involved and guaranteed us that such mistakes would not occur again the the future.

Though Kago could have been held responsible for the actions of his men and punished, I must say in his defense that this type of incident was often very difficult to avoid in the early months of fighting. In many cases the guards posted around the camp of a group of forest fighters wore stolen home guard uniforms. When seeing strangers approach they would signal them in a manner requiring a special response. As sometimes happened, new recruits entering the forest would not know these signals and could easily be taken for enemies and ambushed. On the other hand, if they spotted a guard before he saw them they might open fire on what appeared to be a home guard and so initiate a battle. Later, incidents like this became very rare. But in mid-1953, with the forest fighters not yet well organized, they did occur, particularly with Kiambu fighters who entered the Aberdares several months after our people from Nyeri and Fort Hall had already established themselves there.

During this same month of August I was sent to deliver some arms and food to our fighters in Narok under the command of Generals Nubi and Ole Kisio. I set out with 20 men armed with 12 rifles and six home-made guns. It was about 5 a.m. as we moved from our hideout in the Limuru European-settled area toward Narok that we ran into a Government ambush near Kikuyu station. Before we realized it we were completely surrounded by security forces. Being in a bad position and greatly outnumbered by the enemy I decided we should make a run for it rather than engage the Government forces in an open battle. I directed my group to aim all of our 20 guns at one point in the circle around us. When I gave the signal we opened fire and ran through the hole which our bullets had prepared. Once we made our move the Government forces returned our fire and three of my men fell to the ground dead or injured. The rest of us continued into the bush and lost our pursuers. Without stopping we continued toward Narok arriving the next day and turning over the supplies we had brought to General Ole Kisio.

After discussing our business and spending the night in one of the Narok camps it was necessary for me to return to Limuru with my 17 fighters. We were given an escort of 50 additional fighters and set off through the bush during the day, making sure not to reveal ourselves to the enemy. While traveling I noticed a Government reconnaissance plane overhead but was confident they hadn't spotted us. After a tiring day's journey, as we were sitting on the ground eating, one of our guards ran up excitedly and told me we were being surrounded by a large force of tribal police, home guards and military units.

With a force of 67 well-armed fighters and being in a position well-chosen for its defensive cover I decided to deploy my men for battle. Government forces soon opened fire and a fight began which lasted till dark. One of my fighters was killed but we managed to capture 12 enemy rifles. It was difficult to tell how many men the Government forces lost.

Not knowing where the security forces had withdrawn to for the night it was unwise for us to continue our journey. Instead I sent a couple of my men back to Narok to ask for reinforcements. By the following morning 300 Narok fighters arrived at our camp. The enemy had also built up its forces. A day-long battle began, ending at nightfall with a loss of 11 of our fighters. We had captured no enemy guns and decided to move out.

Midnight found us in the Mount Longonot forests where we met a group of fighters under the command of General Waruingi. We were led to Waruingi's camp and planned to rest there for three days. At the end of the third day as we were making preparations to leave, we were spotted by a military plane which started to bomb the mountain. Government ground forces soon launched an attack on our position. Our own force, in addition to the men who had come with me from Limuru, consisted of 300 fighters from Narok and about 400 of Waruingi's men. After a long and fierce battle we took stock of our position. None of our fighters were killed though six had sustained injuries. Arrangements were made to take the injured men to the Aberdares for treatment and during the darkness of night I started off with my men and an escort of 150 fighters toward Limuru via Kijabe and Lari. When we arrived at Kijabe the fighters from Longonot and Narok bid us farewell and we were provided with a smaller escort by the local leaders for the remainder of our journey. The following day we at last reached our Limuru hideout. Our escort left us but unluckily ran into a Government ambush and lost 25 men.

Shortly after my return to Limuru I was sent off once more with instructions for our people in Gatundu Division. On the way I was stopped by some *askari* who asked to see my travel permit. One needed a permit at this time to move outside his own location and naturally I didn't have one. I was arrested and taken to Githunguri where Government had a police post. It was directly under Central Government control. Close-by was a Home Guard post administered by the local government chief, district officer and district commissioner. Unfortunately I was taken to the police post which held about 400 prisoners and was run by a brutal European officer nicknamed "Kihara".

I was to spend a month in this police post doing forced labour during the day and never knowing which night might be my last. Kihara had a strange and terrifying game which he practiced daily. At any time he might come into one of the cells and read two or three names off the police register. No one knew when his name might be called and all of us lived in constant fear. Those he called were tied up and thrown into a Land-Rover. Kihara would then drive to the home of one of the prisoners, call his family out and in the presence of all, put a bullet through the head of his helpless captive. Leaving the dead body for the family to bury he would drive off to the next house where the same process was repeated. This continued until his car was empty.

Kihara was also famous for his brutal methods of interrogation and for his habit of approaching the hut of a suspect, calling him outside and shooting him right there on the spot. Everyone in Githunguri lived in a constant state of fear, never knowing when Kihara or another killer nicknamed "Kingarua" might arrive. The latter was a European home guard leader and always carried a rifle, *simi* and walking stick. One of his assistants always brought along a huge club. Any Kikuyu whom Kingarua might meet, aside from home guards or other loyalists, was stopped and then held by *askari* while Kingarua got his club. The person was then beaten before even being questioned. Interrogation followed if he survived.

Our work at the police post involved the digging of graves. Early each morning we would be called out under heavy guard and taken to a near-by field to bury the dead of the day before. One day as our guards became a little careless I was able to slip away unnoticed into the bush with a friend. Our absence was apparently not noticed right away as I went without trouble to the home of a Githunguri leader. He gave me an escort and I made my way back to Limuru that same day.

Due to the bad conditions and treatment I'd received at the police post I was not in good health when I arrived at Limuru Headquarters and was forced to rest for about two weeks. Soon after my recovery in late September 1953 I was sent on another mission. This time I went to the European-settled area of eastern Kiambu where I instructed General Kitau Kali to shift his forces from the settled area to Narok. As we talked during the night in his hut we were attacked by a small group of Special Branch men and their *askari*. We returned their fire and when the hut went up in flames under their Sten guns we separated and disappeared into the bush. None of our men were hurt. But since we ran in different directions I had to return to Limuru that night without an escort.

Three days later I learned that Gitau Kali had shifted his force to the area around Kikuyu Station only eight miles from his original position. Here he was acting in violation of district committee rules, attacking home guard and police posts indiscriminately and giving Government an excuse to punish all the near-by villagers. We could not allow these attacks in the reserve to continue and a message was sent to Kitau Kali ordering him to appear before the Kiambu District Committee. When he arrived from Kikuyu he was severely reprimanded. In order to discipline him for not obeying our ruling against fighting in the reserves we agreed that he should receive 50 strokes and be hung by the wrists for an hour from a tree. After being punished Gitau Kali was ordered to lead his fighters to Narok immediately. This order he promptly carried out.

In November while the district committee was still hiding in Limuru a man who had been in close contact with us and who had in fact been one of our major suppliers of food, informed Government of our whereabouts. I don't know what prompted this man to turn informer but luckily for us we were notified by one of our own agents of his report to the Special Branch. Before the security forces could carry out an attack on our position we were able to disperse and find new accommodations. Some members of the committee went to Kikuyu, others to Githunguri, and I remained hiding around my home village. Of the 24 committee members only one ran into trouble. This man, Mbugua Ngahu, was arrested and taken to Githunguri where he was killed by home guards.

By the end of 1953 our fighters in the forests and reserves had become very active, attacking home guard and police posts regularly and with success. Through these attacks they gained arms, ammunition and other supplies necessary for the war we were waging against the Colonial Government. When the new year began our fighters appeared to be in a very strong position and many of us had high hopes of victory over the enemy forces.

Whenever security force personnel were killed, their arms and clothing were taken by our fighters and the bodies left naked. This was done because we badly needed these supplies. Let me tell you of an incident which illustrates one of the uses to which we put this equipment.

In December 1953 some of our men were arrested and taken to the police post at Kikuyu. Putting on a metal home guard armband I had earlier acquired I walked right into the post where the men were being detained. There I found a European officer whom we called "Muru wa Waitina" of "Son of the Fatman", a nickname he achieved because of the size and shape of his father. He spoke Kikuyu very well and I told him I was a home guard from a nearby post and that I'd heard that six of my relatives had been arrested. I said that the men were all decent people and had nothing to do with Mau Mau.

Muru wa Waitina replied that the men stood a good chance of being detained or even killed and that it would cost me a thousand shillings to gain their release. Knowing this might happen I had brought with me a large sum of money. I paid the European the bribe he demanded and walked out freely with my six comrades. Soon we parted ways, the six men returning to their work in the forest as I made my way back to report the incident to the committee.

I should point out that bribes such as this were not uncommon. Many Europeans took advantage of situations created by Mau Mau and became rich men. Some through bribes and theft, others through the sale of firearms and ammunitions to our agents. This corruption is not widely known and is never talked about in European or Government circles.

Unable to defeat our fighters in the forests Government increased its repressive measures in the reserves in an attempt to cut the fighters off from their major source of goods and other supplies. Communal labour was intensified, sweeps and brutalities increased and police and home guard posts went up in almost every location. Restrictions on travel were severely tightened and a rigid curfew was maintained. When all these measures failed to bring about the desired results Government built many detention camps in the hot remote regions of Kenya and began rounding up and detaining thousands of Kikuyu, guilty and innocent alike.

The effect of these measures on our forest fighters was to make contact with their supporters in the reserves more difficult and hence hamper the movement of supplies from reserve to forest. To counteract this our fighters moved their camps closer to the reserves. Daylight battles became much more frequent and our men fought well against their more numerous and better equipped enemy. The continued build-up of military forces from England, however, combined with the strongarm measures taken by Government in the reserves began in early 1954 to take its toll on both the forest fighters and those of us in the reserves. Military posts in the reserves, usually surrounded by barbed wire and staked moats, became more difficult to attack successfully. Arms and ammunition were thus becoming more and more difficult to acquire. Again, these attacks were followed by quick Government action against the local people. Whole villages were burned out, livestock and other possessions looted by the security forces and people beaten, killed or

detained in large numbers. These actions, together with the brutal measures used to extract confessions, also caused greater numbers of Kikuyu to "cooperate" with Government. And this cooperation usually led to more arrests. The tide had begun to turn against us.

Early in January I attended a meeting about 18 miles beyond Kikuyu to make arrangements for 40 fighters who were being sent into the Aberdares. As we talked during the very early hours of the morning, one of our men came in and reported that the entire village was surrounded by security forces. They were making a house to house search for us. This was obviously the work of some Government informer.

Though we had a fairly large force of well-armed fighters we didn't want an open fight in the village, knowing that the villagers would suffer greatly after we left. We made a break for it through the thick coffee groves bordering the village. The *askari* spotted us as we approached the field and opened fire, killing one of our men and injuring another. The rest of us escaped without further trouble. For the villagers, however, things did not go so well. Government arrested every able-bodied man, woman and older boy, accusing them of participating in a Mau Mau oathing ceremony. They were taken to the police post and badly beaten during the interrogations. In the meantime their animals and property were confiscated by the security forces and all their huts burned down. Later I returned to the village to gather information and prepare a report on the actions of Government forces. I had made out several such reports, one being very much like the others. Government, failing to defeat our fighters, took its revenge on innocent men, women and children. Many believed that through its campaigns of collective punishment, communal labour and mass detention, Government was trying to exterminate the whole Kikuyu tribe.

On 7 February 1954 Government *askari* killed my father. He had been living a short distance from my village on common grazing land where people often went to pasture their animals. My father was a very old man and never active in Mau Mau. This made no difference to Government. He was looking after his few animals one day just as he always did, when *askari* came up and started beating him, not stopping until he was dead. They left him lying in the field where I found his body several days later.

Soon after my father was killed, and just before Government's massive sweep of Nairobi – which they called "Operation Anvil" – the Central Province Committee decided to move its headquarters from the city to Limuru. At this time the committee consisted of 16 members: two representatives from each of the five Kikuyu districts plus two each from the Masai, Kamba, and Rift Valley areas. As Government had arrested almost all of the old leaders, the committee chairman, Joshua Mucheru of Kiambu, was the only man on the council with any real political experience.

We prepared a hiding place for these people within one of the Limuru coffee estates. A deep hole was dug, large enough to house the committeemen and some necessary provisions, and a solid covering was made which looked just like the surrounding earth and was very difficult to detect. Supplied with food by our local fighters and supporters, the committee continued its work, which consisted primarily of gathering information from the various regions and attempting to inform the outside world of our struggle and of Government atrocities. The main leadership of the revolution had by mid-1953 shifted to the Aberdares and Mount Kenya, where thousands of our fighters were living and fighting under the command of men such as Stanley Mathenge and Dedan Kimathi.

Kilimani Camp

Very early on 3 March 1954 as I walked toward my home from our hideout in Limuru, I ran into a European district officer (D.O.). He stopped me and demanded to see my travel permit and pass allowing me to be in the European-settled area. Having no such documents, I was placed under arrest and taken to the Karura Police Post near my village.

At the post they found in their records that I was one of the people whose whereabouts were unknown and who were suspected of having gone into the forest. They questioned me wanting to know what I was doing in the settled area. I said I'd gone to look for a job as I was unemployed. The European officer didn't believe this, saying I was probably on my way to take food to the "terrorists" in the area. I denied this strongly. "If I'd been delivering food," I said, "you would have caught me carrying baskets, but when the D.O. found me I had nothing in my hands." After more questioning, which lasted till noon, I was put into one of the cells.

It was about 4 p.m. when two African CID [Criminal Investigation Division] constables came to my cell and called me out. One of these men, Corporal Nguili, was well known in the area for his brutality. He ordered me into an opening behind the building where I saw a four-foot square hole filled half-way with muddy water. They pushed me into the pit and started whipping me with long strips of hippo hide, demanding that I tell them where I was heading when caught and about my connections with Mau Mau. They whipped me for about five minutes then rested

35

and ordered me to confess. Each time they were unsatisfied with my answers and the whipping began again. This continued for almost two hours, when I fell unconscious and they were forced to abandon their game for awhile.

At midnight when I awoke, I found myself back in the cell. I was horribly thirsty and called out for someone to bring me some water. When no one came I frantically yelled again. Still no reply. I had never been so thirsty and I spent the rest of the night in misery. Early in the morning an *askari* came and opened the door of my cell. He had come to see if I was still alive and when I pleaded for water he replied by hitting me in the face with his fist. I fell back onto the floor of the cell. The door was locked and I was once more alone. I had been without water now for over 24 hours.

Another *askari* came at about 9 a.m. and after putting on hand-cuffs opened the cell door and led me outside. They sat me down and again began asking questions. Soon after they'd started, however, three new prisoners were brought in and the *askari* left me to attend to them. I watched as they beat and interrogated the prisoners, eventually taking them into the office to finish up. When they came out the four of us were loaded onto a lorry and driven to CID Headquarters, Kiambu.

Inside the barbed-wire enclosure we were ordered out of the lorry and told to keep away from the other ten prisoners in the compound. Soon a European officer came up and, after looking us over very care-fully, called me into his office. The questions started. At first the easy ones: my name, village, job, etc; then the hard ones about oaths and

Mau Mau activities. After listening to my answers he said they were all a pack of lies and, grabbing my arm, he got hold of my thumb and twisted it as far back as it would go. The pain was so great that I screamed. But he only kept tightening his grip on my thumb till I thought it would break. He said I was a terrorist and that he wouldn't believe anything else. I continually denied this and he finally released my thumb and sent me out of the office. The other three prisoners were called in one at a time and suffered the same treatment. Standing outside I heard each of them scream just as I had.

After we had all experienced this new technique of interrogation an *askari* came over and led us to a cell. Though my thumb still ached with pain I was extremely happy when we were brought some water. It was 6 p.m. before one of the guards came into the cell with a single small bowl of porridge which he put down for the four of us to share. I had only a few bites. I hadn't eaten anything for two days and was glad to have even that much.

Around midnight two new prisoners were brought into the cell. Both had been shot: one having a hole through his leg and the other an arm fractured by the impact of a bullet. They had received no treatment whatever and without even a bandage they spent the rest of the night bleeding and moaning with pain. None of us was able to sleep because of their misery. Finally at 6 a.m. an *askari* came and took them to a nearby hospital. The cell was full of their blood but we had no means of cleaning it up.

A little later we were taken from the cell handcuffed and with our ankles bound in chains. Three of us sat on the ground. The fourth was unchained and ordered to clean up the cell. With this accomplished we were put back inside. In two or three hours I was again called in for interrogation.

I gave the same answers as at Karura and the two African CID constables started beating me with clubs, resting only long enough to repeat their questions and listen to the same answers. After about two hours of this they must have decided I wouldn't change my story. Being only half-conscious, I had to be carried back to the cell. The other three men received similar treatment but only two of them returned to the cell. I believe the third man died under the blows as he has never been heard of since.

When our one bowl of porridge was brought in we were all too weak and battered to eat. All we could do was sleep. In the morning we were transferred to the adjacent police post. The four small cells were so crammed with prisoners that some of us had to be kept outside in the compound under guard.

Each cell, measuring about 12 by 12 feet, contained as many as 60 men and at night I joined them. It was so hot and cramped that none could sleep. There was no room to lie down, or even sit, and there were many desperate screams from the darkness of the cells as men panicked from lack of air and space. A few were hurt as they fell and were stepped on by the others.

There were no sanitary buckets and by morning the cell was littered with filth and the horrible sickening odor of human sweat and excrement. We were removed from our cramped quarters only long enough for it to be hosed out, but as there was still no sanitary bucket the process began all over again until the next morning. During the day, as prisoners were called out for questioning or transfer, there were times when the number of persons in the cell was greatly reduced and I could sit down. Breathing the somewhat fresher air I occasionally dozed off for a few minutes.

Only at noon, when we were given a bowl of porridge (our only meal of the day) were we allowed to leave the cell for an hour or so. We were given some water to drink but none to wash our hands or clean up. As you can see, life at the post was little short of hell itself.

On 14 March I was taken outside with three other prisoners and led over to a lorry containing the bodies of eight men. Though they were fully dressed I could see from their blood-soaked clothing that they'd all died of bullet wounds. The four of us were ordered to remove the bodies from the lorry, wash their hands and fingerprint them. They provided us with the necessary equipment and when we'd finished they ordered us to search the clothing and remove everything we found. Most of the men had some money, a watch or other valuables and we turned this over to the European officer in charge. Loading the bodies back into the lorry, we drove to the hospital morgue, handed over the dead men and were returned to our cell.

Every other day a CID officer and his *askari* entered the cell and searched us for money, cigarettes or other prohibited items and gave us a sound beating. This, I suppose, was designed to soften us up for further interrogation. Several women had been brought into the post since I arrived and three of them were heavy with children. They were kept apart from the men out on the veranda of the building.

In the weeks to follow, the three women gave birth right there on the veranda. They received no medical attention whatsoever. The other women, who delivered the babies, tore their clothing for rags and managed as best they could.

On 30 March I was taken back with seven others to CID Headquarters for more questioning. The old process was repeated but this time my story didn't elicit the usual beating. After returning to the post ten of us were removed from the cell and put into a barrack-like hut made of corrugated iron sheets. Here, though we had more room and better sanitary conditions, we were assigned the miserable job of handling the corpses which were being brought in daily.

Each day I was obliged to wash the hands, fingerprint and search the clothing of the dead. Almost all of the victims had been shot. On one occasion two women were among the corpses we had to handle. None of us felt comfortable doing this filthy work and for three weeks we spoke very little and never laughed or joked.

I was relieved when on 22 April the ten of us plus three women were transferred to CID Headquarters in the Kilimani area of Nairobi. At the gates of the camp I was shocked to see that the prisoners were all practically naked. Passing through the entrance into the compound I learned the reason. We were set upon by a swarm of *askari* who busily started removing all of our clothing and other belongings. One grabbed my shoes, another my watch and two others were fighting it out for my coat. It wasn't long before they'd taken all my garments, leaving me standing there wearing only a pair of under-shorts. With this process completed I was led into an office to be photographed.

At night we slept inside a tent in the open compound, each of us being given only a single thin blanket. I spent the better part of the night shivering from the cold which came up from the earth floor and penetrated every inch of my body. During the next few days a pattern was established which was to last throughout my three month stay at Kilimani. A small bowl of stiff porridge was served on the second day at noon but we were given nothing to eat on the third day. On the fourth day the single meal of porridge was repeated. The fifth day nothing. The sixth porridge. And so on for three long months. We were being systematically starved and after a few weeks we had all reached a very weak, half-starved condition. Added to this were the regular beatings and abuses of the camp *askari* who, having nothing better to do, spent much of their time trying to increase our miseries.

Most of these *askari* were Luo, Kamba or from some other non-Kikuyu tribe. Being jealous and fearful of Kikuyu because of our greater achievements in education, business and politics, they took advantage of their new-found authority by ordering us about and administering beatings. Had we not been defenseless they would never have dared to act so "bravely".

Late in July a detention order was issued for me and I was transferred to the Athi River detention camp about 28 miles southeast of Nairobi in the hot, dry region of Machakos. On arrival I was ordered to squat down in front of the office with 12 other prisoners who had come in the same lorry. We were told not to raise our heads or talk to anyone. After a short time a European officer came out and called ten of us into his office. The other three, being women, were led to another office.

We were thoroughly searched and our identification papers removed. Outside again, we were approached by the camp commandant, Colonel Knight, and a screening team.

"You men have two paths open to you," said the Colonel. "You can cooperate with the screening team and thus considerably shorten your periods of detention, or you can be stupid and refuse to cooperate. If you choose the latter course, the road ahead for you will be a long and hard one."

One by one we were called into the office for interrogation. When I entered I was ordered to squat down on the floor facing the eight members of the screening team. I recognized one man from Gatundu and another from Kijabe. They took turns asking me questions and after the preliminaries regarding my name, tribe, place of birth and residence, etc., the leader asked me if I'd taken the Mau Mau oath. When I replied that I hadn't he commented: "How is it you've escaped this oath to which your whole tribe has been subjected?"

He became quite angry and ordered me out of the office when I said: "You're a Kikuyu. You ought to ask yourself the same question."

The six of us who denied taking the oath were taken to Compound 3. It was reserved for detainees who refused to cooperate and were called "hardcores". Before reaching the compound we stopped at the camp store and were each issued a mat, two blankets and a tin cup and plate. It was 3 p.m. when we were finally shown our barracks within the compound. I saw a few familiar faces and an hour later, when a large number of detainees returned from work outside the camp, I spoke with several old friends.

Most of the hardcores were men who, like myself, had been active in the movement but refused to admit it before the screening team. Some, however, I believe were genuinely innocent, having never taken the oath. Government, on the assumption that all Kikuyu had taken the oath, considered as lies any statements to the contrary.

There were 180 men in the compound. Those I found when first brought in had refused to volunteer for work in the fields. There were four barracks and this latter group was kept separate in one of them. Not knowing whether the new men were willing to work or not, three of us were put in with the non-workers.

Soon after the men returned from the fields we lined up for the evening meal of *posho*, boiled beans and a cup of gruel. The food was cooked in one corner of the cemented area in front of the barracks. There was an overhang beneath which we sat and ate. When I finished I rinsed off my utensils at the lone water tap and took them to the cook who stacked them for the next meal.

At 6 p.m. a gong sounded. It was the signal for detainees to enter the barracks, which the detainees called "clubs". I put my mat in a corner of the room and sat down. The representative of the club called for quiet and ordered all newcomers to stand up. He began asking the three of us questions, most of which were designed to determine whether or not we were stooges placed in the club to gather information for Government. I was asked my name, where I was from, why and where I was arrested and how long I'd been in detention. I said I didn't know why they arrested and detained me since I'd not taken any Mau Mau oath. Thus, while the old detainees of the club were testing my loyalties through their questions, I was also fearful of their motives and careful not to reveal anything in my answers which might prove damaging.

After the questioning the spokesman went over a list of club rules and the penalties for their violation. The rules had been formulated by a committee elected from all clubs in the compound and as I was to find out later were, with slight variation, the same from compound to compound and from camp to camp. They were as follows:

1 No fighting, threats or insults between detainees were tolerated either inside or outside the compound.

2 No intercourse or sexual relations of any kind were allowed between detainees and any of the women or wives of the camp staff or with the women detainees who were being kept in a separate compound.

3 There were two sanitary buckets in the room and each had to be used for its respective purpose, with care being taken not to dirty the floor.

4 Blankets and mats had to be folded properly and stacked in the assigned corner so as to avoid collective punishment by the guards.

5 No one should dirty or urinate in the compound and spitting on the floor of the barracks or in the open area of the compound was forbidden.

6 No one was to butt into the food line and there were to be no second servings. As the number of men in the compound was known and only that number of meals served, second servings meant that some went without.

7 No one was to get close to or touch the inner barbed wire fence surrounding the compound. This might draw the fire of guards who frequently looked for just such excuses to shoot a detainee seen "trying to escape".

8 No one was ever to steal either from a fellow detainee or from any of the camp staff.

9 No one was to disobey the orders of the club leader or the decisions of the club committee regarding the allotment of necessary tasks such as removing the sanitary buckets.

10 No one should loaf in executing any work assigned him or try to avoid the more unpleasant or heavy tasks.

11 No one should ever lie to a fellow detainee or misinterpret any news he might hear or read in the newspapers.

12 No one should smoke *bhangi* or drink any alcoholic beverage inside or outside the compound.

13 Elders must always be treated with respect (never abused or mistreated) and together with disabled detainees must not be given any heavy or dirty work to do.

The penalty for violations varied with the rule. The most common punishment involved walking a specified number of times across the cement floor of the barracks on ones knees. This could be quite painful and depending on the number of laps stipulated often resulted in skinned and badly bruised knees. In addition one always suffered a certain amount of humiliation as the other detainees gathered around to watch and heckle the guilty party. For butting into the food line a person was made to go around the barracks with his hands over his head shouting a confession and repenting. Threats or abusive language to a fellow hardcore required a public apology, while smoking *bhangi* or drinking demanded a public confession plus several trips on ones knees across the barracks.

The four hardcore compounds each contained elected location, division and district committees and were joined by a central committee. Due to difficulties in communication, most cases were dealt with by lower level committees within the compound.

If a person refused to accept the decision of a committee he was usually ostracized and not spoken to for a few days. He was then easily persuaded to accept his punishment.

When the club leader finished reading the list of rules and punishments, we were asked to stand up and repeat them. No one could then claim ignorance in the future. This over, we continued to talk until the 9 p.m. whistle when, in accordance with camp regulations, we stopped talking and went to bed.

At 5 o'clock the next morning there was a pounding on the barrack's door and an *askari* shouted out his order that we move outside and line-up in twos to be counted. It took about an hour. Standing in line, I figured the aim was to determine whether anyone had escaped during the night. The count for each of the barracks was checked against that of the preceding evening. We were next ordered to form a queue for the morning meal – a single cup of hot gruel.

A European officer came into the compound half an hour later and the volunteers were led out to their places of work in the field. I waited with the other new detainees until called for further questioning. We kept separate from the hardcores who remained in the compound.

When a guard approached and asked that our sanitary buckets be brought over to the gate the club leader asked two of us to go fetch them. A lorry drove up, containing twelve detainees and four guards. They picked up the buckets and drove on to the next compound.

Soon the six of us were led to an office by two *askari* and called in one at a time for questioning. Inside I found a European officer and his *askari*. The European told me to turn over any money I had, saying I might draw on it to purchase sugar, tea or butter – the only items we were allowed to buy at the camp store. Unfortunately I had no money as the little I had with me when arrested was taken at Karura. Smoking was prohibited, he said, and being in the hardcore compound I could write home only once every three months. If I wanted anything from home I should fill out a chit and my family would be contacted. I took advantage of this offer sending a note to my wife requesting some clothing and stamps. Before leaving the office I was advised to get smart and cooperate with the screeners. Detention could be much worse, he said, than imprisonment. A man at least knew when he would be released from a prison.

It was midday by the time the six of us had been interviewed and returning to the compound we got into a queue for the noon meal of stiff porridge and boiled beans. We weren't asked to work and spent the rest of the afternoon sitting and talking in the shaded corner of the compound. When the detainees returned from the fields we had our evening meal and at 6 p.m. with the sound of the gong, I entered the barracks.

I found a meeting of the club committee going on. A member had been seen talking to one of the camp rehabilitation officers and a lengthy discussion was taking place to determine the proper punishment. The crime, though not on the list of rules, was considered serious. It placed in grave danger the other hardcores of the club. Many of these men had been together for a long time and each knew a good deal about the others. Anyone showing signs of weakening was a threat. Thus a great deal of loyalty was both felt and demanded within the hardcore groups.

Finally a decision was reached. The man was sentenced to a year and a half imprisonment. On hearing this I was somewhat surprised, but soon learned that in club language a year imprisonment meant one lap of the barracks on ones knees. As it took at least a three year sentence to make a man's knees swell badly, and hence made walking the following day difficult and painful, the guilty person had been let off lightly.

The next morning, tired of just sitting in the compound and feeling a need for some physical exercise, I decided to volunteer for work in the fields. This was, I discovered, a serious decision. I was now considered by those who refused to work as a "softcore" – a man willing to cooperate with Government. After the evening meal I was separated from the non-workers and put in with a club of volunteers within the same compound.

Early the next morning I marched out with the others to an assigned place in the field. The work consisted of preparing a field for the planting of vegetables. Clearing an area of rocks, stumps and weeds and turning the soil was hard labour, but since we'd volunteered the guards didn't push us too much. We were each given a daily assignment and it was fairly easy to finish by 4 o'clock in the afternoon. But this was not to last very long.

After about two months Colonel Knight decided to give the hard-cores a more difficult task – that of digging a moat around the camp. Having once volunteered, there was no changing ones mind; even though the conditions of work were radically altered. Under the new arrangement we were formed into work teams of six men with each group assigned the daily task of digging an eight-foot-long section of the trench, which was twelve feet wide and six feet deep. It was very difficult to complete this within the normal working hours and for the first few weeks my unit didn't finish until 7 or 8 o'clock at night.

In addition to the increased and more difficult work we were having to forego our midday meal. The camp commandant thought it best that we work straight through until the daily assignment was completed. The whole maneuver, of course, was designed to increase the pressure on us to confess. I deeply regretted my earlier decision to volunteer and many times seriously considered refusing to work. We were threatened, however, with severe disciplinary action for any such action.

Shortly after we started on the moat I was transferred to Compound 5. Each day a small number of us would be kept back from work for interrogation by the screening team. Under the pressures of hunger, forced labour and the brutal techniques of our screeners, about 50 hardcores confessed during this period. They were moved to a different compound, where their statements were recorded.

When my turn came, I entered the office determined not to change my story. It wasn't long before the screeners discovered this and began their attempts to force a confession. When the usual beatings failed they tried a new technique. I was suspended upside down at the end of a long rope tied to one of the rafters. In this position I was whipped with strips of rubber cut from old automobile tires. Along with the whipping came demands that I confess. My only words were that I'd told them the truth and could say no more. Becoming more furious each time I said this, they brought their whips down on me with increasing strength. I don't recall how long it was before I finally lost consciousness.

I remember waking up one afternoon in the camp dispensary, where I was to remain for over a month recovering from the lacerations and bruises caused by the rubber whips. I was luckier than some, however. Six of my comrades were to die from such beatings during my stay at Athi River.

Once able to work again I returned to Compound 5 and took up the old routine. Long, hard hours of work, abuse from the *askari*, poor and inadequate food; these were the common features of my daily life.

The camp rehabilitation officers gave instruction in the reading and writing of English or Swahili. Those of us in the hardcore compound, however, refused to cooperate and we set up our own classes. We were lucky to have several educated hardcores. Two of our teachers, Kimani Ruo and Henry Muli (who later confessed and cooperated and is now a Member of Legislative Council from Machakos) held B.A. degrees from Makerere College. I started learning to read and write English and continued these studies whenever possible in the other camps.

Finally one evening late in August 1955 about 200 of us were called out and told not to report for work the following day. The next morning a number of lorries arrived and we were instructed to pack our belongings. After being lined up and ordered into the trucks, all the while being cuffed about and generally mistreated by the *askari*, we were driven to the Athi River station and put on a train heading east toward Mombasa.

Mackinnon Road

I had no idea where we were going, though I'd heard of several camps near the coast. When we boarded the train each of us was handcuffed to his seat and ordered not to look out of the windows. Anyone who took his eyes off the floor or was seen glancing around received a heavy blow from one of the many guards standing about.

The following morning the train pulled into Mackinnon Road station. The camp was a quarter of a mile away and getting down I noticed two long rows of *askari*. Each man held a rifle or a baton and they formed a pathway to the camp through which we had to pass. We were ordered to hold our belongings on our heads and run through, being hit by rifle butts and night sticks over the entire distance. Holding tightly my few possessions, I ran along trying to avoid or ward off the blows of the *askari*.

By the time we arrived at the camp my head was cut and bleeding and my shoulder was swelling and full of pain. All of us suffered some injury from this senseless brutality and the assault continued as we sat ourselves in rows of five as ordered.

Shortly, a European officer came up and ordered us to remove all of our outer clothing. Those of us who weren't wearing under-shorts had to tear our pants off at the knees. When all our belongings had been taken we were led into an empty compound, still being abused by *askari* who seemed intent on causing us the maximum discomfort and misery.

The 200 of us were put into a single barrack and the door was locked from the outside. We remained here for the rest of the day and night with neither clothes, bedding nor food. I had not eaten since we boarded the train two days earlier.

Next morning the European in charge of the camp came into the compound and we were called outside the barrack to hear his instructions. "This camp," he said, "is called *Kufa na Kupona*, which means in English, 'Life and Death'. It is well named. Those who cooperate with the screening team and the rehab officers leave here alive. Those who fail to cooperate usually die at Mackinnon Road."

With this brief introduction over, the European left the compound and we were taken to the camp store and provided with the usual equipment. After washing the utensils we were served a morning meal of hot gruel.

The camp commandant returned when we'd finished and gave us further instructions. No one was to touch the barbed wire fence surrounding the compound. This might arouse suspicion and the guards had orders to shoot anyone trying to escape. We were also warned never to speak abusively to the African rehabilitation workers in the camp. These men wanted to "help us" and anyone abusing them would be dealt with severely.

These rehab-assistants were detainees who, after demonstrating their willingness to cooperate, were allowed certain liberties in the camp. They were used by Government to try and convince us of the merits of cooperation and often preached the benefits of Christianity and Moral Rearmament.

During the noon meal, which never varied from the horrible porridge and beans, I sat thinking about what the camp commandant had said and wondering if I'd ever leave Mackinnon Road alive or see my family again. I also thought about the possessions I had brought with me from Athi River, doubting very much if I would ever see them again. As it turned out, I was right. All the things my wife had sent me at Athi River – my shoes, clothes, utensils and even the box I brought them in – became the property of Mackinnon Road *askari* on that first day.

On the third day we were provided with thin cotton shorts and a shirt, the standard clothing of Mackinnon Road detainees. Throughout this first week we remained in the compound receiving treatment for our wounds and not being forced to work. When my head injury began to heal toward the end of the week I was given some light sanitary work to do around the compound, such as picking up papers and cleaning the drains.

After three weeks of recuperation and light compound work we were told that a group of home guards chosen from our home areas had been brought in to screen us. As they entered the compound I noticed that one of the men was my old enemy, Kamithi, the headman. I was surprised to see him with a man named Nganga, who had previously been a member of our locational committee and had taken and even administered the *Batuni* oath. He knew a great deal about my early activities in the movement and his presence was surely a grave threat to my life.

The 200 of us were lined up facing the home guards, who passed slowly up and down the rows of detainees, looking each man over carefully and identifying those from their home areas. Each detainee identified was classified into one of three categories. Those thought to have no record of Mau Mau activities, and toward whom the identifying home guards held no personal grudges, were classified "White". These men would be moved through a series of camps ever closer to their homes – a process known as the "pipeline" – and finally, if all went well, would be released under a restriction order confining them to their villages for six months. Another group, about whom little or nothing was known, were classified as "Grey". These were detainees whom the home guards

suspected but had no information on regarding previous Mau Mau activities. The third group, into which I was placed, contained men whose activities in Mau Mau were fairly well known or against whom a particular home guard held a personal grudge. We were classified "Black" (a term ironically fitting) and, due to the fears of the local loyalists, would not be pushed through the pipeline toward our home locations.

It was on the basis of Nganga's statement that I was classed a Black and with the others so classified, separated from the main group, beaten and put in a different compound. Inside the new compound, beatings were intensified and continued until nightfall. After this onslaught by club, rifle butt, boot and fist, I was so badly battered and bruised that the next two months found me once again in the camp dispensary recovering from the wounds so senselessly and brutally inflicted by Government's "good boys".

Though I still suffer constant pain in the side, where several of my ribs were kicked in by one of the guards, I consider myself lucky to have survived at all. Nine of my comrades died from these beatings – some right away, others after being taken to the dispensary.

When able to move about I was put back in the compound with other Blacks. For the next month life was a virtual hell. The 120 of us were put on half-rations, receiving food only every other day. For any minor infraction of the rules these already slender rations would be cut severely, and on one occasion we went without food for 7 days. We were so weak when food was finally brought in that we had to be spoon-fed by other detainees. Mackinnon Road is about 85 miles from the coast and the hot, arid climate of this semi-desert region added greatly to our miseries.

Ill treatment by the guards and beatings continued – on the whim of the camp commandant or as punishment for some petty violation of the rules – despite our generally weakened condition. Usually the guards would separate out those men in a really grave condition and dispense their justice only to those of us considered "relatively healthy".

As in the other camps, we elected a committee and a spokesman. Our rules were similar to those at Athi River, but under prevailing conditions few men received disciplinary punishment. Mwaura, our committee spokesman, frequently voiced our complaints to the camp commandant, but with little or no effect. Only when someone died from a beating or as a result of some disease easily contracted while in a weakened condition, did the treatment and food improve for a short time.

Within the compound we were assigned various jobs such as cooking, washing the dishes and sweeping up the open area. Though not regularly forced to work long hours outside the camp as at Athi River, we were sometimes taken out and made to dig useless holes in the sand which we were later ordered to fill up.

After four miserable months at Mackinnon Road 80 of us who had failed to confess were taken by truck to Manyani, a camp 50 or 60 miles closer to Nairobi but still in the hot, dry region of the Taita district. Since the camp was located in a tsetse fly area we were all forced on arrival to go through a deep trough of water, similar to a cattle dip, which supposedly contained some medicine. I hadn't realized how deep the water was until suddenly I was completely submerged. On the other side we were lined up and led into Compound 6. As was customary with new prisoners, we were abused and given introductory beatings.

Manyani

Manyani is a large camp containing 30 compounds and, during my stay, about 26,000 detainees. There were 280 of us in Compound 6, which was reserved for "Blacks" or hardcores who refused to cooperate through useful confessions. After being assigned to barracks and issued the usual camp equipment, I had a chance to talk to several old friends from Athi River. I noticed that there were no mats in the barracks and soon learned that Manyani hardcores were made to sleep on the floor with only two blankets for bedding. I was introduced to the club committee and leader, told the rules and spent the rest of the evening learning from friends about the peculiarities and special conditions of life at Manyani.

Those of us in Compound 6 were kept locked up within the barracks except for sanitary duties and one hour of forced running around the compound. One day, after I'd been at Manyani for six or eight weeks, my name was announced over the loudspeaker. Soon an *askari* came, unlocked the bolted door and led me to the office of the Special Branch officer. It so happened that my name was mentioned in the confession of another detainee and I was wanted for further questioning.

In the office I found two European officers and three African *askari*. I was told to sit down on the floor. One of the *askari* asked me if I'd ever taken a Mau Mau oath and when I gave my usual "no" answer the *askari* standing behind me kicked me sharply in the middle of the back. As I lunged forward from the blow one of the European officers hit me in the face with his fist. This started an hour-long beating with brief intervals for the same old questions and answers. When finally convinced I wasn't going to change my story, they ordered me out of the office. Instead of being returned to the compound, however, I was put in a small cell containing two other prisoners.

There was only one small, barred window which let a little light and air into an otherwise dark and musty room. On the floor was a single sanitary bucket and nothing more. We were given neither mats nor bedding, and to keep from freezing during the night and early morning hours the three of us slept huddled closely together, trying to gain a little warmth from one another.

I was kept in this cell for four days with no food and very little water. On the fifth day we were given the normal camp meals and the following morning I was taken to the office and confronted by the same interrogators.

"Are you ready to give us a truthful confession?" asked one of the Europeans.

"What I've told you," I said, "is the truth. Do you think I'd continue suffering like this if it weren't?"

They didn't believe me and just kept asking the same questions in different words. Finally, and with no beating this time, I was sent out and led to another cell where I was kept in solitary confinement for four days. The guards were instructed not to beat me but also not to provide any blankets or water. For food I was given a bowl of stiff porridge each day.

On the afternoon of the fourth day I was called again to the Special Branch office. The old process was repeated, with the same questions and answers and no beating. When it was over I was taken to Compound 5, containing men who'd refused to confess or whose confessions were rejected. My ankles were chained together like those of the other 190 hardcores. Movement was difficult and painful and soon my ankles were sore and irritated from the heavy manacles I was forced to drag along wherever I went. Food was served every other day and consisted of a single meal of porridge and beans. As another calculated punishment our sanitary buckets were not removed till late in the afternoon and a sickening stench pervaded the barracks all the time.

Several people not directly connected with the camp – priests, civil servants and high ranking rehabilitation officers – were brought in to try to convince us of the benefits of an honest confession. They all stressed the point that cooperation with Government was necessary to our very survival and pleaded with us to repent and make a fresh start in life. All of these fine words, however, had little effect on us and to my knowledge none of the hardcores was moved closer to confession by their arguments.

Though we had an elected committee spokesman in the compound, the harsh conditions of life made enforcement of the rules difficult. The main duty of the leader was to present our grievances to the camp commandant and other camp officials. There were not many cases in which this brought results, but the occasional successes kept us trying.

I must, at this point, mention one Health Inspector who was sent to Manyani after several reports had reached Central Government officials and the press about conditions in the camp. During my six years in Kenya's detention camps this man was the only European I came across who was genuinely sympathetic and fair-minded. He had a deep sense of duty and did his best to improve sanitary conditions and protest against the inadequate food being given the detainees. All of us liked him, though his actions on our behalf brought him nothing but scorn and dislike from the camp officials.

Despite this man's efforts conditions remained poor. Beatings were fewer but those who received injuries were given neither medicine nor medical care. Due to infections resulting from untreated wounds three prisoners died during my four months in chains in Compound 5.

Death at Manyani surprised no one. An early typhoid epidemic had taken many lives and an even greater number of detainees met their death through beatings, starvation or avoidable diseases. Government tried to cover up its brutalities by claiming that these men also died of typhoid, but no one who has been detained at Manyani will ever believe this.

Manyani was a place of great heat during the day, cold nights and millions of insects. Many of us in Compound 5 had been dispossessed of our blankets and were forced by the desert's early morning cold to sleep bundled together on the cement floor. Sand was always blown or tracked into the barracks during the heat of the day and at night we would brush it up, forming little walls of sand and exposing the warmed cement. Sleeping two or three men in each small hollow we tried to protect ourselves from the worst extremes of cold. This didn't save us, however, from the mosquitoes, scorpions and other insects whose bites caused constant discomfort. The scorpion bite is poisonous and had to be treated. As soon as someone was bitten he would cut open the skin and rub in a little snuff, which somehow managed to remove the worst effects of the poison. None of us was lucky enough to avoid this treatment for long.

All of us were classified or re-classified at Manyani and once more I was deemed a "Black". In accordance with Government's pipeline process many of those classified "White", or the middle category "Z", were moved to camps closer to their homes. Those of us classified "Black", however, were destined to even remoter areas of Kenya than Manyani.

Lodwar

On the morning of 30 June 1956, after six long months at Manyani, I was put on the train for Nairobi with 60 others. We arrived late in the evening after a 250 mile trip and spent the night in the large Nairobi dispersal camp. The next day we were taken to Eastleigh Airport and put in two planes. After taking off we headed toward the Northern Frontier and a camp named Lodwar, 300 miles from Nairobi in the land of the Turkana tribesmen.

We covered the distance in a few hours, landed on the small airstrip and were led to the D.O.'s office. Here, we were surrounded by Turkana whom the D.O. had called in to have a look at the "Kikuyu cannibals" – a fiction invented to prevent the local people from befriending us. They inspected us closely and because of what they'd been told, made several threatening gestures. The D.O. warned us that anyone who tried to escape would end up in the hands of a Turkana band and be killed. I'm sure these men would have done away with us right there on the spot if given the word by the D.O.

The landing strip, administrative offices and detention camp were located very close to one another and after this brief meeting with the D.O. and his Turkana, we were led in two columns toward the camp. With our ankles still chained, this was a slow, painful trip made worse by the great afternoon heat of the northern desert.

56

Unlike the other camps, Lodwar was administered by the local D.O. Shortly, he came over and said a few words. "I know you're a bad lot of men," he said, "but you're a long, long way from home here at Lodwar. You won't be abused or mistreated as long as you obey the camp rules, do the work demanded of you and live peacefully among yourselves."

It was about 3 p.m. when he left. A guard was ordered to remove our ankle chains and show us the camp shower where we could wash. An hour later the evening meal was served and to my great surprise it contained a portion of meat. Large numbers of cattle and sheep are herded by the Turkana and I imagine it was cheaper for Government to feed us meat than to ship up large quantities of grain from the southern regions. Nonetheless, it was good to taste the flavor of beef again after more than two years of nothing but gruel, stiff porridge and boiled beans. During my stay at Lodwar meat constituted the major part of our diet.

We all went to sleep early that first night being very tired from the long, two day trip. Next morning the D.O. came by again, telling us we'd be given four days to rest and regain some strength before starting to work in the rock quarry, cutting stone for the construction of new buildings in the administrative area.

Lodwar had previously served as a prison for convicted Mau Mau prisoners. Now it was just another detention camp. When we arrived there were already 100 men in the camp but the 60 of us were kept in a separate compound. Before the four day rest period was over we elected a committee and spokesman, and when the D.O. came to see us our representative told him our decision and some of our fears.

"We are all willing," he said, "to cooperate with you regarding work, the camp rules and keeping at peace amongst ourselves. But since the 60 of us have always maintained our innocence concerning Mau Mau and its oath, we fear that here at Lodwar as in the other camps we'll be interrogated and punished for failing to give acceptable confessions to the screeners."

The D.O. sought to reassure us: "I'm not concerned with whether you've taken the oath or not. All I care about is your willingness to cooperate and perform the necessary work of the camp." He went on to say that there would be no beatings or other punishment as long as we did what we were told. Our leader expressed his appreciation for this guarantee and the meeting ended.

The 100 detainees in the other compounds were all cooperating in the quarry work but shortly after our arrival a new group of 240 detainees, who considered themselves political prisoners, were brought to Lodwar and refused to work, claiming that only convicted criminals could legally be forced to work while serving their sentences. According to the Geneva Convention, they said, political prisoners could not be made to work against their will. The D.O. told them that regardless of the Geneva Convention a new Kenya law gave him legal power to put all detainees to work and, if they refused, to use all the power at his command to bring about their cooperation. "I'm not going to play games with you," he said, "either you work or you'll die trying not to."

The new men were put into a separate compound and given a few days to make up their minds. After much discussion they finally decided to do the work required but to passively resist all other forms of cooperation. They were given the difficult work of chipping quarry stones and carrying them to the D.O.'s office while the rest of us were assigned the lighter tasks in the quarry and the jobs of collecting firewood, cooking, and cleaning up the camp. The new men at first considered us "softcores" and had nothing to do with us. As time went on, however, our relationship improved.

Lodwar was in many ways a real pleasure compared to the other camps I'd been in. Not only was the food considerably better, but there were no beatings, no chains and no mistreatment by the guards as long as we did our work and obeyed the rules. We were also freer in another sense. All of the camp *askari* and staff were Turkana and didn't understand a word of Kikuyu. We could thus speak quite openly among ourselves without any fear of being overheard and reported. While working we sang many songs which, had we been at Manyani or Mackinnon Road, would have brought us severe punishment. These songs, two of which I have recorded below, did much to boost our morale and increase our feelings of brotherhood and unity.

This first song expresses our feelings toward Jomo Kenyatta and our attitude toward both the European and the African loyalists:

O God, we who used to carry a shield, a spear and a sword
Are no longer allowed by the foreigners to have them.
Our enemies cannot sleep
For thinking how they can kill
Our great leader, Kenyatta

But they will never succeed.
O God, we used to carry a shield, a spear and a *simi*
Now the foreigners have taken all these away
You, God, know where they were kept
O God, take them and beat our enemies with them.
Warrior of Kikuyu, awake
Ye who cannot see that the old man grows older
If you sleep the foreigners will seize our wealth
And then what will the children of Mumbi feed on?
In the last fifty-two years
All have seen what the foreigners have done
And you, you foolish men, have taken money
And you are selling your country for money
You, foolish men, go and take a thousand shillings
And when you finish that, what will you get?
And now I tell you, friends of my age-group
You have been shown the wrong way in the daytime
By a foreigner who will desert us tomorrow.
You cannot build on the work of a foreigner
His word should be drowned in deep waters by God
His rule should be brought to an end
In this country of ours, Kenya
Let the black people govern themselves alone."

A second song, which was very popular, was called Song of Africa and
went like this:

God gave to the black people
This land of Africa
Praise the God who dwells in the high places
For his blessings

Chorus
We will continue in our praises
Of the land of Africa
From East to West
From North to South
After much suffering
The country of Egypt
Was delivered from bondage
And received its freedom

Chorus
Abyssinia saw the light
Shining down from the North
Her people struggled mightily
And rescued themselves from the mire

Chorus
Now we do loudly rejoice
To hear the story of Ghana
The flag of Great Britain
Has been lowered for all time there

Chorus
If you look around the whole of Kenya
It is only a river of blood
For we have our one single purpose
To lay hold of Kenya's freedom

Chorus
Listen to the sobbing
Of our brothers in South Africa
Where they are being tormented
By the tribe of the Boers

Chorus
We shall greatly rejoice
In the unity of all the black people
Let us create in our unity
A United States of all Africa."

After about three months at Lodwar I was growing accustomed to the horrible weather and had regained the strength and health I'd lost at Athi River, Mackinnon Road and Manyani. Though the desert heat was excessive and sand got into everything, including the food, we were provided with sandals and light clothing and were not overworked.

Classes were set up within the compound and I was again trying to learn some English. During the late afternoon, inside the barracks, some of the more educated detainees gave instruction in English and a few other subjects to those who were interested. Wherever conditions allowed, this kind of instruction was carried out. Among "hardcores", however, it was often the case that we had no educated man to teach us in a particular compound or barracks. Few educated detainees remained hardcore for very long in the tough camps. However, we greatly respected those who did, not only for their efforts to educate us but because they sometimes expressed our grievances through letters smuggled out through friendly guards to important people in Kenya and England. Often, as in the case of Josiah Mwangi at Manyani, these men were severely punished for their efforts to inform the outside world about conditions in the camps.

My teacher at this time was a very clever man though he had only a high school education. He was called "Njoroge the D.O." because of his exploits before being arrested and detained. For over two years Njoroge posed as a D.O. and loyalist while secretly assisting Mau Mau. He gained the confidence of local Government officials by repeatedly bringing poll tax evaders and Mau Mau suspects into the police post. Government didn't know that most of the people he brought in were loyalists and that he escorted fighters into the forests and made deliveries of arms and ammunition to the forest leaders. He did a very good job for our people until his game was discovered in 1955.

Everything went well at Lodwar until the end of the fourth month. A screening team was sent up from Nairobi made up of the same men I had encountered at Athi River. They asked me if I had any desire to see my wife and children again or return to my own country. If I did, the shortcut to achieving these ends was to confess my Mau Mau activities. I replied, "If you want the truth, I can only repeat the statement I gave you at Athi River. I have never taken a Mau Mau oath and know nothing about the activities of that organization." The screeners were considerably softer than they'd been earlier. They just recorded my statement and sent me out of the office. For a change my answers didn't provoke the usual beatings. Perhaps it was because our forest fighters, by the end of 1956, were no longer a military threat to the colonial government.

In early December 1956 after almost six months at Lodwar, by far the best camp I was detained in, 45 of us were flown to Nairobi, loaded into lorries and driven to Marigat, a camp near Lake Baringo in the Rift Valley. It was a 25-hour journey by road and we arrived late at night.

Rift Valley Camps

The camp was located in the region of the Njemps people who, like the Masai, carry on a pastoral form of life. It contained about 300 detainees, all of whom had confessed. Here the detainees were allowed a certain amount of freedom. Paid 25s. a month, they had to provide their own clothing, cooking utensils and other household items. They were not closely guarded or supervised while at work in the fields and could go to the shops in Marigat township.

The 45 of us from Lodwar had neither money nor the necessary personal belongings for life at Marigat. When the camp commandant spoke to us that first morning, he said everyone in the camp was self-supporting. Government provided nothing save a small *posho* allotment. When one of our men informed him that we'd brought nothing from Lodwar and had no money, he said he was sure the other detainees were willing to help us through the first month. Continuing, he told us that Marigat contained only good men. Since we were sent there we must have proven our worth to Government. There was a rehabilitation officer at the camp and anyone wishing to have an interview could sign the register indicating he would not work that day. This was not compulsory, however, as no one at Marigat was interrogated or forced to confess.

We were given a two-day rest before starting work and inoculated against typhoid and other diseases prevalent in the area. Luckily I met two men from my sub-location and they offered to take me in and help me through the first month. There were no barracks. Detainees lived in huts large enough to house five or six people. The camp area was surrounded by barbed wire and a deep moat and had only one guarded gate. We were given permission to visit Marigat town after our day's work was completed – having to return by 11 p.m.

Starting work on the third day, I noticed very few guards. It wouldn't have been difficult to escape, though I never seriously considered trying. In the fields we prepared irrigation canals for water to flow through into experimental fields of maize, sugar cane, bananas, ground nuts and rice – crops not usually grown in this region.

Rising at 4 in the morning, we worked till 11 a.m., then returned to camp for lunch. The afternoon work was from 12:30 until 3 p.m. Though these were long hours I considered Marigat a good camp. There were no beatings or interrogation and I enjoyed some freedom of movement. I also appreciated not having to live in crowded barracks. The detainees who had been at Marigat for some time usually saved enough for a few chickens and sheep and cultivated small *shambas* of maize and vegatables. For newcomers like myself the *posho* provided by Government – plus the generosity of my friends – had to do until I was in a position to buy additional supplies.

In January I received my first token-money payment and life became a little easier. I bought some provisions at the local shop and my diet improved considerably. After a time I began to reconsider the value of continuing my resistance to confession. The treatment I received at Lodwar and now at Marigat made me wonder whether a minimum confession might not increase my chances of release or at least insure continued placement in the "good" camps. It would be easy enough to make an appointment with the rehab officer and confess to taking the oath. I could give a few details of my Mau Mau activities which would neither endanger me nor implicate anyone else. The confession wouldn't be forced and I could give just as much or little information as I wanted and not be tortured for more.

I can't say whether I'd have confessed or not, for while still in the process of making up my mind the decision was made for me.

One evening late in June 1957 an announcement came over the loudspeaker that the 45 of us who had arrived in December were not to report for work the following day. We were lined up in front of the office and paid the token-money due us, being told to pack our belongings and be ready to move to our home areas the next morning. Wanting to spend my 45s. in camp money before leaving I went to the shop and purchased a pair of pants, an undershirt, two plates and a cup and a small packing box.

Eagerly awaiting the lorries I felt a confidence, slightly dampened by doubt, that I was at last going home. During a sleepless night two lorries drove up and I shared an unbelieving excitement with the others. Early in the morning we were called out singly by name to board the trucks. When all of us were on we headed south toward Nairobi. Approaching the city after a long and tiring ride, however, my dreams were quickly shattered. Instead of turning onto the Kiambu road the two trucks continued along the south-bound road leading, I feared, to Athi River.

It was mid-afternoon when we finally arrived at Athi River detention camp. A message had been sent ahead informing the camp commandant and he was awaiting us at the entrance with 20 rehab men, a screening team and 40 or so guards.

Getting off the lorries we were told to form ranks of five and the *askari* began grabbing our belongings. Colonel Knight was gone and the new camp commandant sharply ordered his men to leave our things alone and return what they'd already taken. After this reprimand he told them to search us for cigarettes, money or other prohibited items but not to remove the token-money we might have brought from Marigat.

With the search over, the camp commandant left and we were marched toward Compound 7 being knocked about and generally mistreated by the *askari* on the way. Hearing the commotion the commandant rushed from his office and ordered the guards in no uncertain terms to stop abusing us.

Ordered into one of the compound barracks we were shown where to put our things and then taken to the camp store to get the usual two blankets and utensils. I was assigned identification number 3303.

After the evening meal I went right to sleep. Next morning they were already calling us out by number for interrogation. Early on the fourth day 3303 rang out over the loudspeaker and I got into a queue awaiting interrogation.

There were six screening teams and I was led into the office of team number 1. I recognized the five men inside, two of whom were converted ex-detainees. The leader, a man from my location, knew me long before the Emergency was declared. On seeing me they started to chuckle and the leader mockingly asked if I'd not been there before. I must really like Athi River, he said, to have returned so soon. He then asked in a more serious tone where I'd hidden my firearms, how many loyalists or 'turn-coat' Mau Maus I'd killed and what oaths I'd taken. I replied asking if Government had any real evidence regarding the two capital charges: murder and the possession of firearms. If they did I wanted to know about it before discussing the matter of oaths. He didn't answer my question; instead, he turned to one of the other screeners and said: "This Karigo Muchai is a very bad man. Take him into the back room and give him a chance to think things over."

I soon discovered that what they had in mind was forced thinking. In their efforts to extract a confession they used rubber tire whips. The beating lasted for over half an hour and whenever I tried to scream out a hand was clasped over my mouth. Finally I was taken back to the office and asked if having thought things over I was ready to answer some questions.

I was too angry to speak and one of the screeners "bravely" slapped my face. The leader ordered me returned to the compound. I was suffering so much from the pain of the whipping that I crawled between my blankets and slept, passing up the noon and evening meals and not arising till the following morning.

For the next few weeks I remained unmolested in the compound. Every time the loudspeaker blurted out a number I stiffened, fearing it might be my turn again. It took three weeks to interrogate the 45 of us from Marigat and out of this number only one man confessed. The other 43 had, like myself, been whipped and beated but persisted in their refusal to confess or give the screening teams the information they wanted. One of my comrades, a man from Kithiga named Mungai, was blinded in one eye during the whipping.

There were six barracks in Compound 7 but five of them were empty. The 44 of us were to be kept separate from the other detainees. We elected a spokesman, Mr. Njenga from Fort Hall, and he made several protests to the camp commandant about the treatment we'd suffered at the hands of the screeners. It did little good, however, as these men were apparently acting on instructions, or at least with the consent of Government.

Njenga also allocated the routine sanitation jobs in the compound and barracks and presided over meetings. We spoke at great length about the man who confessed and had been removed from our compound.

We had all been together for some time now and each man knew quite a bit about the others. Those of us who were close to the confesser feared he might give the screeners damaging information about our pre-arrest Mau Mau activities. There was nothing we could do, but it helped to talk things over.

Three times a week all the detainees were gathered together in the main compound. Here we were addressed by screening team leaders and rehab officers – advised over and over again about the merits of confession, cooperation and Christianity and told of the good work being done by the rehabilitation team.

The 44 of us were kept separate at the meetings from the main body of detainees and on one occasion, shortly after our ex-comrade's confession, the speaker asked if anyone knew anything about us. Everyone should stand and speak his mind, he said, as this made confession easier for hardcores still not convinced about the merits of cooperation. This technique was practiced in almost all the camps. Government tried to use the information and persuasion of softcores at public meetings to gain confessions from the hardcores. It was a sort of collective pressure.

A man from my village named Kiruku stood and said he'd seen me at a sub-location meeting discussion Mau Mau activities. Kiruku had confessed some time earlier and probably implicated my in his statement. I rose before he'd finished and asked him to tell us the kind of meeting it was, what sort of activities were discussed and what I had said or done. We were both ordered to sit down and soon an *askari* came over and took me to one of the small cells.

These "cells" were actually small rooms within one of the compounds. There were 12 prisoners when I arrived and each of us was isolated within one of the tiny, dark rooms. No mat was provided and I slept on the cement floor wrapped in a single blanket. I could see and speak to the other prisoners only during meal time – each day at 4 p.m. After two weeks of this solitary confinement I was again called before the screening team.

The leader reminded me of what Kiruku had said and asked me what kind of meeting it was and what I was doing there. "If Kiruku has anything to say about me," I replied, "he should be called in and made to confront me with it personally. After all, he's admitted being at the meeting and should know all about it. As for myself, I don't recall any such meeting."

They agreed and Kiruku was called to the office. He was asked to describe in detail the meeting he claimed to have seen me at. "It was a sub-location meeting of Mau Mau," he responded, "at which plans were being discussed regarding the formation of a patrol of fighters. These komereras were to patrol the sub-location at night, investigating Government activities, eliminating loyalists on instruction from the district committee, and fighting if necessary."

After a few questions Kiruku continued: "While the meeting was in progress Karigo entered the hut, stayed for a while and then left." The screening team leader wanted to know if Karuku thought I had heard what was being discussed and he replied that I had. He was then asked if I had taken the Mau Mau oath.

"I've never seen Karigo at an oathing ceremony." he said, "but there were rumors he was a location committee member. He would never have been allowed into the meeting had he not taken the oath and been a member of Mau Mau."

At this point I asked Kiruku if I said anything when I entered the hut where the meeting was being held. He said I hadn't. The sub-location leader was there, he said, and was conducting the meeting. Addressing myself to the screening leader I said, "Don't you think that if I were attending this meeting as a location committee member I would have led the discussion, or at least exchanged a few words with the sub-location chairman?" When no one replied I continued, "I'm beginning to recall the incident we're discussing. One evening I entered a hut in the village looking for a friend. I noticed a number of people sitting around in silence. As it was dark I remained a few minutes trying to see whether my friend was there. Finally I decided he wasn't and left. I recall being surprised by the silence in the hut but as you can see I had no idea that this was some sort of meeting."

Kiruku and I were ordered out of the office. The screeners wanted to discuss the matter in private. About 15 minutes later Kiruku was called back. I don't know what they discussed in my absence but a short time later they called me in too.

Starting out pleasantly enough they tried to convince me of the benefits of confessing. Even if I hadn't taken the oath myself, they said, I must know something about the activities of Mau Mau in my area. "You have many experts on these matters," I said, "including many detainees who have already confessed their Mau Mau activities. I don't see how the little hearsay knowledge I have can help you and I refuse to invent stories about Mau Mau just to please you."

This seemed to anger the team leader and he asked if I had no concern for my family or ever wanted to return to my village. "Why don't you tell us the truth," he said, "and go home to your wife and children?"

"I have great concern for my family but I won't confess to lies simply to gain my release!"

"You deserve all the beatings you've gotten!" he said, "and soon you'll be sent to a place built especially for bad ones like yourself." I was ordered out of the office.

I wasn't taken back to the cell but instead to Compound 10 where my 43 comrades had been moved. My old friends were glad to see me and relieved to learn that I'd not confessed. The following morning after a breakfast of hot gruel we were taken to the rock quarry and began our day's work. It was very early in the morning when we started. The skies were just beginning to lighten. Each of us had to crush a ton of rock, just enough to fill a large oil drum. This work began when I was in the isolation cell and the others already knew their task. Those who worked hard and fast could fill their drum by 4 p.m. and return to the compound. Many, however, didn't finish till 7 p.m. and there were usually a few who hadn't completed their task even by that time. On several occasions during the first week, when I failed to finish by 7 p.m., my drum and enough rock to fill it were loaded into a lorry and taken into the compound. Here under guard I worked till 9 or 10 p.m., finally filling my drum to the top. After the first few days my hands became so bruised and calloused that I actually slowed down instead of getting faster.

Only when we'd completed our daily assignment were we given our second meal of the day. With breakfast gruel served before 4 a.m. and no lunch, I was extremely hungry by late afternoon and when I'd completed my work in the evening I was starving but almost too exhausted to eat. After a few weeks we decided to assist our slower members so that we could all leave the quarry and return to the compound together. In two months my hands had toughened and I could finish the work as early as most.

We were joined in the quarry by about 40 new detainees whose confessions had been rejected. They were put in our compound but within a short time more than half gave adequate confessions and were moved out. While there were no ill feelings between ourselves and the new men, the fact that they'd confessed made us unwilling to take them into our confidence or speak openly in their presence.

Hola

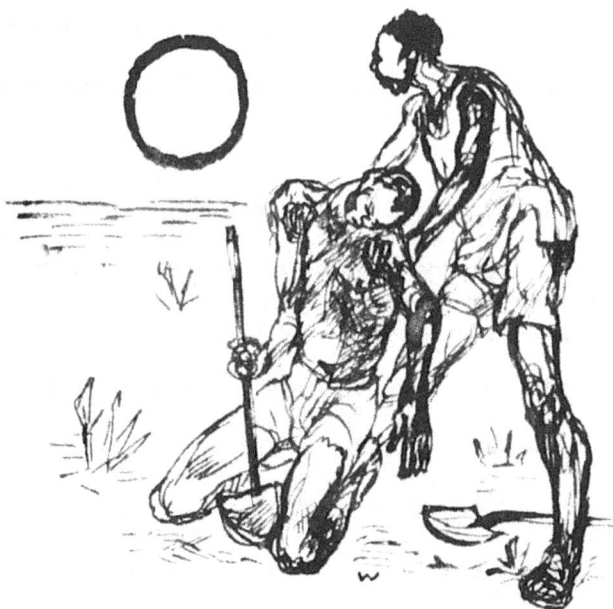

With the addition of 20 hardcores from the new group our number rose to 64. We continued in the established routine until one morning early in October 1957 when we were told to remain in the compound. Two nights later we were awakened at 2 a.m. and told to pack our belongings. After being lined up and counted we left Athi River before sunrise in three lorries. I didn't know it at the time but we were heading toward Hola. Each of us was given a loaf of bread and half a pound of dried meat for the long journey. As usual we were ordered not to look around and were guarded closely by five *askari*.

The 325 mile trip took us northward through Nairobi then east to Mwingi and Garissa and finally southward along the Tana River to Hola. About 60 miles from the Indian Ocean in Pokomo country, Hola is situated in the hot, mosquito-infested desert of the Tana River Valley. The rainfall is very slight in this region and most of the Pokomo are settled in small villages along the flood plains where they cultivate small *shambas*. Every few miles we would pass through one of these villages and having never seen or heard of these people before, I stole many glances trying to see what they looked like and how they lived.

During the early part of the trip we ran into heavy rains and several times had to get out and push the lorry out of a ditch on to the swampy road. Arriving at midnight 22 hours after we'd left Athi River, we were met at the entrance by the European in charge of the camp. There was no electricity and he was accompanied by several *askari* holding hurricane lanterns. We were led into a part of the camp still under construction. The barbed wire enclosure was not yet erected though several watch towers could be seen around the perimeter. We were told that escape was easy but useless as the wild *"askari"* in the bush, the faithful lions, always took good care of anyone walking through their territory at night.

The barracks were very small measuring about 12 by 15 feet and we were locked in for the night in groups of six or eight without being searched. The camp commandant arrived at 8 o'clock in the morning and told us to wash all our clothing. He said he knew we were tired from the long trip and that he would return in two days to talk with us.

Though not subjected to beatings, we suffered greatly from the extreme heat and mosquitoes those first few days. When the camp commandant returned he said he'd studied our files and discovered that many of us had refused to confess our Mau Mau activities at the other camps. This didn't bother him, he said. Hola was an exile camp and the men sent there wouldn't be leaving for many years, if at all. We were once more warned against the dangers of trying to escape and told that we would begin work the next day.

On the following morning we were shown a piece of land about four acres in extent and told that it was our job to clear and level it for a new village. We were paired-up and each two-man team was assigned a certain area to be cleared during the day. This piece-work was difficult to complete before dark and most of us didn't finish until 7 or 8 o'clock at night. The work also contained an element of danger. One of the plants we were uprooting in the field contained a poisonous liquid which, if it got into the blood through an open cut, caused a great deal of swelling and pain. One day during the first week as I wiped the sweat off my brow with my forearm, I accidentally got some of this liquid in my eye. I spent the next several days in the camp dispensary receiving treatment and waiting for the swelling and pain to subside.

The afternoon desert heat was extremely oppressive. It was a real struggle just to keep from collapsing while working under the blinding sun. Soon after we'd completed clearing the village site a medical officer arrived to inspect the camp. He reported that the afternoon work was beginning to have a serious effect on the detainees' health and suggested that a new work schedule be arranged. The camp commandant, noting our generally weak physical condition, agreed with this advice and established new working hours. We were to start at 4 a.m., two hours earlier than usual, and continue working straight through the cooler morning and early afternoon hours until our daily assignment was completed. This turned out to be anywhere from noon to 2 p.m. We would then return to the camp for lunch and have the rest of the afternoon off.

As compensation for the work we were paid 30s. a month in token-money. With the site cleared we began the job of erecting 22 large barracks to house the detainees. This took us 10 weeks after which, though the new camp was not quite finished, we were transferred to work on the irrigation scheme. Government was attempting to bring a large area of desert land under cultivation by bringing in water from the Tana River through a network of canals and irrigation ditches.

Each two-man work team had to dig a section of the main canal four feet long, ten feet wide and two and a half feet deep every day. While some of us worked on the main canals others were digging the smaller irrigation ditches or preparing the fields for planting.

During my third month at Hola, in January 1958, we were told that a D.O. and some tribal police were coming to stay at the camp. We had to build 25 houses for these people and were told that we would be under the D.O.'s charge for the remainder of our stay. There were then about 400 of us at Hola – a number which was soon to swell to over 2,000 – and we had all been previously classified as "Blacks". It took us less than a week to finish erecting the buildings for the new staff and a few days later the D.O. and his men arrived.

For several weeks the D.O. went about his business without coming to see or speak to us. Finally at the beginning of the fourth week he called a meeting of all the detainees to inform us of a new camp plan. The detainees who were to live in the new village we had constructed would be completely under his jurisdiction. Those who chose to stay in this camp, to be called the "Open Camp", would no longer be paid in token-money. They would receive a salary of 30s. a month in regular currency which could be spent as they wished at the Arab *dukas* (shops) in nearby Hola trading center. Later when a new and larger village had been built these men would be allowed to bring their wives, dependents and children under 13 to Hola to live with them. A certain amount of freedom would be given these men. They would not be closely supervised in their work and could move around within a one-mile radius of the camp, having only to do their jobs and be present for morning and evening roll call. It was up to us, he said, whether we wanted to remain in the old "Closed Camp" administered by the Superintendent of Prisons or volunteer for the Open Camp under his jurisdiction. He would come back later and record our decisions.

I thought about the choice we were given very carefully and talked about it with other detainees. Finally I decided on the Open Camp. Since I didn't know how long I would be at Hola, it seemed wise to accept the best living conditions offered in the situation. When the D.O. returned in four days I was one of the 127 men, out of over 800, who volunteered for the Open Camp. Most of those who refused did so out of misunderstanding. They thought as long as they remained within the barbed wire of the Closed Camp that they would be considered "detainees" rather than "exiles" and retain a chance of some day being released and sent home. Their mistake was to think that volunteers for the Open Camp were accepting permanent exile. In fact all of us were legally classed as exiles and it made no difference which camp we were in.

The following morning lorries arrived to take our belongings and bedding to the new camp. We were all given beds to reduce the chances of scorpion bites. These insects, together with mosquitoes and a host of others, were everywhere at Hola and presented a constant source of annoyance and irritation.

On the first day we elected a committee of 24 and a spokesman. We also elected cooks and allocated the various jobs involved in cleaning up and maintaining the camp. Next morning after the usual breakfast we started off toward the fields and our respective places of work, this time without the usual escort of armed guards. Since our assignments had not been changed, however, we found ourselves working alongside the men of the Closed Camp under the same conditions of supervision.

After two weeks our spokesman suggested to the D.O. that we be separated from the others as we had been told that volunteers for the new camp would not be forced to work under close supervision. Our purpose in making this request was not to avoid working with comrades in the Closed Camp, but to avoid the abuses of *askari* who grew restless and mean standing out in the fields watching us work.

The D.O. agreed and the next day we were sent to a different part of the scheme where we worked alone with only a few guards scattered around the perimeter of the area.

Those in the Closed Camp, seeing that we were having an easier time and enjoying much more freedom of movement than they were, began volunteering for the Open Camp in growing numbers. Within two months there were over 600 of us. We were divided into two groups, one of which continued to work on the irrigation scheme while the other began constructing houses for a new village for detainees planning to bring in their families.

I continued working on the scheme. Though I'd volunteered for the Open Camp I never seriously considered bringing my family to live with me at Hola. As much as I wanted to see them I didn't want to subject them to the heat and insects of this desert hell.

Most of the old rules carried over to the Open Camp. Poor food continued to be provided by Government and all of us had to be back at the camp by 6 p.m. for roll call and the evening meal. Nevertheless once our daily piece-work assignment was completed we were free to engage in certain other activities. I continued classes in English and began learning the tinsmith craft. Many took up other crafts such as blacksmithing and carpentry. When I got good enough I took old cans and other tin scraps and made tin cups which I sold for 20 cents each. Later I made charcoal stoves, used very widely in Kenya, and sold them to other detainees, *askari* and sometimes to Arab traders. In a single afternoon I could make two or three of these stoves and the 2s. I got for each greatly increased my monthly earnings.

After I'd been in the Open Camp three months the Ministry of Works (MOW) started a project in the area and was in need of skilled workers. They asked whether any of the craftsmen wanted to work full-time for the MOW at a salary of 75s. per month. Along with one other tinsmith and several blacksmiths and carpenters, I volunteered and thus stopped working on the irrigation scheme.

It was a few months later when I heard that a screening team was coming to interrogate Hola detainees about their Mau Mau activities. The little pleasure I'd been able to enjoy in the Open Camp and in my job as tinsmith disappeared on hearing this news.

The arrival of a screening team was always bad news, particularly for hardcores. It always carried the threat of beatings, torture or

even death. The team came in April 1958. It was made up of headmen and chiefs from various districts and locations of the Central Province. About 50 men in the Open Camp were kept back from work each day for interrogation. Due to the heat interrogations were conducted in the shade of the few large trees in the camp.

When my name was called the screeners said I must hate the thought of going home since I kept refusing to cooperate. "You're quite wrong," I said. "I want to go home very badly but I can't give information I don't have and won't confess to a pack of lies."

Screeners never tire of asking the same questions and their techniques of persuasion varied little from one team to another. This team sat with my file before them and bombarded me with the old allegations, questions and threats. Finally, when they realized I wasn't going to change my story they ordered me to leave.

After ten days the chiefs and headmen left the camp but three months later, in July, another team came and the whole process was repeated. My life didn't change much during this period. I remained in the Open Camp working for the MOW and still trying to learn English. Many detainees confessed to the screeners and were moved to camps in their home areas. I resigned myself to spending the rest of my life at Hola. I knew I wouldn't be released before confessing and also that I'd never confess what was wanted by the screeners and Special Branch men.

In this frame of mind I was very surprised when, in August 1958, my name was included on a list of those to be transferred to camps in their home locations. For the first time I was to enter Government's "pipeline", which often ended with release from detention and eventual freedom. I had managed to save over 600s. and was pleased with the thought of returning to the cool highlands. Many detainees, however, had already been through the pipeline to their home locations only to be rejected by the headman or chief and returned to exile. I feared this might be my own fate and this thought dampened my hopes.

There were 150 of us and we were put in eight lorries. The truck I was in drove straight to the D.C.'s office in Kiambu. It was about 10 p.m. when we arrived. We were lined up, counted, given blankets and put into a single barracks.

In the morning a group of detainees who had already been rejected by their headmen and chiefs at the divisional works camps were put into the lorries we had arrived in and taken back to Hola. It was not difficult to picture myself in a similar position.

We all brought provisions and primer stoves with us from Hola and weren't forced to eat the miserable gruel provided at the post. We asked for water and prepared our own meals. This was just a stopping-off place before going to the works camps and we weren't made to do any work other than cleaning up the camp.

Somehow my wife got news of my arrival in Kiambu and with our home only eight miles away she decided to come visit me. She was not allowed to enter the camp but asked an *askari* to go tell me to come over by the fence. She couldn't see me from where she was standing and when I heard of her presence I was both pleased and upset. She know about my Mau Mau activities and I'd informed her in many letters of my unwillingness to confess.

While I wanted to see her very much I was afraid she would try and persuade me to confess. Her telling me of the hardships she and the children were facing at home might weaken my resolve not to give in to the screeners. Deciding not to see her till I'd been released, I asked the *askari* to say there was no one in the camp named Karigo Muchai. My wife, though with some doubts, accepted the story and walked off sadly toward our home.

I remained in the Kiambu D.C. camp for three weeks. The food I'd brought was used up within a few days and, refusing to eat the horrible weevil-infested *posho* and beans we were served, I spent some of my money to purchase food from the camp store. Early in the fourth week I was sent to Githiga Works Camp in the Githunguri division about 6 miles from my village.

On arrival, toward the end of September, 11 of us whose files showed we'd never confessed to taking the oath were put in a separate cell. All of our possessions were taken in return for receipts. I unhappily handed over my post office savings book and 56s. in addition to my clothing and other belongings.

In the cell we received the usual food and the following morning I was called before the screening team. After I'd given my story an *askari* was called in. I was handed a bucket filled with wet sand and told to put it on my head and start running around the compound. Soon there were 20 of us undergoing this torture and whenever someone slowed down or stopped he was whipped with long slender sticks. This continued till noon. I was completely exhausted.

After lunch we were called out once more and made to run in circles around the compound. The bucket seemed to grow heavier and heavier on my head. Unable to continue many men faltered, being whipped until they rose and started running again. This went on for the rest of the afternoon.

That night I slept very deeply. Early in the morning when ordered into the compound for more running, my legs were so stiff that I could hardly walk. We'd been provided with thin, red-striped shorts and shirts and when thoroughly exhausted the *askari* ordered us to lie down in the wet grass and roll over. At 7,000 feet above sea level in the Kenya highlands it gets very cold in the early morning hours and I was shivering and wet when finally led in for breakfast.

There were about 800 detainees at Githiga Works Camp. When those who had given adequate confessions returned from their day's work they gathered in the compound forming a circle. We hardcores would be called to the center of the circle one at a time and collective persuasion was employed in an effort to gain confessions.

The screening team tried to shame us into cooperation with abusive language and by calling us savages and wild animals. Those who failed to cooperate, they said, were rightly considered less than human. After this "introduction" the screeners would call other detainees to stand up and tell the crowd what they knew about the hardcore in the center and try to convince him of the benefits of whole-hearted cooperation.

The morning running routine and public interrogations continued till one day during the second week. Slowing down while on a forced run I was struck sharply by an *askari*. Hit with the butt of his rifle from behind, I lost my balance and lunged forward across the gravel surface of the compound, scraping the skin off my chest and bloodying my nose. My shoulder was badly bruised and already beginning to swell. I wasn't taken to the dispensary however; the *askari* just threw me into a cell.

The next day I was very ill. They had to take me to Kiambu hospital where my shoulder was operated on and my chest treated against infection. I remained there under treatment for 18 days, finally being moved back to Githiga with my shoulder bandaged but still not completely healed.

Githiga was divided in two sections. One was fenced and contained the detainee barracks and a small cell for those who committed minor offences. The other contained the offices of the screening team, the camp staff and rehabilitation officers plus a cell where the worst hardcores were kept separate for more severe types of persuasion and punishment. Returning from the hospital I was put in a cell within the detainee compound. In a week I was called to the office of the screening team where I found my location chief, the screening team leader and a European Special Branch officer. As I entered the chief was talking to the European. He said he'd known me a long time, being from the same sub-location, and didn't think it wise for them to release me; particularly since a new subversive organization, the KKM or *Kiama Kia Muingi* (Council of the Community) was active in the location. It would be dangerous, he said, to have a man like me back in the location. I might be a bad influence on his people. It didn't matter whether I confessed or not, he simply didn't want me released. Asked by the Special Branch officer about my character before the Emergency, the chief said that to his knowledge I had been a good man.

Opening my file the European turned to me and glancing over my records, remarked that I'd been in several camps and still hadn't confessed. He asked the chief why he thought this was so and the latter said he didn't know – many other detainees, some of whom had committed serious crimes, had already confessed and been sent home. Perhaps, said the European, this Karigo has committed such grave crimes that he's afraid to confess them. Then he asked me if I really wanted to return to my home and family. I said "Yes", but when he next asked if I'd taken the Mau Mau oath, I replied "No".

I would have confessed if I thought there was a chance of being released. But having heard what the chief said about me I decided it would be wiser to remain silent.

With my negative answer to the oath question the European officer retorted that I'd never be sent home before confessing and would probably be sent back to one of the other camps.

I was then led to the small cell. Because of my shoulder injury they gave me light work around the camp while the others were outside breaking rock. Toward the middle of December my name was read off as one of 25 men to be transferred. I was given my belongings but the cash was returned in token-money. Two lorries drove up containing 35 detainees from the other works camps in the district, Ngimia and Wait-haka, and together we were taken to Kiambu Headquarters. Here we were joined by 30 more prisoners from Gatundu, the end of the pipeline for Kiambu detainees, and taken away by lorry.

We arrived at Hola at 5:30 p.m. on 9 January 1959. I was placed with the others in a compound for new entries. After two weeks I was given the choice of living in the Open or Closed Camp. I was disgusted and angered at being returned to Hola and when the D.O. came for our answers I told him I wanted to stay in the Closed Camp. As long as they considered me an evil man, I thought it best to be with the others so classified and live within the barbed wire of the Closed Camp.

Few changes had been made since I left, though the village camp for men who brought their families was now completed and the old Open Camp was enclosed with barbed wire and used to house hardcores. The former Closed Camp was being used for new entries like myself who would stay there a few weeks before being sent to one of the other camps.

The 20 of us who refused the Open Camp joined 90 others behind barbed wire. We were given prison uniforms and blankets and were not allowed to use our own belongings or bedding. There wasn't much change in the camp routine except that during the first three weeks we were badly treated and beaten by *askari*. As for the work, I now had to plant cotton and maize in the fields I had earlier helped prepare.

As was the practice in Kenya's detention camps, we were served a hot cup of gruel each morning. Not wanting to drink anything hot in this desert region we left the gruel to cool, putting it in a tin can or other container until later in the day when we'd return from work and drink it cold. Some of us accumulated gruel for several days, liking it best when slightly soured.

One day an *askari* looked into a tin and thought we were brewing *pombe* or "native" beer. He reported the matter and an investigation was carried out. The so-called beer was sent to a laboratory in Nairobi for analysis and found to be just what it was: sour gruel.

The camp commandant was angered by his own frustrated suspicions and by the fact that we were proven right. He ordered us to drink the gruel in the morning when it was served and not to save it. Through our spokesman, Kiburi, we informed the camp officials that if we couldn't drink the gruel later when it had cooled we didn't want it at all. This notice was not received kindly by the camp commandant who insisted on having his way. Each morning the gruel was served, only to be poured down the drain when we failed to drink it.

Angered sorely by his apparent defeat over the gruel the commandant increased our daily piece-work until, after a short period, we were forced to do almost double the previous work. Instead of finishing at noon as before most of us had to remain in the fields until 6 or 7 p.m., working without food under the blazing afternoon sun. The midday meal, to be eaten when the day's work was done, was simply put aside and served to us for dinner.

With our spokesman and elected committee we discussed at length the possibility of going on strike. All our efforts at negotiation with the camp commandant had failed to bring a satisfactory settlement regarding the gruel and piece-work disputes and many of us felt that refusing to work was the only weapon we had. A vote was taken and it was unanimously agreed that we should go on strike until our grievances were satisfied.

When informed of this the already infuriated camp commandant came storming into the compound. Remaining calm, Kiburi told him that we'd voted to strike and would not return to work until satisfactory agreement was reached regarding the gruel and piece-work. Though we explained our grievances in great detail the camp commandant merely turned on his heel shouting that our strike was illegal and that he'd return after deciding what to do with us.

For a week we remained in the compound without working. There were no incidents. Each day we refused the hot gruel, eating only the noon and evening meals. On Monday, seven days after our strike began, the camp commandant together with the District Superintendent of Prisons and medical officer entered the compound. The latter started examining us, separating the weak, sick and disabled from those he considered physically fit. The former were moved to a different compound. After completing this ominous procedure the officials left.

Nothing happened for two days though we noticed several lorries leaving the camp heading toward the nearby prison. We soon discovered that they were going to pick up the prison warders we would meet the following day.

It was 7 a.m. Wednesday morning when the camp commandant and superintendent with four members of his European staff entered the compound. A few minutes later a battalion of warders moved up in lorries and took positions near the gate. The camp commandant left without saying a word. More *askari* arrived and I noticed a truck full of farm implements heading toward our usual place of work in the fields.

Seeing about 200 *askari* from both the camp and prison we quickly and quietly held a meeting. It was obvious an attempt would be made to forcibly break our strike. And once the *askari* started to "work" on us they wouldn't stop before inflicting a good deal of damage. Knowing this and wanting to avoid fatalities we decided that if threatened with violence we would volunteer to work. We could plan further types of passive resistance later.

The camp commandant returned at 8 o'clock. He asked us if we were still prepared to carry through our strike. Kiburi replied that if force was going to be used we would call off the strike and go to work.

This reply seemed to shock the camp commandant, who had apparently made elaborate preparations for much greater resistance. He might have considered it a personal defeat if we were simply allowed to return peaceably to work after our nine-day strike. However that may be, for I don't pretend to have read his mind, he ordered us to form two files and march out of the compound.

The place in the field where we normally worked was about 600 yards from the camp. *Askari* were standing in two lines facing one another and forming an aisle or passageway through which we were ordered to walk. About 150 yards from the camp they started beating us with batons and rifle butts. We tried to hurry through using our arms in an attempt to ward off the blows but none of us could avoid being hit for long. By the time we reached our place of work many were already badly bruised and bleeding. One of my 80 comrades lay dead on the path. But the worst was yet to come.

The camp commandant ordered us to sit on the ground and once again asked, in a tone sarcastic rather than sincere, "Well, are you ready to work now?" Kiburi answered, to no avail that we were prepared to return to work peacefully.

As we sat we were surrounded by two rings of *askari*. The inner circle was armed with clubs and shields while the outer group held rifles which they kept trained on us. Moments later the camp commandant blew his whistle and the guards and warders set upon us like wild animals with their clubs, feet and fists. They continued to beat us for quite some time; I don't know exactly how long it was as I was too busy trying to protect myself against the club-swinging madmen to be concerned with time.

I had a strong urge to fight back but knew that if any of us resisted, the outer ring of *askari* might open fire on us with their rifles. There was no chance of escape from the beating which was brutally and calculatedly being carried out under the orders of the camp commandant and Superintendent of Prisons.

After what seemed an eternity the camp commandant finally blew his whistle as a signal for the *askari* to stop swinging. All of us were by then lying flat on the ground. When ordered to stand up only 50 or so of the men rose slowly to their feet. Though not unconscious I just couldn't raise myself off the ground. With 19 others I was carried to the camp hospital, which had been constructed with detainee labour.

Soon we were joined by some of the men who'd managed to walk back to the compound but had sustained more or less serious injuries. I was injured on the right knee, in the ribs and at the base of my spine. Though these wounds bother me to this day, I was certainly much luckier than the 11 men who died under the clubs.

After three days in the dispensary I was moved back to the compound to make room for those suffering more severely than myself. Somehow, news of this Government atrocity reached the outside world. As I lay in bed a number of Europeans came to question us about the incident. At first I was so bitter that I refused to speak. The others refused also. Three weeks later, however, when we learned that a commission of enquiry had been assigned the task of investigating the "Hola Massacre" – as it had become popularized in the press – we took a vote and decided to give statements to the commission's representatives.

At the end of the fourth week I was moved to the camp for new entries with 20 others. Government now wanted to separate us and the remainder of our hardcore group were sent in groups of five or ten to other camps. The D.O. came and asked us if we wanted to return to our old compound or move into the Open Camp. We held a lengthy meeting and after much discussion finally decided in favor of the Open Camp.

The new Open Camp was much larger than its predecessor. Little else had changed, though several men now had their families with them. Most of us refused to bring our families to the heat and bad living conditions of Hola.

Soon after getting settled I met a European with the MOW whom I'd previously worked for. He liked my work and offered me my old job. I accepted and again becam an MOW tinsmith. Salaries had been reduced from 75s. to 45s. per month but it was still better than working in the fields.

The D.O. came by a few weeks later and asked if any of us wanted a small shamba to work for ourselves. Many detainees accepted this offer, but having a full-time job and no family with me I decided against it.

Toward the beginning of April 1959 a screening team was formed, led by the D.O. and containing several rehab officers. When I went before it the D.O. mentioned my previous refusals to confess and then asked if I'd ever taken a Mau Mau oath. I asked if he would be good enough to open my file and read aloud the allegations made against me by Government. He agreed and began reading off a long list of charges and suspicions, some supported by statements from other Kikuyu and some merely rumor.

It was alleged that I had taken part in the murder of both Government loyalists and dissident Mau Mau members and that I had been in possession of firearms and ammunition. Added to these serious charges was one alleging that I'd taken at least one oath.

I asked the D.O. if it was possible to investigate the first three charges and determine whether Government had sufficient evidence to prove them in a court of law. I said I would be willing to discuss the question of oaths after these more serious charges were looked into.

I felt sure that Government didn't have enough evidence to try me. If they did I would have been tried and hanged long ago. I wanted them to withdraw these capital charges before I confessed anything about oaths or Mau Mau activities. Otherwise, what I confessed might support statements made by others containing more serious charges against me.

The D.O. said he would look into the matter and I was ordered out of the office.

For the next several months I carried on my work as tinsmith hearing nothing from the D.O. and losing practically all hope of ever going home.

I was living in a single room with seven other detainees. We prepared our own meals and shared the housework. Though life might have been worse, coming from the highlands I could never get used to the oppressive heat and mosquitoes of Hola and longed to be with my wife and family. I hadn't seen my children for over five years. I couldn't even remember or imagine what they looked like.

The months passed and in December 1959 the D.O. called me into his office. He said the results of the enquiries he'd made about me had finally arrived. An intense investigation was carried out in my home area and while several people said I had been a leader of Mau Mau, none could give any detailed information connecting me with particular murders or the possession and delivery of firearms.

"Most of the people who implicated you in their statements," he said, "did it only to help get their confession certificates. The evidence against you is not sufficient to bring a conviction in the courts. The fact that many people agreed about your being a location leader of Mau Mau, however, is strong evidence that you've taken the Mau Mau oath."

We talked further and he made it clear that a confession regarding the oath and my activities as a location leader could not, at this point, do me any harm. The fighting had ended several years earlier and very few people were now being taken to court on Mau Mau charges.

My fears regarding a capital charge were greatly reduced on hearing what the D.O. had to say. It was very late in the game and being promised that no further interrogation or investigation would be carried out concerning the allegations of murder and arms possession, I decided to give a minimal confession. By this time most of the detainees had confessed and been released and there was little danger of any more information about me falling into Government hands.

Return to Kiambaa

A few weeks after my confession, in January 1960, the State of Emergency was declared officially over. I continued to work as usual until 21 March when I was finally given my release from Hola. They let me return directly to my home and family in Kiambaa location. The works camps and pipeline system had since been abandoned.

I was driven from Hola to Kiambu District Headquarters where I spoke with the local D.O. He told me to go see my location chief. On 25 March 1960 I entered my village for the first time in six years. My wife and children were very excited and happy to see me. The traditional Kikuyu cleansing ceremony was performed and a feast was prepared to celebrate the return of a warrior from battle. A he-goat was slaughtered and cooked and we ate a meal to commemorate my "rebirth" into the family. Special types of herb were gathered and boiled in water. My wife insisted on my drinking this so as to regain my lost strength and vigour.

After spending a few days at home I went to see the chief. He hadn't been told I was coming and was surprised and alarmed to see me. Though he'd rejected me before he had no choice now but to accept my presence in the location. After a brief and cold conversation I left him and returned to my family.

Being at home didn't mean that I was altogether free. I was restricted to Kiambaa location and had to report weekly to the D.O.'s office seven miles away. This was, in fact, a semi-detention which was to last for 11 months. Having neither land to cultivate nor a job, I found it increasingly difficult to provide even the minimum requirements for my wife and five children. I was glad to be back with my family and friends but poverty is never enjoyable, even under the best circumstances.

In my absence Kiambaa had changed considerably. People had been forced off their *shambas* into small, crowded villages. Our old house had been demolished and my wife had struggled to put up a small hut in the new village. Soon after my return we were again ordered to move, this time to a slightly larger village site a short distance away.

I was ordered to destroy my hut but I had neither a plot in the new village nor the money and equipment necessary for building a new home. Not wanting to leave my family without a place to sleep, I failed on the appointed day to burn down our little hut.

Government was not concerned with my reasons. I was arrested and taken before the court. The fine was 60s. or six months imprisonment and, but for the generosity of friends, I surely would have landed in prison.

When my restriction order was finally revoked in February 1961, I was still without a regular job. I earned a few shillings making and selling charcoal and with this money erected a small, inexpensive hut on a plot provided by a friend.

Allowed to leave the location, I entered Nairobi in search of employment. Thousands of men were out of work in the city and I was lucky to find a job driving a lorry for a dairy firm. This lasted for only two months, however, as the company decided to cut its staff and I was given notice.

It is now February 1962 and I am still without regular employment. My wife works on a European farm in Limuru for 2s. a day and I've been trying to build up a small trade in produce and charcoal. With almost no capital this has been a great and not very profitable struggle.

I am at present unable to provide adequate food and clothing for my family and have had to borrow money for my eldest childrens' school fees. I was arrested not long ago for failing to pay my poll tax. Again I needed the help of friends to save me from imprisonment.

I don't know what the future has in store for me. I can only hope that with Kenya's independence my suffering of the past ten years will somehow be rewarded. I want only a decent job or a piece of land to cultivate so that I can provide for my family and see to it that my children go to school and have an opportunity for a better, richer life than my own. These are the things we Kikuyu fought and died for. I only pray that after independence our children will not be forced to fight again.

MAN IN THE MIDDLE
The Story of Ngugi Kabiro

Introduction

The British colonial and white settler regime in Kenya offered few avenues for upward mobility to those Africans fortunate enough to complete a Standard 8 education but unable to compete successfully for the few openings in Kenya's two secondary schools. Hundreds of such rejected students each year entered the towns, especially Nairobi, seeking jobs which were increasingly outnumbered by their applicants. Educated or, perhaps, miseducated enough to spurn the daily toil of the peasantry, or being from families whose lands were insufficient to provide them a livelihood, many Kikuyu – whose shrinking reserve surrounded the ever-expanding Nairobi on three sides – entered the capital to become part of a growing rural-urban lumpen population. Young girls with a Standard 8 certificate often found their only employment in prostitution, while young men not infrequently became petty thieves or con artists. Fear of falling to the level of menial laborers led to a fierce competition for scarce white-collar and semi-skilled jobs, which often enough went to the most clever and opportunistic elements.

It is into such an urban situation that Ngugi "Solomon" Kabiro, aged 17, entered in 1947 to seek employment and means to further his education. Working first as a dispatching clerk, briefly trying his hand at a South African correspondence course, living in over-crowded rooms, Ngugi drifted through a number of jobs and periods of unemployment over the next few years, eventually settling into the con-jobbing work of an insurance salesman. Racial abuse, the "culture" bar, discrimination in wages, and that pervasive and unsurpassed contempt with which the British relate to "inferior races", moved Ngugi toward a hatred of the Europeans which was combined uneasily with a craving for the outward material comforts and privileges of that dominant class-caste vis-a-vis the masses of African peasants and workers. And it is this contradiction, this colonized mentality embracing resistance to a hated and oppressive colonial-settler system alongside a narrow petty-bourgeois self-interest and opportunism, which led Ngugi to "join" the underground movement in 1950, play out his role as gun-runner, petty broker and go-between for "Mau Mau" guerrillas after the fighting started, and finally to accept employment as a member of a government "rehabilitation" team in a detention camp.

The opportunism of Ngugi Kabiro, a "man in the middle", is vividly revealed in his comment about an early gun transaction: "Mau Mau fighters had acquired six weapons, the Asian and his European partner had earned 800s[1], and I was both 200s. richer and an active participant in the Kikuyu struggle for land and freedom." For colonized Kikuyu of Ngugi's class and experience, this type of opportunism was in no way unusual; if anything, it was the norm of conduct for "intelligent" people. In Kenya as in other "independent" ex-colonies this opportunist legacy of colonial rule and brutalization pervades the new "elites" making up the bureaucrat, comprador and national bourgeoisies and accounts in no small way for the relative ease with which Africa has been re- or neo-colonized by the advanced capitalist countries of the imperialist system.

1 approximately US$114.25. [seven East African shillings was equivalent to one U.S. dollar].

PART 1

In the evenings we often sat in my old grandmother's hut and listened to tales about the coming of the Europeans and how they stole our land and burned down our huts. These stories of the "White Bwana" take on a much deeper meaning as a man passes into adulthood and responsibility.

Ngugi Kabiro

On the 19th day of May 1929, I was born. My parents were living in the Kiambu District. My father, who had earlier trained as a carpenter, was employed on a European farm as a first assistant. Our homestead was about a mile and a half from his place of work, located on a plot of land he had acquired from a close relative on tenancy terms. As a *muhoi*, or tenant, my father had the right to erect his huts and cultivate a small piece of land. Though no rent was paid, we had no ownership rights over this land and could, with due notice, be made to vacate it. This position was forced on our family by the fact that my grandfather's land, located in the fertile highlands of Limuru, had been alienated for exclusive use by European settlers.

I remember that when I was a young boy most of our neighbors dressed in animal skins or blankets – though a few, who had joined the Christian church and acquired some education, dressed as Europeans. Life at this time revolved around the tilling of land, herding of goats and sheep, and the traditional Kikuyu customs. I recall many of the Kikuyu dances, circumcision and marriage ceremonies that I observed during this period.

I was the oldest child and son of my father, and while he was at work I assisted in herding our goats and sheep under the supervision of a neighbor. I found myself in the company of many other boys, most of them older than myself, who were performing similar duties. With the work went the usual children's play and the excitement of chasing the animals who strayed into the surrounding bush and forest. This was not an unpleasant time.

Our home was some three miles from the only church and school in the area. My father was nominally a Christian and with his trade and job he had acquired an important position within the community. He did not, however, break with the Kikuyu traditions practiced by the others. According to our custom, and to the great displeasure of the church, he married two more wives in 1935. My three mothers rotated the job of assisting me with our 200 head of goats and sheep. One at a time, for two-week periods, they would instruct me where I should graze the animals and relieve me at midday so that I might return home for lunch. My job became increasingly enjoyable as my younger sisters and stepbrothers grew old enough to be of assistance. Being the oldest, I felt much pride in having a band of little ones to command.

In 1937 the Kenya Government decided it needed more of our land for European settlement and we were once again told to leave our homes and fields and seek new places to live. The people strongly resisted this Government move and for a long period refused to leave their *shambas*. Finally, Government moved in and started pulling down and burning the huts of those who refused to obey the eviction notice. My father had arranged to buy a piece of land some seven miles from our home and so at the beginning of 1938 we shifted to the hastily erected huts on this new *shamba*.

Life in the new location was considerably different from what I'd experienced during the first nine years of my childhood. Here, most people had been converted to Christianity and took a great interest in education. The Kikuyu dances which I so much enjoyed were a rare sight, and most of the men dressed in European-style clothes.

There was a mission school about two miles from our home and, according to my father's wish and instruction, I started schooling. Though my oldest stepbrother was only six years old, he joined me in the second term of Standard I.

When most of our sheep and goats died – due largely to insufficient grazing land – my father bought ten head of cattle. I used to wake up early in the morning and milk them before preparing for school. Returning from school at 1 p.m., I would take the cattle to a stream one and a half miles from our home, where I was joined by other boys from the village. Here, as the cattle grazed, we played and occasionally fought. Kikuyu-land is very hilly with streams running in the valleys between the ridges. One of my favorite games was sledding down the slopes of the hill on a thick banana stem. On these sleds, about three feet long and six inches wide, we achieved high speeds on the slippery wet grasses of the slope. My father, and the parents of the other boys, didn't appreciate this game at all, as one afternoon was sufficient to wear out the backside of a new pair of khaki shorts.

In the village there was an older boy who had been to school and knew how to read and write. He was hired by my father to tutor my stepbrother and me in the evenings. Having the advantage of this extra teaching during the first three years of school, I managed to lead my classes in the terminal exams. In 1940 I began attending both morning and afternoon classes and had to give up the work and fun of watering and grazing our cattle.

My father had just resigned his job and set up a carpentry shop in the trading center near our home. On my return from school at 4 p.m., and on the weekends and holidays, I assisted him in the shop, planing and cutting the wood from which he built chairs, tables and other items of domestic use to the villagers.

In 1943 I ranked near the top of my Standard VI class and the time approached for a very important examination – which one had to pass in order to move on into the secondary school. There were about forty students in my class and a preliminary test was given to determine which of us were most qualified to sit for the Common Entrance Exam. I was extremely happy when my name was among the five students selected as having the best chance.

The day arrived when the children from thirteen schools were to meet for the final examination. My father presented me with a new fountain pen and five shillings for food on the eight-mile journey to the central mission controlling these schools. On arrival, the five of us, including three girls, spent the night in the house of a friend. When morning came, we joined the other students at the mission and the examination began.

It is necessary to point out that the number of secondary schools in Kenya was, and still is, very small. Because of this inadequacy, only a very small percentage of African students were permitted to pass beyond Standard VI.

When the day-long examination was over, we all went back to our villages to await the results. At home I waited impatiently for the longest month of my life and as the days passed, hope and confidence were overcome by despair and the certainty that I'd failed. Finally, as I approached his shop one day, I saw my father talking to my teacher, who held the long-awaited letter from the education authorities. With an air of excitement and pride, my father announced that I was the only one of the five students from my school who had passed the exam. My heart filled with joy and I relaxed for the first time in several months. The only damper to my happiness was the fear that I'd not gain admission to the secondary school.

Two weeks later I received a letter from the principal of the school I hoped to attend asking me to meet him at the D.C.'s office on 10 January 1944. Here, on the appointed day, I learned that I was among the eleven students, out of the fifteen who had applied, who were accepted into the school. Three boys were rejected because they were too old and I felt I must have only narrowly escaped this misfortune myself.

The new school was 90 miles away from home, in the Nyeri district, and I had to go there by train. My father bought me one of the half-price tickets given to students with Government concession letters and, when the day for my departure arrived, took me to the station 12 miles from our village. I had mixed emotions as we parted. This was to be my first train trip, my longest journey from home and the first time I would be away from my family for more than a day or two.

Though my father had provided me with fruit, candy and other food for the journey, it was not a very pleasant trip. It was the practice of returning students to put newcomers through a rather brutal initiation. We were knocked about and punished in various ways and I remember

94

spending most of the day crying. Reaching the Karatina station late in the afternoon, we got off the train and prepared to spend the night in the tea rooms of some local traders. The following morning we began our fourteen-mile journey on foot to the Kagumo School, being led by the older students. On the way we crossed the Tana River near the falls and, heading westward, reached the school after a gruelling five-hour walk.

Kagumo is a boys' school and during the first week the ninety of us who were new were divided into three classes of thirty each and given space in one or another of the school's nine dormitories. We were each provided with a small steel bed, two blankets (but no mattress), two school uniforms and a spoon and were then shown around the campus.

Though all of us were Kikuyu, the language of the school was Kiswahili – all instruction and reading was to be done in this language. The principal was a European and our teachers were all African. They administered the school with severe discipline and some of the boys had a difficult time adjusting to the new conditions. Several, in fact, deserted the school. For myself, knowing the harsh reaction I could expect from my father if I quit, I stuck it out and finally made the necessary adjustment.

Apart from its classroom work, the school ran a farm and raised a number of pigs, chickens and cattle. Each class had six hours of practical agricultural training a week. After the day's class work, all of us would go to the recreation field where competitive games were organized among the nine dormitories. I learned to play football, volleyball, cricket and several other sports. For the first two years I was on the junior team of my dormitory, making the senior squad only in my third year. The winning dormitory would be presented with a shield and I was lucky to be in one which had a very strong football team and retained this school trophy throughout my three-year stay.

Without hesitation I can say that the three years I spent at Kagumo were the happiest of my life. Even my holidays during this period were exceptionally pleasant. When I returned to my home in Kiambu all my relatives and friends treated me as a guest and went out of their way to make my vacation enjoyable.

At the end of 1946 I sat, with the rest of the seniors, for the Primary School Examination, which I had to pass if I wanted to continue my education in one of the two high schools in the Central Province. Competition for entrance into these schools was fierce and only a few students with excellent marks were permitted to enter each year. Though I did fairly well on this examination, I failed to rank high enough to continue my education. Returning home when the school closed in late November 1946, I sadly awaited the inevitable news that I was not to enter the high school.

I was by this time already 17 years old, the proper age, according to Kikuyu custom, for a young man to be circumcised and initiated to adult status within the tribe. Although I had attained a higher-than-average education and had long attended the mission schools, I could not dream of being circumcised in a hospital, as was the practice with most Christians and mission-educated boys. This, I felt, would be considered a cowardly act and would strip me of the pride rightfully attached to boys circumcised in the traditional Kikuyu fashion. I wanted very much to become an adult in the manner of my forefathers.

Other youths in the village were also ready for circumcision and our fathers began making all the necessary arrangements. Clothes had to be provided and a lodging place found for us to stay after the initiation ceremony. Only certain individuals qualify to provide the huts for recuperating "circumcision patients". They must be of the ruling generation (either Mwangi or Irungu) and have to possess both the knowledge and paraphernalia required by the ceremony and the wealth necessary to take care of the initiates for one or two weeks after the operation. These people enjoy a high status in the community and whenever there are youths ready to be initiated, their fathers go to them and request accommodation for their children. My father succeeded in making arrangements with one such person and a date for the ceremony was set.

Beer was prepared by all the fathers and a great feast was held with much singing and happy conversation. The twelve of us to undergo the ceremony were to spend the preceding night in a particular hut where female relatives of each boy came and enjoyed the practice of shaving our heads. This was a sleepless night for me, and in the very early hours of the morning we were led to one of the large perennial streams. It was about 4 a.m. when we were instructed to remove all our clothing and bathe in the icy waters. We then began the two-mile walk to the initiation site, shivering and completely naked. All interested neighbors attended and were anxious to see which among us would stand up to the painful operation without fear. At 6 a.m. we were seated in a field surrounded by about 500 spectators. Numb from the cold, which tended to reduce the pain, all but one of us went through the operation without displaying

any signs of fear. This one boy who had shown signs of cowardice was much talked about in the village and brought shame to both himself and his family.

When all of us had undergone the operation, we were led to a small hut where we were to spend nine days. Very early on the last morning we were instructed to burn our bedding of fried banana leaves and walk directly to our respective homes without looking behind us. When I returned home my father had to slaughter three goats for me. To have a child circumcised according to Kikuyu custom is quite an expensive affair. Each boy's father was to kill as many goats as he could afford and prepare a feast for the initiates. Beer was also provided, and the man who put on the largest and most successful feast was held in high regard by the villagers and was proud to be thought "not a poor man".

When I was a child, back around 1939, I used to see people crowded into lorries, singing as they went to age-group meetings. At the time of my own circumcision these age-groups were competing with one another to see which could contribute the most money for the construction of the Kenya Teachers Training College, Githunguri.

Within my location, the boys who had just been initiated organized themselves into an age-group club and I was elected secretary at the first meeting. Dues were collected and after several meetings the question was finally raised about our contributing to Githunguri. I argued that we should each give more money and contact boys from the other Kiambu locations so that we might join together and have our name recorded on the roll of age-groups contributing to Githunguri. Though several others agreed with me, the majority seemed to feel that we could not compete with the age-groups of our elder brothers and fathers and that it would be embarrassing to give only a few shillings while the other groups gave thousands. They suggested instead that we take the little money we had and hold a large feast.

While I realized that most of the boys in my age-group were young and not earning a cash income, I felt very strongly that we should contribute what little we could to the college. I argued so hard for this position that the majority voted to remove me as secretary and exclude me from the feast and from all future meetings regarding it.

Being disillusioned by the whole affair, I had little further to do with the organization of my age-mates. I was happy, however, that despite our reluctance, the training college at Githunguri was making progress. Having begun in 1939, the school now had a beautiful stone and tile dormitory for girls, a church and large wooden classrooms. Its main purpose was to act as a high school and training center for African teachers and it had an enrollment of almost 600 students. These were drawn mainly from the independent Kikuyu schools attached to either the Kikuyu Karinga Education Association or the Kikuyu Independent Schools Association. Between them, these bodies grew to over 300 schools and 50,000 students by 1952 and, being born out of revolt against the mission schools' rejection of female circumcision and polygamy, demonstrated what the Kikuyu could do for themselves if given half a chance.

In January 1947, when I learned that I hadn't passed the Primary School Examination, I went to Nairobi to seek employment. I found, however, that there were few jobs available to men without some kind of special training, and rather than become a menial labourer I decided to enroll in a commercial college for classes in English, typing, mathematics and bookkeeping.

By October of this same year I found a job with a law firm as a junior dispatching clerk. It was a fairly good post and I was given a starting salary of 60s. per month – not bad considering that many Africans were earning as little as 5s. What upset me, after being on the job for a time, was the fact that an Asian, doing the same work as myself, received more than twice my salary. It is a bitter fact to Africans that however competent a man might be in his work, he receives for the same work, only a tenth of what a European gets and about half as much as an Asian.

In Nairobi, I was staying with my uncle. He had been a Government employee for some time and had managed to get a two-room flat in the workers' quarters. Luckily, he had a small table, a hurricane lamp and a book shelf and I was able to study in the evenings. As I hadn't lost my interest in education, I enrolled in a South African correspondence school. Though I worked hard, it was difficult for me to study well after putting in a full day at the office. Even when I found a job with an insurance company at an increased wage of 90s. per month, life in Nairobi wasn't very pleasant or comfortable.

My uncle was refused permission to house me and so I went to the City Council to apply for a room, putting my name on the waiting list. As an indication of how difficult it is for an African to obtain housing in Nairobi, I waited four full years before getting a room in one of the African locations. To this day, though the City Council builds and rents rooms to Africans, there aren't nearly enough to go around. Some of the big firms provide housing for their employees but, while this arrangement may sound good, it in fact tends to bind many people to very low paying jobs: if they give up their jobs, they also have to give up their houses and, in many cases, are forced to return to their homes on the reserve.

On leaving my uncle's place I moved in with a friend. He had only a single, 10' by 12' room in which eight of us were to live. We had two beds, each sleeping three people, while two others slept on the floor. I soon became very dissatisfied with these accommodations and decided to go back to Kiambu. I used my father's bicycle and started making the 24-mile round-trip journey to and from work each day. Travelling over the steep hilly countryside was very tiring and, added to the fact that study conditions at home were extremely bad, this contributed to my decision to give up the correspondence school courses.

During this period I had gotten into the habit of buying the daily newspapers. In the morning I could only glance over the headlines before

going to work. But in the evening I would go through the paper intensively, with a growing interest in the reports on African political meetings and activities and the African contributions to the correspondence columns – where criticism was often made against the white man and his treatment of Africans.

Since I left school, my feelings against the European and his Government in Kenya had grown more intense. I knew that it was the will of the European which caused African salaries to be so low, and I had now personally experienced the life made necessary by these starvation wages. Again, I was increasingly aware of the damage done to my family when several acres of my grandfather's land were alienated for European settlement. Today on what is rightfully our land sits a European who, with African labour, grows coffee and raises cattle. He is very rich and prosperous while we in my family cannot raise sufficient money to pay the school fees for our children. In the evenings we often sat in my old grandmother's hut and listened to tales about the coming of the Europeans and how they stole our land and burned down our huts. These stories of the "White Bwana" take on a much deeper meaning as a man passes into adulthood and responsibility.

In my village we often passed time in the early evenings and weekends in the nearby tea room. I often went there with the English newspaper and translated the political sections into Kikuyu for the old men, who were always happy to see me enter, paper in hand.

Sometimes I cycled long distances on the weekends to visit friends and relatives, who in turn made frequent visits to my home. I had become a very good cyclist and used to enter the competitions sponsored by the schools. I usually came in first or second and won many prizes, such as bicycle tires, ties, etc., in addition to winning a certain amount of popularity amongst my people.

Along with working, earning my small salary, and finding enjoyment in cycling, reading the newspapers and visiting girlfriends – whose company I came increasingly to appreciate – I was becoming more aware of political events and could observe the great influence of the Kenya African Union in raising the level of political consciousness among the Kikuyu. KAU was a Kenya-wide organization which was registered with Government and held many public meetings and rallies. Led by Jomo Kenyatta, KAU was rapidly increasing its membership and popularity among Kenya Africans. Though not a member myself, I used to attend the public meetings that were held in Nairobi and Kiambu.

May this Oath Kill Me

I had become aware, through a friend, that another organization existed which sought the return of all land alienated for Europeans. With my family having claims to such land, I was very keen on joining. It was not, however, a registered society and I didn't know (or so I thought at the time) any of its members. Though I tried, I could not make contact with the organization and my desire to join it waned. In fact, this organization was the old Kikuyu Central Association which was formed in 1926, proscribed by Government at the beginning of the Second World War, and now operating underground with a very select membership.

Toward the end of 1948, I managed to get a slightly better paying job and took up my new employment in January 1949. Shortly thereafter, however, I came down with severe bronchitis and had to leave the office each day at 10 a.m. for treatment at the Government dispensary, the only clinic in Nairobi serving the African population without fees. Since this clinic was completely inadequate to serve the many Africans who needed medical attention and couldn't afford to go elsewhere, there were always long queues of people waiting – often the whole day – to be seen by medical assistants who, if they felt a case to be serious, would direct the patient to one of the qualified doctors.

After standing in the queue for several hours the first day, it was my misfortune to be seen by a medical assistant who wrongly diagnosed my illness as malaria. Every day for the next two weeks I was given medicine for a disease which I didn't have and my bronchitis continued to get worse. Finally, after a brief but bitter argument with an assistant, I was allowed to see the doctor who, finding that I had a temperature of 104°, had me admitted to the hospital. I had arrived at the dispensary at 9 a.m., was seen by the doctor at 3 p.m. and was taken to the hospital by ambulance at 4:30 p.m.

On arrival, I was provided with hospital clothes, a bed and an evening meal. At about 6 p.m. I fell unconscious and remained in that condition for almost five days. When I finally awoke I was extremely weak and, not

102

knowing I had been asleep more than one night, couldn't understand why my watch had stopped. The nurse came by and seeing me awake asked me how I felt and whether I wanted something to drink. Shortly, the doctor and several of the medical staff came in and expressed their happiness over my recovery: most of them had thought I would die. The doctor told me how long I had been unconscious and gave me a glass of orange squash. As opposed to the dispensary, where one received indifferent treatment from poorly qualified and overworked medical assistants and doctors, the King George VI Hospital was, and remains to this day, the only place where an African can expect individual care and sound treatment.

After nine days, I was released from the hospital and instructed to remain at home and not work for three weeks. Gradually I regained my strength and returned to the office during the third week. The attitude of my employers had changed noticeably. They disliked and seemed to resent the fact that my illness had kept me from the job for such a long period. There is a mysterious belief amongst Asians and Europeans that only they have the "privilege" of being sick. When this happens to an African, they feel cheated somehow and comfort themselves with the thought that the person isn't really sick: he's simply drunk or downright lazy. Within a month my employer gave me notice, with the usual excuse that they were reducing their staff.

I remained unemployed for the next few months, eventually finding a job with another insurance company as both clerk and agent on a salary of 150s. per month plus commission. For the first time in my working career, I began to earn 200s. or more a month. I abandoned cycling to work each day from Kiambu when a friend of mine, who was leaving Nairobi, allowed five of us to remain in his house and be responsible for the rent.

It was at this time that I once more began to hear of the existence of the banned Kenya Central Association. A friend, who knew I wanted to join the organization, promised to take me to the next ceremony. This never came to pass, however, and it was only later that I managed, without help, to gain admission to the KCA.

Throughout this period, I continued to think about and make plans for furthering my education. I was very much disturbed on seeing other boys my age entering Makerere College or going overseas for university training. I made up my mind to diligently pursue my private studies and try to save sufficient money to enter high school. I managed to save a considerable amount from my small salary but the crowded conditions where I was staying made things difficult. I couldn't study and at the same time do my share of the domestic work. It was thus an unhappy situation in which my studying bred ill feeling amongst my roommates.

One evening in February 1950, I decided to go home and visit my girlfriend who was staying in the house of a relative in our village. When I arrived at the hut at about 7:30 p.m. I found that, while she was not there, a number of people from the village had gathered and were sitting about talking, laughing and telling tales. Curiosity made me stay to find out what sort of meeting this was and I joined into the conversation. At around 9 p.m. a man entered the hut and said he was looking for a couple of strong young men like myself to assist him in some work he was doing in a nearby hut. Three of us arose and, volunteering our services, followed the man out into the darkness. The hut was only a few yards away and inside I saw about fifteen people. My father was there assisting some others in slaughtering a lamb. In the course of our conversation I asked one of the men what sort of occasion this was and he replied that they were awaiting the arrival of an important visitor. I knew all of the people present and felt no cause for alarm, even though I was somewhat bewildered by the situation.

In a matter of minutes, I was once again called outside and led with six others to a hut located beneath the black wattle trees and separated from my home by our kei-apple fence. I felt a little scared at this point because I knew this third hut had been vacated long ago and could see no point in going into a deserted house. Again, the people who were accompanying us behaved as if they were guards – which in fact they were. I was also upset by the fact that my clean clothes were getting wet and soiled by the high grass made wet by the early evening rain.

As we approached the door, I saw a dim light inside and heard people whispering. But as we entered, the light went out and there was complete silence inside. We were all somewhat frightened at this point and entered with some reluctance on the insistence of the guards. It was pitch dark inside, but I could hear the whispered voices of many people who soon began asking us, in turn, who we were and other questions about ourselves. I remember suffering a few minutes of terror while being held around the neck and arms by three or four people. Moments later, however, someone ordered the lights to be turned on and shortly

three hurricane lamps illuminated the inside of the hut. What struck me at first was the sight of an arch made of banana leaves and the fact that three men stood guard armed with *simis*, or Kikuyu swords. The door of the hut had been firmly bolted and glancing around the room I estimated that there were some forty solemn-faced people inside. (Later, I discovered there were also people outside, guarding the approaches to the hut.)

One of the men in the room ordered the seven of us to form a queue by the arch, take off our shoes and remove any coins, watches or other metal objects we might have in our possession. It was at this point, as I relaxed a bit and saw that most of the people in the room were familiar to me, that I realized this ceremony was probably the one I earlier wished to undergo in order to become a member of the KCA. Though the people were stern-faced and would surely have harmed any who resisted, I was unafraid from this time onward.

The man who had us remove our shoes and coins then instructed us as follows: "We want you young men to join us in the struggle for freedom and the return of our lands. That is why we have brought you here to swear an oath binding you with us in this struggle. Mind you, this is no joking matter. Any who refuse to take this oath will be killed and buried right here in this hut."

At this juncture, one of the persons to undergo the ceremony said he had never heard of such an oath and was not willing to take it. Before he had completed his statement, however, he was hit very hard in the face. This convinced both him and the rest of us that this was, in fact, no joking matter. The man pleaded to be allowed to take the oath and have his life spared.

At this point I had better explain just how these oaths were arranged and the equipment used in the ceremony. I know these things not only from having taken the oath, but from having attended dozens of such ceremonies in the months following my own initiation.

I mentioned above that in the second house I entered a goat was being slaughtered. The meat was roasted to be eaten later and the skin cut into thin ribbon-like strips which were twisted and joined to form rings. The eyes of the goat were removed together with the thorax and *ngata*, a bone which connects the head and the spinal column and contains seven holes. The eyes were stuck on either side of a 15-inch-long piece of banana stalk which was hollowed out lengthwise so that it might function as a container. Also attached were clusters of seven kei-apple thorns (from a particular tree known as *Muthuthi* or *Mugaa*) and sodom apples which were fixed to the three sides with these same thorns. This container was to hold a liquid formed by a mixture of goat's blood, soil and crushed grains, such as maize, sorghum and beans.

The arch, which stood about five feet high, was constructed of long banana stalks dug into the ground and joined at the top by tying or intertwining their leaves. On this frame were put other plants and shrubs, such as sugar cane, maize stalks, etc. The ngata of the goat and the thorax, or large chest-piece of meat, were suspended from the top of the arch near the center.

Throughout the ceremony, each initiate wore a ring of the twisted goatskin around his neck and held a damp ball of soil against his stomach with his right hand. This latter was a symbol of the person's willingness to do everything in his power to assist the association in regaining and protecting the land belonging to the Kikuyu people.

Standing thus before the arch, I passed through it seven times while the oath administrator uttered and I repeated the following vows:

1 If I am called upon at any time of the day or night to assist in the work of this association, I will respond without hesitation;

   And if I fail to do so, may this oath kill me.

2 If I am required to raise subscriptions for this organization, I will do so;

   And if I do not obey, may this oath kill me.

3 I shall never decline to help a member of this organization who is in need of assistance;

   And if I refuse such aid, may this oath kill me.

4 I will never reveal the existence of secrets of the association to Government or to any person who is not himself a member;

   And if I violate this trust, may this oath kill me.

Following this, and repeating these vows again on each occasion, I was instructed to take seven sips of liquid from the banana-stalk container, seven small bites of the goat's thorax and – performing each act seven times – to prick the eyes of the dead goat and insert a piece of reed into the seven holes of the ngata. The administrator then had me take a bite of sugar cane, poured cold water over my feet and made a cross on my forehead with the blood and grain mixture. When this was completed, I was surrounded by a number of spectators who took hold of the skin ring around my neck and started counting. Reaching the number seven, they all pulled, breaking the ring and saying: "May you be destroyed like this ring if you violate any of these vows."

The oathing ceremony was thus completed and I was led into another hut with the others. A lamb, slaughtered earlier, was now roasting over the fire and we sat down to eat and talk till about midnight. Over fifty of us had undergone the initiation ceremony by this time and before departing we were all gathered in a single hut for final instructions. The administrator entered and told us we were now members of KCA and linked by an oath of unity which would extend brotherhood to all members of the Kikuyu tribe. The white man, he said, was our enemy and we should have nothing to do with him. The land stolen from our people by the Europeans must be returned; and this could only be achieved through an irresistible unity of all Kikuyu, who would act as a single man with a single purpose. We were then asked to pay an entrance fee of 2/50s. and told that an additional 62/50s. plus a ram were to be paid as soon as we were able.

This, then, is how I took the KCA oath. The ceremony was similar to the dozens I attended as spectator or assistant in the months to follow. It was the one which Government later, after the Naivasha trial in May, 1950, labeled "Mau Mau" and banned.

As I made my way home with my father I was very happy and excited about the evening's proceedings. My wish to join the secret organization was now fulfilled and I was confident that some of the friends who had recently been avoiding me (I now know it was because I hadn't yet been initiated) would henceforth accept me as their comrade in the new brotherhood fashioned by the oath of unity. I also felt relieved of the burden of doubt and curiosity about the organization which had plagued me for so long.

I overslept the following morning and arrived at the office quite late. Luckily, they accepted my excuse about missing the early bus. Right after work I went to see the friend who had earlier promised to take me to an oathing ceremony. I told him of the preceding night's activities and he was very pleased to hear that I too was now a true son of Gikuyu and Mumbi.

My life at this time was a happy one, except for the minor discomforts caused by my studies and consequent failure to perform my share of the domestic duties in the little room five of us had rented in Nairobi.

One Friday evening in March 1950, after I'd been in the underground organization only a month, I went home to spend the weekend with my family and friends. On arrival, I met a friend of mine in the trading center who advised me that there was to be a meeting in the village that night. He said I should try and bring a mutual friend whom we had talked of earlier and who had as yet not been initiated. This is the usual way in which members of KCA communicated with one another and indicates the manner in which most new members were recruited. News of meetings and oathing ceremonies passed from person to person by way of whispers and the use of certain key words (which I shall speak of later) that only a member could understand. Recruitment was accomplished by individual members bringing in friends and acquaintances whom they trusted and who had expressed views sympathetic to the organization or its aims.

I found the man I was looking for in his hut and asked him to come home with me. On the way we passed the house of a neighbor and dropped in to chat. As the oath was to be administered nearby, my intention was simply to pass time until all the preparations had been made. After a while, I left my friend at this house and went to find out exactly where the ceremony was to take place. I found that my father had opened my room and was making preparations for the oath to be conducted there.

By 8 p.m. there were several hundred people at my home, some unknowingly about to be initiated, others ready to take up their duties in the organization as guards, messengers or merely spectators. I spent more time in the house than I had planned and when I hurriedly returned to where I'd left my friend I found he'd grown tired of waiting and left. I felt sorry that I'd failed – at least for the time being – to bring this friend into KCA.

Nevertheless, several dozen people were initiated in my little room that night, the ceremony lasting until dawn. Being very young in the organization, I was surprised to learn that Saturday and Sunday were also busy days in administering the oath. On Saturday the oathing ceremonies were conducted in someone else's house, but on Sunday it was held again in my small room.

Since the oaths were always administered at night and often lasted into the early hours of the morning, I returned to work Monday morning having had very little sleep since the preceding Thursday night. I could barely keep my eyes open and finally asked for the day off so that I might go to my Nairobi room to sleep. When I arrived I found the door locked. Without a key, but unable to resist the urge to sleep, I stretched out on the grass in front of the quarters and lay there like a dead man until my friends returned from work in the early evening. I was surprised to learn that I had many unknown spectators as I lay on the grass. People gathered around me, not knowing whether I was sick, drunk or perhaps dead. Most decided that I must be drunk and left chuckling to themselves.

For the next three months, I continued my routine of work, living in my Nairobi room with four others and returning to Kiambu on the weekends to participate in oathing ceremonies. My father was a very old and trusted member of the organization, having joined KCA as early as

1933, and our home was often used for meetings and the administration of oaths. Compared to other homesteads in the village, ours had the advantage of being well fenced and easy to guard.

It is interesting to note that while my father had been a member of the organization for many years, he never once revealed this secret to me or to other members of the family. It was only after we'd become members ourselves (all of the adults in my family had by this time been initiated) that he was willing to discuss these matters with us. The vow of secrecy, you see, extended even to the most intimate members of one's own family.

Before Government forced the Kikuyu into small over-crowded villages during the later stages of the Emergency, Kikuyu peasants used to live on their own small-holdings or shambas. Those who lived close to one another and shared a common stream were known as an itura. These neighbors helped each other in case of emergencies. Everyone within an itura was easily available in the event an alarm was raised. Again, these people could call on one another for assistance in domestic tasks and could be counted on for help in the event someone ran out of salt, water or firewood. This group, often referred to as a "village", was the smallest and basic unit within the KCA organization.

Two or three matura make up a Government administrative unit known as the sub-location, under the administration of a salaried "headman" approved by Government. A combination of four or five sub-locations make up a location under the administration of a Government "chief". Next, following this same principle of grouping small units into larger ones, comes the division, then the district, under its district commissioner (DC) and his district officers (DO's), and finally the province, headed by a provincial commissioner (PC).

Though I held no office in the KCA organization – and know about it from experience only on the sub-location level – it is my understanding that our association was organized on levels corresponding to the Government administrative units. Each level, beginning with the village and ending with the province, was headed by an elected council or committee which sent a certain number of its members to represent it on the next highest level. This, at any rate, is what I believe to have been the way the underground KCA was organized up to the time the State of Emergency was declared by Government on 20 October 1952.

Tightening the Noose

In May 1950, while I was still working in Nairobi, the Transport and Allied Workers' Union staged a strike. Trade unionism in Kenya was still very young at this time and the Government did its best to discredit the movement and its central body, the East African Trades Union Congress. The EATUC was refused registration as a trade union and now, supposedly because it had called for a boycott of the February celebrations conferring city status to Nairobi, it was brought to court. When a general strike was called by the Congress on 18 May, Fred Kubai, a leading member of KAU as well as president of the EATUC and secretary of the Transport and Allied Workers' Union, was arrested along with the organizer of the Congress, Makhan Singh. Kubai was fined 110s., but Makhan Singh, because he admitted to being a communist, was deported and restricted to a small trading center in the far north where he was to remain for nearly 13 years.

The general strike, as a political protest against these Government actions, had the sympathetic support of virtually all African workers in Nairobi, regardless of whether or not they were themselves members of a trade union. In the insurance office where I worked, I succeeded in getting the other employees to sign a circular informing our employer that we were joining the strike. Seeing to it that everyone signed and was out of the office, I left the circular on the manager's desk and returned to my home in Kiambaa, where I remained until the strike was officially over eleven days later.

Back at the office I found that some of my colleagues had returned to work on the eighth day and that my employer was extremely bitter toward me. Though he didn't want to dismiss me due to the competence I had demonstrated in my work – he insisted that I apologize to him and promise never to do such a thing again. Thinking I had done the right thing, however, I refused absolutely to comply with his demands and resigned immediately.

Being now a fairly good typist, I found a new job within a week with another insurance firm. My salary and commission were better and my savings continued to grow. After receiving a lump sum of money through chain letters, I remember having as much as 3,000s. in the bank – a considerable sum for a man of my age. My earnings enabled me to enroll in an Asian-owned commercial school in Nairobi, which I attended one hour each day after work, and to abandon my over-crowded room in the city. I could now afford to live at home and take buses to and from work. I would rise early to catch my bus and be at the job by 8:30 a.m., leave the office at 4:30 p.m., go to my class and then take the last bus back to Kiambaa Location.

Oathing ceremonies continued in the village and, being at home in the evenings, I was in a position to assist in the preparations. Reading the newspapers every day, I kept myself informed about current political affairs and could observe the growing political awareness of the Kikuyu and their increased hatred of British colonialism and European settler domination.

Whenever Africans spoke of the Kenya white man they expressed resentment and bitterness toward the loss of land, discriminatory legislation, low salaries and ill-treatment they had suffered since the coming of the European. Keeping pace with this growing hatred of the white man and his evil deeds, membership in both the underground KCA and the registered KAU continued to swell day after day.

With their great interest in politics, Kikuyu joined the Kenya-wide KAU in larger numbers than any other tribal group. On the basis of this, many misinformed Government spokesmen assert that KAU and the secret KCA (later known throughout the world as the "Mau Mau") were one and the same organization.

This confusion was brought about by several factors. Since the KCA was banned in 1940, the Kikuyu people had had no registered political organization through which to air their mounting grievances. When KAU came into existence, they flocked to it in large numbers, creating the false picture that it was a Kikuyu tribal organization. Again, many leaders of the underground KCA, being competent politicians in their own right, gained positions of importance within KAU. This has led certain people to conclude that KAU was simply another name for the banned KCA, while in fact KAU was nationwide and drew leaders from most of the large tribal groups and areas in Kenya. The logic used by these Government spokesmen is simple: "If KAU was predominantly Kikuyu in membership, and if the KCA or Mau Mau were Kikuyu organizations, then KCA or Mau Mau and KAU were one and the same body."

While it is correct to say that KCA and KAU were linked by persons who held membership in both and by the fact that the two organizations had many similar political aims, it is false to say that they were identical. Many thousands of KAU members – including many Kikuyu and some of the top leaders – were totally unaware of the existence of KCA. Again, KAU was Kenya-wide and not tribally based, while the KCA was almost entirely a Kikuyu organization. Finally, KCA was banned and operating underground, recruiting members through an oath of unity, while KAU was an open, registered society trying to unite all Kenya tribes into an effective national force to achieve their political ends.

Turning to the term "Mau Mau" and its origin, there is also a great deal of confusion and misunderstanding. Some people claim that the term was brought back from England by Jomo Kenyatta in 1947 and that it originally referred to the "Mau Revolt" staged by some Oceanic people. Others believe "Mau Mau" was formed by changing the order of letters (a pastime often engaged in by Kikuyu children) in the expression "Uma Uma", which in Kikuyu means "Out, Out", and that this refers to the Kikuyu desire that Europeans leave (or be put out of) Kenya. I don't agree with either of these views.

In mid-1950 I remember reading in a vernacular newspaper about the Naivasha Trial, in which a number of Africans were convicted of illegal oathing after having been arrested during an initiation ceremony on a Naivasha farm. One of the defendants testified that the oath was administered by the "Kiama Kia Mau Mau", or the Council of Mau Mau. Being a short, easy-to-say term, it was picked up by the reporters attending the trial and the following day's newspapers carried head-lines referring to Mau Mau and Mau Mau oaths. The term then spread, gaining popularity, until finally it was used throughout the world to describe the Kikuyu revolt against the Kenya Government and British colonial rule.

"Mau Mau" was not a well-known or widely used term amongst Kikuyu. The only literal meaning it has in Kikuyu is "greedy eating", most often used in reference to children. In my location the term was also sometimes used as a derogatory expression referring to certain elders who, when called in to hear a case by the chief, were more inter-ested in the few shillings (or goats, as is the Kikuyu custom) paid to them by the defendant and his accuser, than in dispensing justice. These elders often magnified the seriousness of the case they were hearing in order to obtain from the guilty party a fine of a goat or lamb, which they would then slaughter, roast and eat under the guise that they were merely carrying out traditional Kikuyu legal practices. Earning a reputation for being greedy, these elders were sometimes referred to as "Kiama Kia Mau Mau", meaning the "Association of Greedy Eaters", or as "Ndia Nyama", which simply means "Meat Eaters".

It is my belief that the defendant at the Naivasha Trial who used the term "Mau Mau" in referring to the association he had joined, was only doing so in an attempt to conceal the fact of his membership in the banned KCA. It is also my opinion that other persons arrested during oathing ceremonies in the following months (i.e., up to the time Mau Mau was proscribed by Government in August 1950) made use of this strange expression in their statements to protect themselves and cover up the existence of KCA. It is in this way, I feel, that the term "Mau Mau" originated as the name of the underground KCA and gained currency in the Kenya and world press.

1950 ended with an increasing number of arrests for illegal oathing. I remember one night in December when, as we were conducting an initiation ceremony in one of the villager's huts, one of our guards rushed in and informed us that a squad of police had just driven into the village and parked their car by the roadside. Within a matter of minutes, the arch was destroyed, the fire put out, all the rest of the oathing paraphernalia removed, and the people dispersed to their own homes. Even if the police had arrived five minutes after our warning they would have found nothing unusual or suspicious in the hut where the oath was being administered. As it so happened, they merely looked around the village a short while and then left without having entered the initiation hut.

Toward the end of this same year, our organization seemed to radically alter its principles of recruitment. After it was banned, KCA was kept alive by a small group of its leaders who continued to meet secretly in one another's huts. Later, after the Second World War, its membership increased but still remained a small group of trusted and respected men. In late 1950, however, the association threw open its doors to all – men, women and young people alike – in an attempt to become an organization embracing the whole of the Kikuyu people. While the strength of the organization increased with its ever growing membership, this change had the negative effect of allowing into the association active or potential Government informers, morally corrupt individuals seeking their own personal gains, and many persons who lacked sufficient understanding of KCA's political objectives. Nevertheless, the strength and popularity of the underground movement grew by leaps and bounds.

In the beginning of 1951, I began to think seriously about going overseas for further education. I wrote letters to high schools in five countries, but the only favorable response I had was from a school in the Union of South Africa. Considering at length the bad relations I heard existed in South Africa between Europeans, Africans and Coloureds, I decided against going there. Instead, since I couldn't get into high school in Kenya either, I made up my mind to drop the whole idea and use my money to construct a house in Kiambaa and seek a wife.

I began withdrawing my money from the bank for this purpose but, unfortunately, found the cost of bad habits and romance very high. Before my house was even completed, I had spent all my savings on drink, dances and the cinema, which had replaced my evening studies. This compelled me to postpone my marriage which I had planned for the end of the year.

I continued working throughout this period and, finding that my recently acquired taste for beer and movies had cost me my savings and were making achievement of my aims difficult, I decided to adopt a more serious attitude and get down to the important business of completing my house, buying the minimum amount of furniture and saving for my marriage.

For the remainder of 1951 I continued working, attended the many KAU rallies held in the area, visited my wife-to-be once or twice a week and took part in the initiation ceremonies held in the village. My regular attendance and enthusiasm at the oathing ceremonies earned me a certain respect by the elders and toward the end of the year I was given some minor responsibilities, such as registering the new recruits, collecting their dues and sometimes going out to gather the necessary shrubs for the arch and other items used in the oathing ceremony.

Membership continued to expand, as did Government arrests for Mau Mau oathing, and life was becoming very difficult for people in the village who had not yet been initiated. It was the tendency of members to disassociate themselves from persons who hadn't taken the oath. Thus, non-members found themselves more and more alone and isolated from their former friends and neighbors. One such man in my village, for example, made a large quantity of beer and as is our custom invited everyone in the neighborhood to come share it with him. No one showed up at his home, however, and the man was very disturbed and unhappy. With almost everyone in the village being members of the secret society, non-members were coming more and more to be considered, along with the obvious traitors, as enemies of the people.

1952 did not begin very well for me. Hard pressed for the money I needed to cover the expenses of marriage and having been with the same insurance firm for over two years now without receiving any increase in pay, I decided to ask my employer for a raise. When he offered me only an additional 20s. a month I became furious with him and resigned on very short notice. My anger was due mainly to the belief that it was entirely unfair for an employer not to consider raises for his employees until asked, and then to offer only token increases.

I was not worried about getting another job, having gained experience in automotive insurance and being popular with most of the African transporters. In a few days I was hired by another insurance firm, with a higher salary and commission rate. At the same time I worked as an agent for another firm selling life insurance. Though my new job was not

Oathing ceremonies were more frequently interrupted by police raids and arrests of oath-takers mounted.

a bad one, I was bitter over the fact that the Asian whom I replaced was earning 700s. a month, while I was to start at 250s.

In the meantime, as it expanded to include the vast majority of Kikuyu in the Central Province and white highlands, our underground movement was being infiltrated by ever larger numbers of Government informers. Many of these people had joined the organization out of fear or intimidation (usually in the form of social ostracism) and found it profitable to cooperate with the Criminal Investigation Department (C.I.D.). Through these informers – who were often church-goers or Government employees such as teachers, headmen and chiefs – Government gained an increasing knowledge of the secret movement. Oathing ceremonies were more frequently interrupted by police raids and arrests of oath-takers mounted.

Again, Government was becoming increasingly suspicious of all Kikuyu gatherings, whatever their purpose, and it became dangerous for a Kikuyu even to slaughter a goat. I recall one instance when a man in my village killed a goat for his in-laws who had come to visit him. A police informer observed the man slaughtering the goat and reported to his superiors that an oathing ceremony was being prepared in the man's house. As a result, the police arrived, seized the meat and threw the man in jail. Though he finally convinced them of his real reason for killing the goat, he was obliged to spend the night in a damp cell.

While some informers honestly reported the facts, many others used their position to gain wealth and land, create difficulties for neighbors of whom they were jealous, or merely to amuse themselves at others' expense and prove their worth to Government.

Though I had been promised a raise in salary after six months, when the time came for this increment no mention was made by my employer. I decided against asking for the increase, fearing to jeopardize my job on the eve of my wedding. When my savings reached a sufficient amount in mid-1952, I reported my intention to marry to my parents, who began making the necessary arrangements. According to Kikuyu custom, I was required to contribute toward the making of native beer for my prospective in-laws, while my father was responsible for paying the bride-price.

I bought 120 lbs. of sugar and 70 lbs. of honey, which I took to my father, asking him to begin the proceedings. I was extremely disappointed when, after continued efforts to gain administrative approval, my father was refused permission to brew beer for the marriage. Government was steadily tightening up its restrictions on the brewing of native beer. And so after waiting two months in vain for the traditional practices to be carried out by our parents – which couldn't be completed without the beer – we decided to go ahead with our plans and be married without the customary Kikuyu formalities. The established amount was paid over to my in-laws and the wedding was enjoyed by all.

This was September 1952, when Government started repatriating Kikuyus who were found in the towns without employment. The newspapers carried frequent stories of "people arrested during Mau Mau oathing ceremonies" and increasing numbers of Kikuyu were being sentenced to seven years hard labour for administering the "Mau Mau oaths". Instead of diminishing political activity, however, these initial repressive measures by Government only served to increase political interest among the Kikuyu and demonstrate the need for greater unity. At the same time, KAU was growing in strength and popularity and was holding huge rallies all over the country. In addition to voicing African grievances regarding land, political representation, wages, educational facilities, etc., many KAU leaders, under increasing pressure from Government, started to condemn Mau Mau in their speeches and called for their members to disassociate themselves from secret societies and oathings. Some of these men were serious in their condemnation of Mau Mau; others, however, were saying words simply to please Government, often using expressions or sayings in Kikuyu which had more than one meaning.

It is important to note two things about these public condemnations of Mau Mau by KAU leaders during this period. First, you will remember that the term "Mau Mau" was popularized by the press and wasn't used by members of the secret society to describe their organization. Thus, denouncing Mau Mau was not in itself interpreted to be a denunciation of the underground (KCA) movement. Secondly, most Kikuyu realized that Government was forcing these leaders to denounce Mau Mau and, believing strongly that some of these men were themselves members of the organization, took their statements with a grain of salt, always looking for double meanings which would alter the apparent intentions of the speaker. What must be clearly understood is the fact that the Kikuyu people as a whole, almost without exception, believed beyond a doubt that men such as Kenyatta, Koinange, and other important Kikuyu leaders of KAU were strong supporters, if not leaders, of the underground movement. Hence, anything these men might say was interpreted on this assumption.

In this same month of September, I once again changed my place of residence. Marriage had increased my financial responsibilities and I decided to move in with a friend in Nairobi so as to save the daily bus fares to and from the city. My wife remained in Kiambaa and each Friday evening I would return in order to spend the weekend with my family. This was not a happy situation, to be sure, but was one forced on most African men in Nairobi by the low wages and shortage of adequate housing.

PART 2

Seeing that the six pistols and ammunition were there, I walked behind the hotel to meet Kinyua, stopping just long enough to tell him everything was going well and to accept a packet containing the 1,000s.

State of Emergency

On the night of 20 October 1952, Government declared a State of Emergency. The weeks prior to this had seen an increase in violence on both sides: Government was stepping up its repressive measures and arrests, while Mau Mau was beginning to use force in an effort to eliminate Government stooges and informers. When Senior Chief Waruhiu, one of the foremost Government supporters, was assassinated by Mau Mau fighters, the scene was set for the long, bitter and brutal struggle which was not to end officially until 1960.

When I read about the Emergency declaration on my way to work on the morning of the 21st, however, I had no idea of the terrifying events which were to follow. As I walked back to the office after lunch, thinking about the large number of KAU leaders who had been arrested the night before, I noticed a group of African policemen on the next street who, with bayonets fixed, were forcibly directing all passers-by along a route leading (as I discovered later) to the Caledonia sports grounds.

Before I realized it, an *askari* was coming toward me swinging his rifle butt furiously. I avoided the blow but the unfortunate African next to me was knocked to the ground. Seeing the dangers of continuing along this street, I retreated and took a longer but safer route back to the office. Through the office window I observed the scene being enacted below. Streams of Africans were being indiscriminately pushed and bullied onto the playing field where the first mass check-up, or sweep, was being carried out by police and Government Special Unit teams.

Following closely upon the declaration of the Emergency were a series of Government restrictions, such as curfews and travel permits, and an accelerated number of arrests, sweeps and harsh Government practices. In these early stages, it seemed to most of us that men were being arrested and detained or imprisoned largely on the basis of their holding positions of leadership within KAU and certain Kikuyu welfare societies. Though Government often acted on information gathered by informers, many innocent people were being arrested, mistreated and detained.

*I avoided the blow but the unfortunate African next to me
was knocked to the ground.*

Strong feelings were developing towards those Africans who were neutral or were thought to be assisting Government as informers, and every effort was being made to administer the oath to everyone not yet initiated. Here it must be stated that while most educated Kikuyu did not believe in the magical features of the oath, the majority of illiterate peasants felt a person would in fact die if he violated the oath. With this belief, one felt a certain pride in tricking unsuspecting non-members into an oathing ceremony.

At the same time, Kikuyu who openly worked with Government, or were known to have acted in a traitorous fashion, were blacklisted and every effort was made to eliminate them. In most cases their crimes were discussed by councils of elders, which then passed sentence and made arrangements for the traitors to be killed. Though not a member of any such council, I fully agreed that Government agents, informers and brutal loyalists should be killed.

By the end of 1952, many such traitors had been eliminated and dozens of Mau Mau leaders had found their way into Government detention or concentration camps.

As for myself, 1953 began with my asking for a raise, being refused, resigning and finding another insurance office job. I also managed, at long last, to get a house from the City Council. It was located in Bahati and consisted of one small room, barely large enough to contain a single bed, a small table and two chairs. This one room had to serve as bedroom, living room and kitchen. The toilet and shower, which served several rooms, was located outside. Not wanting to bring my wife into these conditions, I decided to allow her to remain in our larger house in Kiambaa.

In Nairobi itself, life had become very dangerous. Street shootings of Government informers and loyalists, daylight robberies and the theft of guns and ammunition were common occurences.

It was in May 1953 that I had my first opportunity to assist the Mau Mau fighters in their desperate struggle for arms and ammunition. After eating lunch one day, I was standing in front of a sporting goods shop on Government Road looking into the window at the various items on display. There were some guns in the window and as I peered in an Asian salesman stood by the doorway watching me intently. After a few minutes he asked me in a pleasant voice to come inside and have a look around. He seemed extremely friendly and was curious about my interest in the shop. Sensing his real motives, I was quite willing to talk. We spoke about a few pieces of sports equipment and bicycles and then the conversation turned to more personal matters. I told him where I lived and worked and before leaving agreed to meet him for lunch the following day at a nearby restaurant.

As we sat at the table, feeling each other out over a cup of tea, the Asian kept bringing the discussion back to firearms. The conversation was not direct; it didn't have to be. He knew I was a Kikuyu and I knew what he was driving at. There was suspicion on both sides, however, my own caution deriving from a fear that the Asian might be a Special Branch man.

When he finally revealed that he was in a position to get me firearms if I wanted them, I hesitated, seeking a moment or two to weigh the matter. The dangers were obvious. If I agreed, it might mean walking right into a trap. He could simply hand over the weapons, accept my money and then call in his Special Branch comrades to arrest me. Since being found with even a bullet in one's possession was a capital offence, I would certainly be tried and hung.

On the other hand, our fighters urgently needed arms and this could be a big break for both Mau Mau and myself. No one could expect me to run these risks for nothing and I could certainly use the commission money made possible by such a deal. I had to take the chance and told the Asian I could use one pistol. After a brief discussion we agreed on a price of 150s. and arranged to meet the following day.

We met at the same restaurant, had lunch and then went out to his car and got in. As we talked about the weather and other trivial subjects, he slipped the pistol into my pocket and I handed him the 150s. We parted and since the money I'd given him had come from my own savings, I now had to make arrangements with a buyer.

Knowing several of the Nairobi fighters, I asked one of them to contact the appropriate persons and inform them that I was in a position to buy firearms. A few days later I was approached by a Fort Hall man nicknamed Kinyua. He was a leading fighter in the city and the elders assigned him the task of handling these matters. I told him I could get large quantities of arms, mainly pistols (the sporting goods store didn't handle heavy arms), and that the price would range from 150s. to 250s. We agreed on a price of 200s. for the one pistol I'd brought and then went to his Bahati house for further discussion. This is where I could always contact him, Kinyua said, and handing me the money he instructed me to arrange for a larger purchase of both guns and ammunition.

When I left Kinyua I went immediately to see my Asian friend. Telling him what I wanted, we arranged to meet a few days later on Latema Road in front of the Green Hotel. He was to bring me six pistols and some ammunition for an agreed price of 800s.

Returning to Bahati, I informed Kinyua of the arrangements, telling him to meet me behind the Green Hotel and to bring 1,000s. He was pleased, offering me a cup of tea before we parted. As yet he didn't know where I was getting the guns or what price I was paying for them. It was sufficient merely to get them at a reasonable price.

On the appointed day I was waiting in front of the Green Hotel when the Asian drove up in his car. With him was a European whom

I'd seen earlier in the shop. They were obviously partners and, though a little concerned at seeing a white face, I wasn't really worried. During the course of the fighting many Europeans took advantage of their positions in business or Government to become rich men. Some sold arms, others took bribes and many appropriated Kikuyu livestock, which they disposed of for cash. This is an aspect of the revolution which none of the white man's books on the subject seem to mention, though it is a well known fact among Kikuyu.

As arranged, another car, containing two of Kinyua's men, pulled up behind the first. I had approached the Asian and was checking the contents of a sack in the trunk of his car while his partner sat poised behind the wheel. Seeing that the six pistols and ammunition were there, I walked behind the hotel to meet Kinyua, stopping just long enough to tell him everything was going well and to accept a packet containing the 1,000s.

Back in front, after removing my 200s. commission, I gave the money to the Asian and went inside the hotel to watch as the sack was transferred to Kinyua's car. This completed, both parties drove off hurriedly, as I sat over a cup of tea. Mau Mau fighters had acquired six weapons, the Asian and his European partner had earned 800s., and I was both 200s. richer and an active participant in the Kikuyu struggle for land and freedom.

However, I was in a rather dangerous position. On the one hand, Kinyua might somehow find out about my self-calculated commission (though I'd arranged with the Asian not to disclose our price to anyone), putting me in hot water with Mau Mau fighters and thus endangering my life. And on the other hand, the CID or Special Branch might get wind of our transaction and I knew what that meant.

Thinking the matter over carefully during the next few days, I decided that the risks were too great for the little money involved. Arranging for a meeting with Kinyua and the Asian, I put buyer and seller in direct contact and stepped out of the picture entirely. Some time later, I ran into Kinyua and he told me they had obtained considerably more arms from the Asian – and at a surprisingly better price. Not wanting to hear any more, I told him I was in a hurry and left.

At this time Government was carrying out extensive checks on all Kikuyu, Embu and Meru (the KEM tribe) in the African locations and on the streets of the city. Movement restrictions were imposed on all KEM tribesmen and written permits, issued at Government offices, were required for anyone wishing to travel outside Nairobi. Kikuyu in large numbers were being repatriated from the towns and European Settled Areas back to the reserves. It didn't seem to matter to Government that many of these people had never lived in their home areas – or hadn't been back for 10 or 20 years – and that most had neither homes nor land to return to.

Any African, and especially a Kikuyu, who was caught in the city without the proper passes and work card was tried in the courts and imprisoned. A close relative of mine suffered this fate. He had lost his job two days earlier and was arrested while seeking other employment.

In an attempt to undermine the effects of the oath, Government organized what they termed "cleansing ceremonies" throughout Kikuyuland. Christians were not forced to undergo these ceremonies but were obliged to confess in their churches. I continued spending my weekends in Kiambu and one Sunday all the people from my location were gathered by the stream near my house to be "cleansed".

Unlike our traditional cleansing ceremonies, these were forced rather than voluntary and each person was made to pay the administrator anywhere from 2s. to 10s. Government had hired a number of witchdoctors, often referred to as "Her Majesty's Witchdoctors", who cleansed people ten to twenty at a time. This mass cleansing was, again, opposed to Kikuyu traditional practices.

In view of the fact that most Kikuyu were members of Mau Mau, many of the witchdoctors employed by Government were themselves members, and in some cases leaders, of the underground movement. It was my strong feeling that the man employed for the ceremony I attended had arranged with leaders of our organization to conduct the cleansing ceremony in a manner deemed utterly ineffective. I first became suspicious when I noticed people coming out of the ceremony smiling and observed the rather light-hearted manner in which the medicine man conducted the ceremony. Normally, this being a serious matter to Kikuyu, the administrator remains very solemn and straight-faced. Again, as I was being cleansed, I was surprised to hear the witchdoctor use words and expressions which conveyed a meaning different, and in some cases opposite, to that which was intended by Government.

For my part, as I didn't believe in either the magic of the oath or the curses used in the cleansing ceremony, it wouldn't have mattered whether the witchdoctor performed the ceremony correctly or not. All I wanted to do was obtain one of the Government certificates and avoid the trouble which befell those who refused to be cleansed. My personal feeling is that these ceremonies had little, if any, effect even on those who believed in magic. The ranks of Mau Mau continued to swell despite all the "cleansing", and Government finally abandoned the entire project.

With movement restrictions tightened even further by Government, it became difficult for me to go home on the weekends. But I managed to convince my employer that I'd given up my room in Nairobi and he wrote me a note, through which I obtained a Road Pass. Retaining my Nairobi pass, I now had two passes – allowing me to stay in Nairobi or go home, as I pleased.

Arrests in both Nairobi and the reserves continued to mount, with Kikuyu being detained as Mau Mau suspects or imprisoned for not having poll tax receipts, employment cards or residence permits. Government sweeps in the Nairobi African locations also became more frequent. Occasionally I was lucky enough to get wind of a sweep planned for Bahati and would take the bus for Kiambaa right after work and spend the night with my family. It is in just this manner that I escaped the three-day Bahati lock-up. Early one morning security forces entered the location and bolted all the doors from the outside, forcing the inhabitants to remain in their rooms without food or water for three full days, not even allowing them to go to the outside toilets. While Government carried out an intensive check of each and every room, people who hadn't stocked up on food went hungry.

Government was obliged to take such drastic steps because of its failure to win the cooperation of the KEM tribesmen and, to a certain extent, other Africans in Nairobi as well. If someone were shot, or a gun stolen, on the streets of the city, Africans present on the scene would either keep walking as if they hadn't seen the incident or assist the fighter in making his escape. Most did this as a sign of open support for the revolt, others because of their fear of being earmarked as traitors and hence putting their own lives in jeopardy.

In the reserves, Government faced the same problem. With over 90% of the Kikuyu people being members of Mau Mau, Government found it increasingly difficult to protect its African informers, Christian supporters and loyalist chiefs and headmen. I recall one headman in Limuru who was shot by a Mau Mau fighter in the hospital after he'd been wounded in his home. The fighter simply entered the hospital dressed as an attendant, shot the headman in his bed and disappeared into the darkness.

After the above incident Government put into effect another restriction, according to which patients were not allowed to receive any visitors. In addition, all the hospitals were to be heavily guarded. This particular measure affected me directly in July, when my wife entered the hospital to give birth to our first child. During the three days after my son was born, I tried very hard to get permission to visit my wife, but this failed. However, being determined to see her anyway, I decided to try to get in without a pass. On the fourth day I put on my best suit of clothes – so as to appear an important person – and asked my Asian employer to drive me to the hospital. He agreed to do this and let me off right in front of the guarded gate. From there I simply walked through the gate, paying no attention to the two armed guards, and entered one of the hospital wards. As I had planned, the guards assumed from my dress and manner that I wasn't a Kikuyu.

Inside the ward, I went up to a European matron and asked to be directed to my wife. She obliged, not thinking to ask for my pass as I couldn't – or so she must have thought – have gotten in without one. She called a Kikuyu nurse who led me to see my wife. As no Kikuyu had entered the hospital as a visitor for such a long time, this nurse couldn't believe her ears when she heard us speaking our native tongue. It was an amusing sight to see her confused expression as she left the ward.

Conditions in the reserves were deteriorating rapidly. Police, military or home guard posts were being built in every location – with the forced labour of the local peasantry – and Government initiated its brutal and inhuman scheme of collective punishment. All able-bodied adults and young people were forced to work on the "communal labour" teams, building camps, roads and bench terraces. In addition, with Government unable to win the voluntary support of the people, it began to beat and torture them into confessions and used every method at its disposal to intimidate and terrorize the Kikuyu into cooperation.

As examples of some of the techniques used to extract confessions, I might mention the following: men were castrated; boiling water, coke bottles or a poisonous shrub were put into the vaginas of women and girls; suspects were dragged over rough roads at the end of a rope. As well there were the more common forms of torture involving beatings and starvation. I know individuals who luckily managed to live through such experiences and am in no way trying to exaggerate the brutalities carried out in the name of law and order. In fact, an entire book could be written on the single subject of Government "techniques and practices of winning cooperation and extracting confessions". My attempt here is only to indicate a few of the crimes committed by Government in its efforts to crush the Kikuyu revolt for land and freedom.

A favorite Government tactic aimed at terrorizing the people into submission was to forcibly enter a person's home at night, call out all adult males and take them into the bush, where they would be shot. While this happened most frequently in the reserves, I recall one incident in which a good friend of mine was killed in just this manner. He was a post office employee who, to my knowledge, wasn't even a member of Mau Mau. One night a group of Kenya Police dragged him from his home and shot him in cold blood. I learned of this from neighbors and felt very bad. The same slaughter of innocent people by the security forces did much to increase the bitterness of Mau Mau fighters and their desire for revenge.

Under these severe conditions, toward the middle of 1953, thousands of Kikuyu young men entered the forests of Mount Kenya and the Aberdares. Others, thinking the risks less great, fled to the towns to live with friends or relatives. I thought about joining the forest fighters at this time but made no real effort to do so.

In Nairobi, the campaign of robbery, stealing or purchasing weapons, and eliminating traitors continued to grow. Being alone in the office where I worked, I was in a good position to assist the men engaged in such activities. On many occasions they would come and spend the entire day in my office hiding from security force personnel. Also, I was able to sell a good deal of stolen merchandise for them, acting as a middleman and working on a commission basis.

It was sometime around July 1953 when one of the office boys told me of some men who had a large quantity of stolen hides and skins but no one to sell them to. He knew I had managed to sell some clothing and textiles and asked if I could help his friends. I told him I might be able to and he ran out of the office, returning minutes later with a man I'd never seen before. He told me they had 650 skins and 100 hides and I said I would do my best to dispose of them. We agreed on my commission and he left.

I then went next door to see an Arab clerk with whom I was friendly. He worked for a hides and skins dealer and, being in the same building, was the easiest person for me to contact. I explained the situation and he showed great interest, wanting to get right down to work on the details of our arrangement and the transfer of the goods. He offered 2s. apiece for the skins and 5s. for the hides, prices extremely low for these items, but with stolen goods one had to take what one could get. After agreeing that I was to receive a 500s. commission from him on the successful completion of the sale, we separated and I returned to talk to the man with the merchandise.

There was a hides and skins license hanging on the wall of my office, I told him, and the deal was settled so long as he could provide the means to transport the goods to the buyer's house. He wasn't too happy about the price but I convinced him that any price was better than none. The goods had been stolen from a railway freight car and were hidden in a corner of the Nairobi African stadium. The gate-keeper was in on the deal and since there were no sporting events until the weekend, the merchandise was safe for the time being.

The following afternoon the man came by with a lorry. I had the license and together we drove over to the stadium. It was about 3 p.m. when the gate-keeper let us in and we quickly started loading the goods onto the truck. I left before the job was complete, not wanting to take any unnecessary chances of being trapped inside by the police with my employer's license.

I waited by the roadside, a short distance away but it wasn't long before the lorry pulled up and I got in. We were safe now. I had a valid license, I was employed by a man who in fact sometimes dealt in hides and skins and the men with me had the proper documents on the vehicle.

We drove past Shauri Moyo location, crossing the bridge to Pumwani and then into Eastleigh where my Asian clerk's employer lived. He was expecting us and opened the gate as we approached. The goods were hastily unloaded and the agreed price was paid. The thieves received 1,800s., out of which I was paid 400s. commission. Added to the 500s. I received from the Asian, this made my total earnings 900s., a considerable sum for a few hours work.

Life in Nairobi, however, was becoming ever more difficult. I thought I was somewhat secure with my Road Pass and Nairobi residence permit, but around mid-1953 Government began issuing a new green card to all KEM tribesmen. Forgery was very common with the old passes, so the new one was designed to avoid this by containing a full-face photograph of the bearer.

To get one of these cards, a man had to obtain a letter from his employer confirming his employment and take this to the appropriate Government office along with his Identification Certificate, poll tax receipts and residence permit. Since thousands of people were flocking to get this new pass, the queues formed around the Government office were huge. When I got the letter from my employer I spent three full days waiting in line to get the card. Others had already waited 10 days and I decided that there must be an easier way. I had noticed a friend working inside the office where the cards were being issued and I asked him if there was any way I could avoid the long queue. Taking my documents and letter, he said it would be easy and moved away to place them on top of the pile which had already been checked.

Within minutes I was called out of the crowd to be photographed. But when the picture was fixed on the green card and the necessary details were added I still needed the initials of the European officer to make it legal. Considering the mob of people waiting, this could have taken another three days. Luckily, my friend called me over and forged the officer's initials on my card.

In this manner, I did in one day what would have taken at least two weeks. Others, by paying a small fee, managed to get green cards in this way without the proper documents or employment letter. Government's new "foolproof" green card system was thus showing great weaknesses before it even got started.

Other laws were also passed, but lawlessness and brutality increased on both sides. When Government killed – whether it be a Mau Mau fighter, a suspect or a completely innocent peasant – it was always done in the name of "law and order" and hence was morally "good". When Mau Mau killed, it was a horrible crime committed by a savage and brutal people. This, at any rate, was the impression the newspapers and Government tried to create. I wouldn't deny that some pretty brutal acts were committed by certain Mau Mau members. But it is ridiculous for the white man and his Government to condemn this as if their hands were clean. Killing with a sten gun, hand grenade or atom bomb is somehow looked upon as "cleaner" than killing with a *panga*. But killing is killing, the way I see it, and most Africans possessed no other weapon than *pangas*. To blow a man's head off with a rifle or to lop it off with a *panga* could make little difference to the man killed. The British and other white colonial powers took more lives violently in their two world wars than the Kikuyu will ever manage to take, so let them not call us savages on this account.

Mau Mau in Nairobi seemed to have the support of almost all the Africans. I remember one morning seeing the usual crowd of city workers making their way into the center of town. What was odd was that they were avoiding a much used foot path along the railway tracks. When I approached, I discovered the reason. There, in the middle of the path, lay the body of a man. It was only about fifteen yards from the main road and must have been seen by literally thousands of people who passed the spot – no one reported it to Government. I learned later that the man was a police informer who had been killed that morning by Mau Mau fighters.

This type of incident was a common occurrence in the streets of Nairobi during this period. As a whole, the African population was very uncooperative with Government. Most were members of Mau Mau, others were sympathetic to the movement and another group remained neutral out of fear. The Government measures to suppress Mau Mau seemed to be having little real effect in the city. In the reserves, however, Government was merciless, applying collective fines and punishment and forcing everyone to put in long hours of communal labour. Under these conditions many Kikuyu families sought refuge in Nairobi.

One of my aunts, finding herself on the chief's blacklist and facing strong possibilities of imprisonment or death, came to Nairobi at this time to live with her husband. He was employed as a driver for a motor company and had been provided with housing. The difficulty was that his single room just wasn't large enough for himself, his wife and their three children. The children were forced to quit school when Government closed down the Kikuyu independent schools. Though two friends were already sharing my small house, I offered to take my aunt's eldest son in with me. We were now four, in a room barely big enough for one.

...suspects were dragged over rough roads at the end of a rope as a method of extracting confessions...

A Good Friend of Mine

Stephen Kamau was, and still is, a very good friend of mine. A slender, medium-sized man from Githunguri, Stephen had taken the first and second Mau Mau oaths. Though he's a jocular fellow, always with a practical joke or good story, he was very serious about Mau Mau, telling me all about the second, or fighting oath and trying to convince me to take it.

He worked as a switchboard operator in the same building where I worked. One day in October he was approached by a man who had a number of typewriters and an adding machine to sell. The machines were stolen, of course, and since Stephen and I never turned down an opportunity for making extra money in this way, Stephen said he thought he could get rid of them and came to speak to me about it. We had worked together on a number of small deals involving stolen clothing and textiles, and so we firmly trusted one another.

It was as we were eating lunch that Stephen told me about the typewriters. He said we might be able to make some money and of course I was interested. I approached the same Arab who had bought the hides and skins and he said he could use a typewriter and an adding machine. We finally agreed on a price of 450s. for both and I asked him not to disclose this to anyone.

I returned and told Stephen to tell his contact that we could get 100s. for the typewriters and 150s. for the adding machine and that we could use one of each immediately. The two machines were brought to the office and I took them over to the Arab, who paid me on the spot. Stephen then took the 250s. to the thieves and was paid his 100s. commission. In all we made 300s. in this transaction and split it equally.

The following day we approached another Asian who owned and ran a tutorial college. He was very excited by our offer and said he needed five typewriters. The agreed on price was 175s. per machine; Stephen and I told our contact it was 150s. The goods were delivered that evening and we took them over to the college and collected the money. Deducting 125s., Stephen took the rest to his friend and was

134

paid his 50s. commission on each machine. We had thus made another 375s. The thieves apparently had no more typewriters and we never heard from them again.

Government at this time was putting ever greater pressure on Mau Mau in the city. Sweeps of the African locations were very frequent and chiefs were being brought in to identify suspects and assist Government in rounding up people who had fled to Nairobi to escape the communal labour in the reserves.

Unfortunately, many chiefs took advantage of this new found power to penalize innocent people on personal grounds having nothing to do with Mau Mau. Some also sought to increase the manpower of their communal labour teams by falsely accusing persons of having fled from their locations. A friend of mine was to suffer this fate when Government bulldozed the squatter village he was living in on the outskirts of town. Because of the great shortage of houses in the city many persons were forced to erect these poor little huts without permission and now Government was demolishing them on the pretext that they were centers of Mau Mau activity. In some cases this was true, but many innocent people were thrown homeless into the streets.

My friend was living in such a village with his wife and two children. When the security forces arrived in the early hours of the morning, he was falsely accused by one of the Embu chiefs. Though my friend was from Kiambu, this chief claimed he had run away from Embu and was highly implicated in Mau Mau activities. Along with others in a similar position, my friend was taken to Embu and subjected to very harsh treatment. In the meantime, his wife and children were homeless and I had to offer them shelter in my little room. There were now three adults and four children in the one room. Luckily, I obtained a pass for the woman on the pretext that she was my wife.

This state of affairs was not at all unique. Many people were living ten or twelve to a room, with the men having to claim as many as three wives with several children each. As more and more men were arrested and detained or killed, this condition grew worse. Many women and children were stranded in the city without friends or relatives to look after them.

After about two months, my friend returned from Embu and took up his old job in Nairobi. He was extremely thankful that I'd taken care of his family, as they would have been in a desperate condition

My friend was highly implicated in Mau Mau activities... In the mean-time, his wife and children were homeless and I had to offer them shelter in my one little room.

without me. Unfortunately, the poor man was arrested once more soon after his return. This time he was sent into detention, where, I learned later, he died from the beatings of his interrogators.

In the meantime, thefts of European and Asian property were increasing. In Nairobi, gangs formed which specialized in this type of activity. One day Stephen introduced me to a member of a group which managed to obtain large quantities of bicycles from Asian shops. Although I was very interested, bicycles were an extremely dangerous item to handle. With the large number of thefts, police were stopping all cyclists to check on their licenses and vehicle registration numbers, the latter being checked against a list containing the numbers of stolen bicycles.

I thought the matter over for a few weeks and finally hit upon an idea. It was somewhat involved but each phase was simple enough. First, I would go to a bicycle shop and purchase an inexpensive spare part. Having the cash receipt, I would simply add a bicycle sale to it. Next, with the stolen bicycle in my possession, I would use metal punches to stamp onto the frame one or two additional numbers. Entering this new number on the cash sale receipt, I would go to the appropriate Government office, present the receipt, have the forged number registered and obtain a license for the usual fee. This done, I could use the bicycle for a few weeks and then sell it for a considerable profit.

Stephen and I began by buying one bicycle each at a cost of 50s. My plan worked to perfection; the road license was obtained with no difficulty and a new and profitable business had been discovered. I sold the first bicycle in about 10 days for 250s. and Stephen also got rid of his. We continued buying the stolen vehicles in units of two and over the next several months I must have sold at least half a dozen at profits ranging from 150s. to 200s. My customers were always pleased to buy virtually new bicycles at a ridiculously low price and several are riding them to this day.

I was still living in my Bahati room during this period and, to my horror, I discovered that one of my roommates had never taken the first Mau Mau oath. Though the man was sympathetic toward the movement, his father was a home guard in the reserves and it wasn't unlikely – considering the great hatred felt toward the loyalist home guards – that my friend's life would be taken in revenge for his father's activities. For harboring such a man, I too was placing my life in very grave danger. I had to arrange for him to take the oath, though this was not an easy task.

Security forces were all over the city, carrying out sweeps of the African locations and checking all KEM tribesmen found on the streets. Anyone found without his Kipande (Work Card), green card, poll tax receipts or residence permit was very lucky to escape arrest and detention. Even with all these documents a man was fortunate to avoid detention in the late months of 1953. Every Kikuyu was a suspect and Government hardly bothered with a man's documents before detaining him.

Under these conditions, oathing ceremonies were arranged only with great difficulty. I approached an Mkamba friend of mine whom I knew to be very active in Mau Mau affairs and asked him if oaths were still being administered in Pumwani. Luckily, he said an oathing ceremony had been planned for the coming weekend and that my friend should come along.

Returning to Bahati, I had a long talk with the man, explaining the dangers we both faced and convincing him of the necessity of his taking the oath. It was a Friday, and after telling him where the ceremony was to be held on the following evening, I left for Kiambaa and a weekend with my wife and family.

On Monday I was extremely relieved to hear that my friend had been initiated. He was now a member of Gikuyu and Mumbi and my fears for both of us disappeared.

I also found myself again in a position to help Mau Mau in its quest for arms. There was an old shotgun lying rusted in one of the upstairs offices and Stephen suggested that we give it to the fighters. I thought it would be quite easy to get away with, so the next day Stephen brought in a fighter nicknamed Nyamu. We discussed the shotgun and asked Nyamu to have a look at it and see if it might not be of some use in the forest. One of his jobs was to arrange for arms to be sent from Nairobi to the forest fighters. We went up to the fourth floor and, locking the door behind us, inspected the gun. It had been badly neglected, for it was covered with rust and a bolt was missing. Nevertheless, Nyamu said he could fix it up and if need be, make the missing part himself. With this old shotgun, he said, we might be able to acquire ten or twelve rifles or a Sten gun.

Next day, he came by in an old Ford automobile during the lunch hour and handed us a sack. I went up to the office, stuffed the shotgun in the bag and walked out with it to Nyamu's car. We made no money on this deal and the fighter left after giving us his sincere thanks. It was almost two years later when I learned that Nyamu had been killed in the forest.

The Christmas season of 1953 came and passed in a most unusual fashion. Formerly, this was a time when I enjoyed the cycling competition sponsored by the schools and the celebrations and feasts in the countryside. On this occasion, however, no trumpets sounded on the sports fields and all gatherings were prohibited by Government. I was home in Kiambaa on Christmas Eve, but there was no singing in the churches and my father feared slaughtering a goat lest it be construed as preparation for an oathing ceremony. I didn't even leave the location to visit friends, since this required a travel permit; and even with a pass, it wouldn't have been wise to go very far. Traveling along the road in places where one was not well-known often led to a man's arrest or even death.

Since Mau Mau prohibited the drinking of European beer and Government forbid the brewing of native beer, there were no drinking parties or dances. This was to be my first dull and unpleasant Christmas Day. The festive gatherings of the past years were replaced by sombre reports of so and so's arrest, detention or death. The usual sound of trumpet and school band found its substitute in the horrible noise of machine gun and rifle fire.

January 1954 started with the arrest of the friend who was living with me. I left him on Saturday morning and the following Monday evening I returned from work to find that he wasn't home. Thinking he would turn up in a short time, I began preparing dinner for the three of us (the woman and her two children had returned to the reserve after the second arrest of her husband). When several hours had passed and he still had not come, I knew that something must have happened.

Recognizing the dangers my friend faced by remaining outside without a pass, I spent a very restless night. The next morning I visited some of his friends but no one had seen him. Tuesday night found him still absent and when he hadn't appeared by Wednesday evening, I just about lost hope. It was simple; he was either arrested or dead.

Then, at about 7 p.m., in he came. He was dirty and dusty and looked very weak and worried. "I was picked up at noon on Saturday just as I was returning to the room," he said. "They took me to Nairobi West where people are being detained and loaded onto railway cars. Luckily, a home guard I knew told the mzungu I wasn't a bad man and the officer told me to get out." He had run all the way home, despite the curfew, and hadn't eaten for five days. I helped him to get off his clothes, which were full of lice and fleas from the Nairobi West station, and when he'd cleaned up a bit, we sat down to eat.

We came to learn a few weeks later that thousands of Nairobi Kikuyu, Embu and Meru people were being loaded onto trains and taken to Mackinnon Road and Manyani detention camps. If a man didn't see a friend of his for a few days, he could rest assured that the man was either arrested and detained or dead.

It wasn't long before it was my turn to disappear and throw fear into all my friends. One morning as I was walking to work, a European policeman stopped me and asked to see my documents. When I gave them to him, he pulled a little piece of paper out of his pocket and was much concerned with my green card. Government, it seems, had discovered some of the forgeries and now this man was looking at mine and comparing it with a specimen of the correct initials.

One look was enough; he ordered me to sit down and began checking the others who passed by. In a while there were ten of us and the officer marched us toward the police station. We were locked in a cell which was so crowded that one barely had space enough to sleep. Here we remained for the first three days without food, suffering the abuses and occasional beatings from the *askari*.

Toward the end of the third day, I asked one of the guards if he would telephone my place of work and tell my employer where I was. This, of course, had to cost money. I took out of my sock the 20s. note I always kept for emergencies and handed it to the man. It was a high price for a 30-cent phone call, but my employer was contacted and he came right over. They told him that I had obtained a green card in an illegal manner and, having no valid permit to remain in the city, I would either be repatriated or imprisoned.

Though he argued for a while, my employer helped little, except that his coming did enable me to threaten the officer in charge. I told him my boss was an important man in Government circles and that he would inform the Governor himself if we were detained any longer without food or if the *askari* continued to beat us without cause.

From that moment on beatings stopped and food was served. We were also brought some water and were allowed to go to the toilet at will instead of twice a day. On the seventh day, however, we were taken to court. It was a long wait, but finally my name was called and I heard the Magistrate read off the charge. I was accused of being arrested in Nairobi without a valid permit. Not hearing any mention of the forged green card, I took heart and began defending myself.

I told the magistrate I had every pass I thought necessary and began handing them one by one over to the Court *Askari*, who passed them on to the judge. First, I gave him my poll tax receipts for three consecutive years, then my road pass, which allowed me to travel between Nairobi and Kiambu, then my employment card. Finally, I asked him to examine my Identification Certificate and green card, both of which were attached to the charge sheet he held in his hand.

The magistrate was dumbfounded. He could think of no other pass or document I might be expected to carry and, after a final glance at the charge sheet, he handed me my papers and ordered me out of the court-room. Thus, due to the carelessness of the police, I escaped at least six months imprisonment.

When I returned to the office, my employer couldn't believe that I'd been set free. My friends had given me up for lost and, luckily, my family in Kiambaa didn't even know I was arrested.

Conditions in Nairobi's African locations had become worse, particularly in Bahati, where I lived. Arrests, shootings and strong-arm methods – by both Government and Mau Mau – were the order of the day. Within a week after my trial, a headman was shot dead by Mau Mau fighters and I knew Government would have its revenge. A sweep seemed inevitable and since every house would be entered and the inhabitants' documents checked, I felt uneasy with my green card. I'd escaped once, but I couldn't get rid of the forged card and the next time would certainly mean at least six months in prison. With this in mind I decided to spend my nights in Kiambaa until I saw what would happen at Bahati. I thought it would be safer this way, but about a week later, as I was shaving hurriedly in order to catch my bus, I heard rifle shots coming from a distant corner of the village. This undoubtedly meant a sweep. I quickly finished shaving and left the house, heading toward the bus terminus two miles away.

After covering about a mile of the distance, I met a woman I knew and she told me a sweep was taking place in the direction I was going. I had to deviate, taking a five mile route which joined the main road I was leaving near the terminus. I think I'd walked about three miles along this route when a group of home guards and tribal police emerged from a maize field shouting: "Look! There goes another one." Before I could think of escape, they fell upon me with clubs, batons and the flats of their *simis*. It was my suit, shoes and wrist watch they were after and I think they'd have killed me for them if it weren't for the home guard leader who, coming up late, recognized me and called off his men.

Bruised all over, my left arm swelling like a balloon, I took off my shoes, tie, jacket and wrist watch and gave them to the leader of the group for safekeeping. This was primarily to make myself a less attrac-tive target for the other home guards I might meet on the way back to Kiambaa.

My arm, which didn't really heal for over a month, was bad enough to keep me out of work for a week. The home guard leader returned my belongings and when I went back to work I decided to take my chances with Bahati.

I found that during my absence a 6 p.m. curfew had been established for the African location. It wasn't long before I was once more in hot water. One evening as I was returning to my room from a Bahati tearoom not more than a few hundred yards away, I heard the 6 o'clock whistle booming out of the nearby police post. Police and home guards were all over the place, arresting and beating anyone they found outside the houses. I knew what I had to do and quickly entered the nearest door.

I'd never met the person who lived in the house, but he understood and let me stay until about 8 p.m. when I thought I should make a break for my own room. I had been watching the streets carefully and failed to see a single *askari*. Unluckily, however, a short distance from my house I ran smack into three constables emerging from the bathroom serving my block.

Just as I was opening my door, one of the *askari* smashed me between the shoulders with his rifle butt. The other two men joined in the beating – my neighbors later told me they didn't think I'd survive the assault. When they had beaten me to the ground, one of the constables stepped back and asked me how much money I had. This wasn't unusual; they were offering to let me live in return for a small monetary consideration.

I handed them 30s., which was all the money I had on me, and threw in my 200s. Roamer wrist watch. They accepted and after kicking me a few more times for good measure, left me to drag my badly bruised body into the room. It was in this manner that many *askari* and home guards became rich men during the Emergency.

These early months of 1954 were very difficult throughout Kikuyuland; curfews, communal labour, beatings, killings and hunger were widespread and increasing. For me this was the worst period of the Emergency.

It wasn't long after I'd been beaten and robbed by the *askari* that I found myself a prisoner of Mau Mau. One of the rules passed by Mau Mau prohibited the use of European buses, beer and cigarettes. Anyone found violating this order, whether he be a member of the organization or not, was lucky to escape with his life. A friend of mine who couldn't stop smoking and drinking was shot and killed by Mau Mau fighters in February.

Nevertheless, I used to smoke in private behind the bolted doors of my room or office. I thought I was fairly safe in this until one day in March. I had just put out a cigarette when there was a knock at the office door. When I opened it, in stepped a man I recognized as one of the fighters in the city. He smelled the cigarette smoke and, seeing that I was alone in the office, accused me of smoking. He left saying he was going to report the matter to the Mau Mau council.

That same night, as I lay sleeping in my Bahati room, I heard someone gently knocking on the door. It was after midnight and when I asked who it was, the men answered: "We are Kikuyu *askari*." I was terrified at hearing this but I got out of bed and opened the door anyway. There was no sense in running.

Two men entered, ordering me to put on my clothes and accompany them. One fighter held a pistol and when I asked him where we were going, he told me that I'd been accused of smoking and that I must go before the Mau Mau court.

As we walked silently through the streets, my fears were great and my heart filled with worry. Smoking was considered a serious offence and I remembered what had happened to my friend. Again, knowing the two fighters were armed, I prayed that we wouldn't meet any security forces. That would mean a battle and could cost me my life. We covered a distance of about a quarter of a mile without incident, however, and then entered a room filled with Kikuyu youths. Most of them were armed with pistols and all were highly intoxicated on *bhangi*, a local opium rolled in a piece of paper and smoked.

Before I could even sit down or say a word in my defence, they passed sentence. One of the young men rose and said: "You were found smoking this morning and will now receive twelve strokes and a fine of 200s." I was then thrown on the floor and lying there face down, with two men sitting on my shoulders and another two holding my legs, received the twelve strokes on the buttocks. When this was finished, they told me someone would come by my office in the morning to collect the fine and sent me back home with a two-man escort.

Because of the strokes, I didn't make it to work the following morning. I did, however, send my friend to leave a message and try to borrow the 200s. for me. He could only get 80s., so when the fighters came by that evening, I gave it to them with a promise to pay the rest later. They left and the matter was closed.

Fear dominated everyone in Kenya during this period, and was particularly great for those who found themselves in neither Government nor Mau Mau forces. The common stories in the newspapers and on the radio were about deaths, killings, houses being burnt down by Government or Mau Mau and people reported missing. Most of the latter had either been arrested and detained, killed by Government or Mau Mau, or had decided to flee to the forests and join the fighters.

To the KEM people, the whole affair had become a miserable nightmare. No one knew what the next day might bring or if he would be alive to see it. For my part, I decided it was time that I joined the Mau Mau fighting forces; life outside was becoming very hard to bear.

I mentioned my desire to Stephen and he directed me to a high ranking Mau Mau official. This man told me I could take the Second Oath but wouldn't be allowed to enter the forest. This, he said, was because the fighters were not accepting disabled or defective persons, or anyone who was the only child of his mother. Since I fell into the latter category, my hopes of entering the forest were shattered.

I did, however, make plans to take the Second Oath. It was to be administered at Pumwani on the next Saturday and the Mau Mau official I'd seen arranged to meet me and take me to the ceremony himself. When the time came, we went to Pumwani only to find that the police had carried out a sweep that morning and the ceremony was indefinitely postponed.

Though I myself was never to take the fighting oath, many thousands took the oath and entered the forests to wage a three-year war against the armies of Kenya and Great Britain. These men were obtaining most of their arms and other supplies from Nairobi – and in order to put a stop to this, Government carried out its "Operation Anvil", which began on 24 April 1954.

On the evening of the 23rd, sensing that something was about to happen, I left to spend the night in Kiambaa. The following morning I got up early, had a cup of tea and set off toward the main stage at Banana Hill to catch the 7 o'clock bus. I took a short cut through the fields, avoiding the trading center near my home.

When I reached the main compound gate, about 600 yards away, I spotted a police reserve officer jumping over the fence and moving toward my house. I watched as he entered my hut and learned later from my wife that he questioned her at length concerning my whereabouts. She told him I'd gone to Nairobi, but he was suspicious on seeing the breakfast utensils spread out on the table. He searched the house thoroughly and then left after taking a cup of tea from the remaining pot.

I continued on my way, not knowing that the village and trading center were undergoing a sweep and that my father, relatives and friends were being loaded onto lorries and taken to the police station some eight miles away. When I reached the bus stage, I was surprised to see all the buses which had left earlier returning to Banana Hill under the charge of policemen. These buses, I soon learned, were taking their passengers to the police station and all roads leading into Nairobi were blocked.

Knowing it was now impossible to get to the city, I decided to stay out of sight. With two friends whom I met at the bus terminus I walked to the nearby market and spent a few hours hidden in one of the stalls. It was about 11 a.m. when, on seeing a lot of people returning from the police post, I decided to go home.

About half a mile from my village I was stopped by a policeman and arrested. He took me to the trading center where I was loaded into a lorry with some others and driven to the police station. It was here that I learned of the massive sweep in Nairobi and Kiambu, in which thousands of persons were rounded up and taken to the detention camps. We late-comers were lucky, as the station appeared to have already filled its quota of potential detainees. By the time I arrived, the cells were filled with those to be deported and I was put with about 600 persons in the open compound under a police guard.

Here we were to remain for the rest of the day and night without food or blankets. Though cold and hungry, however, we were far better off than our comrades in the cells. They were loaded into lorries and taken away to the Manyani or Mackinnon Road detention camps. I was released with the others in the compound the following morning. To my knowledge, the police were not operating on information they had on particular individuals. It seems they had orders to detain so many Kikuyu between the ages of 20 and 30 and they simply took the first people who came along. I was very fortunate to be arrested late, for not only was I not detained, but I managed to escape the beatings and robbery which befell those who were brought in during the early hours of the morning.

In the meantime, while I was in Kiambu, Nairobi was being almost cleared of its Kikuyu population, excepting, of course, those who sided with Government as home guards, informers or staunch loyalists. My roommates along with thousands of others were taken from their homes, placed in a temporary camp within the city and later loaded on waiting trains. Most were taken to the distant camps of Manyani and Mackinnon Road. These people lost not only their freedom, but all the earthly possessions they had with them in Nairobi, from cars and bicycles to bedding and clothing.

Most unfortunately, my belongings also fell into the hands of the *askari*. My little Bahati room had been left unlocked and the home guards came and took all of my books – worth over 800s. – together with my clothing and utensils. All I had left was the suit I was wearing.

This Government operation was to last several days and with it came several further restrictions on KEM people. All those who escaped detention were put into a single location, Bahati, while those like myself who were outside Nairobi at the time of Anvil were not allowed to enter the city without a special pass, which was extremely difficult to obtain. My employer did his best to get me one, but all his efforts failed. He posted me the money I had coming and that was the end of it.

146

April thus ended with continued sweeps and indiscriminate detention of KEM tribesmen. Having failed to uncover the active Mau Mau
members, Government now sought to detain virtually every able-bodied
Kikuyu male of fighting age. For my part, I had no alternative but to
remain in Kiambaa village and allow myself to be recruited for the
communal labour. I was without money, clothing, employment or the
right to leave the village.

Every morning home guards came around calling everyone out of
their houses. Work began at 8 a.m. and ended when the assigned task was
completed. These jobs consisted primarily of building home guard or
police posts, constructing roads or bridges and digging bench terraces.
I was assigned the latter task and, being unaccustomed to this manual
labour, my hands were sore and full of calluses after the first few days. I
remember being so slow in this work that one day, when I hadn't finished
my piece work assignment by 3 p.m., the supervisor gave me a tongue
lashing. Everyone had finished already and I was delaying him.

Though I hated the idea that I was being forced to work without any
compensation whatsoever, chances of escape were slim and dangerous.
Anyone who tried to evade the communal labour was arrested and
taken to the guard post. Here, after interrogation and beatings, people
were tried and usually fined or imprisoned or both. With this in mind, I
remained in Kiambaa and worked along with the other adult members
of my family.

Life in the reserves had become worse than ever. Working most of
the day on the communal labour projects, people had little time to cultivate their own shambas. Since my family had to do without the cash
income I had been earning and found little time to work on our six acre
plot, we began to suffer the horrible pains of hunger. Added to this was
the ever present fear of arbitrary arrest or death at the hands of home
guards or settlers. Mau Mau fighters were becoming more active in the
area – raiding guard posts, attacking Government patrols and making
off with the livestock of loyalists – and security forces stepped up their
campaign of intimidating the people.

Every able-bodied Kikuyu male ran the risk of being called out of
his hut at night and shot by revenge-seeking settlers or their *askari*. For
myself and my family, nights were a time of fear and restless sleep. I kept
a panga by my bed and decided that if visited at night by Government
forces or settlers; I would die fighting rather than be dragged to the forest

edge and used for target practice. My wife was pregnant with our second child at this time and lived in constant fear. Hard work and insufficient food and sleep had made her tense, nervous and apprehensive. I've often wondered if this had an effect on the child who now seems very insecure and withdrawn, not playful and talkative like the others.

Two months under these conditions were all I could bear. I decided to run the risk of entering the European settled area of Limuru without a pass and seek some kind of employment. The first place I tried was a European hotel. When I approached the proprietor for a job, he told me his manager had resigned earlier that month and, as he ran two other businesses in addition to the hotel, he was in desperate need of a good clerk. He offered me the job and I accepted without even inquiring about the wage or conditions.

I worked that day in his office and in the evening he drove me over to the chief's camp to make some enquiries. The chief was honest, saying I was a man of good character but that he couldn't comment on my activities regarding Mau Mau. Though my employer pressed him on this point, the chief would say no more either for or against me.

Being desperate for clerical assistance, the European hired me despite his doubts. My salary was to be 100s. per month and I started work immediately. Before the month was over, however, he hired another European manager and informed me that he would no longer need my services. His fears that I might be a Mau Mau fighter in disguise apparently outweighed his desire to save money through the use of African rather than European labour.

Without employment, I was forced to return once more to Kiambaa and resume the thankless task of digging bench terraces on the communal labour team. After another two months, however, I again left without a pass and entered the settled area. This time I went to a different hotel some seven miles from my home. An African labour supervisor had been arrested that same week and the hotel manager reluctantly decided to give me a job. Once again I was lucky. I accepted the job not caring what the salary might be – it had to be something, and anything was more than I made digging bench terraces.

My work entailed keeping account books, typing correspondence and filling in details on the pass book applications which were required from all the workers. The green cards were at this time abandoned in favor of a passport-like booklet which contained a mass of detailed information about its bearer. Being impressed with my ability to handle the work, the manager upped his original salary offer to 180s. a month and entered my name in the books as a labour supervisor. It seems he had no allocation for an African clerk.

Every morning I rose early, typed out several copies of the day's menu and went to the labour quarters to distribute the daily chores. By 8 a.m. I was back in the office to work on the account books and labour records. After a short time, when one of the European secretaries resigned, I also had to work in the reception office dealing with customers. Though I was working more than ten hours a day and had to work till 2 a.m. in the bar on Saturday nights, I never complained for fear of losing the job. As bad as it was, it was better than life in the reserves.

Monday was my day off, but without a travel permit I was unable to go home. Passes were becoming harder than ever to obtain, being issued only under very special circumstances. Thus, on Mondays I had little alternative but to remain at the hotel and rest in my room or converse with fellow workers. It was difficult being so close to home and not being able to see or visit my family.

It was after I'd been at the hotel for two months that misfortune struck again. A man with whom we shared a common boundary reported to Government that my father was very active in Mau Mau affairs. As a result, my father was arrested and taken to court, where they found him guilty, fined him 400s. and imposed a one-year prison sentence. This sad news reached me through my eight-year-old sister, who, being young enough not to require a pass, was the only person my mother could send.

There wasn't much I could do to help other than contributing my 150s. savings toward the payment of the fine. Luckily, my father had sufficient money to pay the rest. Otherwise, his prison sentence would have been increased.

It wasn't more than a day after my father began to serve his sentence, than our neighbor began uprooting the motoka plants which served to demarcate the boundaries of our shamba. He had long felt that a strip of our land about five yards wide rightfully belonged to him. Apparently he had arranged for my father's arrest with the thought that he could just move in and take possession of part of our land.

When I heard about this, I asked for a pass and with the support of my employer managed to get one. Hurrying home, I accused our neighbor before the chief and began making preparations for the case.

Since Kikuyu land disputes require expert knowledge, I called upon a close relative who was both skilled in land cases and knew the history of the piece of land in question. He spoke on my father's behalf and was successful in winning the big case heard by the chief and a jury of elders. Our opponent not only failed to acquire the disputed land, but had to pay the costs of the case.

This was not the end of our troubles, however. In less than a week, Government passed a ruling that all Kikuyu in the district were to be concentrated in villages. This was a radical change for people accustomed to living in homesteads located on their scattered shambas. Government calculated that we could be more easily controlled if forced to live right on top of one another.

Everyone was ordered to pull down or burn their huts and move into the new village which, to my great dismay, was to be situated on our six-acre shamba. Everyone serving on the communal labour teams was now put to work uprooting our crops, tearing down the fences and leveling the whole area for demarcation into small, household plots. My family, numbering 19 persons in all, was left without a good garden or huts to sleep in and there was no place to keep our few goats, cows and chickens.

With my father in prison, I was now responsible for the family and had to make the necessary arrangements. We were allotted four 25 by 50 foot plots on which to build our huts. Luckily, my stepbrother is a carpenter and with the materials I bought, we managed to erect two small houses in a fairly short time. Mud walls were fixed onto wattle tree frames and flattened oil tins were used for roofing.

Not wanting to lose my job, I returned immediately to the hotel and resumed work. It was the time when the new pass books were being issued and had to be filled in for all employees. Because of conditions in the reserves, many of these men had various relatives and children living with them in the workers' compound. They were all claimed to be the wives and children of the male employees. I remember that one man claimed to have three wives and five daughters with him. Without passes, these women and girls would have been sent back to the harsh conditions on the reserves.

Not wanting to see anyone ejected from the hotel, I vouched for these people and saw to it that they received passes. This not only won me the confidence of the employees, but also put me in good standing with my employer, who marvelled at the good relations I was maintaining with our labour force of 150.

One day he introduced me as his assistant to a visiting administrative officer in the area. This confidence allowed me to assist the workers in still another way. Whenever Government planned a general check of the labour quarters, I was informed by the manager. When I passed this information on to the workers, they had time to remove any suspicious items from their rooms and temporarily get rid of any arms or ammunition they happened to be hiding.

Mau Mau attacks and Government countermeasures intensified toward the end of the year. It was in December 1954 that a group of security force personnel came to the hotel on a Saturday night as I worked at the bar. At about 9 p.m. I heard shots and went out with some others to check. Not too far from the hotel, we came across the body of a Mkamba employee.

Later, through the bragging of a policeman, I learned what had happened. It seems that the Mkamba had a dispute with this *askari* over a woman and when he left the hotel for his quarters that night, several *askari* were waiting for him hidden in the bushes. The Mkamba was with a friend and both of them were pounced upon and dragged a short distance away onto the golf course. After shooting the Mkamba, the *askari* took the other man to the nearby home guard post, where he was beaten and tortured for almost a month. It was possible during this period for a loyalist serving with the security forces to get away with almost anything. Anyone killed, beaten or robbed was simply classified as a Mau Mau gangster and that was all there was to it.

1955 began with a new feeling in the air. Throughout the first two years of the revolution, there was a widespread belief amongst Kikuyu that our fighters in the forests would be victorious and that the war would end with the return of our stolen land and political independence. However, the mass arrests early in 1954, followed by the concentration of Kikuyu peasants into the villages, gradually diminished this hope of victory. Instead, there came despair, poverty and starvation.

Because of the communal labour, people had few crops to harvest. Most of the shops and businesses had closed down and money was virtually absent from the reserve. Fines, robberies and the seizing of livestock had left the people penniless, hungry and ill-clothed. Added to this was the fact that Government imposed a 23-hour curfew in many areas, so peasants were allowed outside their homes only one hour a day to collect food and water.

Under these severe conditions, starvation and disease swept the countryside, hitting hardest the elderly men and women and the young children. Hope vanished and in its place came the daily prayers that the terrible struggle end. The million or so Kikuyu had had their fill of revolt and wished now only for peace and bread. The fight in the forest came to a halt with a temporary agreement on a cease-fire. But while negotiations went on between our fighters and Government, thousands of detainees were suffering or dying in the detention camps. This, at any rate, was how the early months of 1955 appeared to me.

My Confession

I continued to work, but I was now the sole supporter of my large family on a wage of only 180s. per month. My father was still in prison and my two grown stepbrothers could not leave the village to seek employment. To make things worse, Government increased its pressure to gain confessions and anyone who wished to obtain a travel permit had to have a signed confession certificate. To get such a certificate, a person not only had to confess his Mau Mau activities, but also had to pay a heavy fine. I know of one household whose members were fined a total of 1,500s. In regard to my own family, the figure was to reach 820s.

Failure to pay these fines resulted in prison sentences. However, Government eventually had to reduce them, seeing that people were going to prison through failure to pay even the smallest amounts. They simply had no money, and the prisons were already overflowing.

In April 1955, I once again joined the ranks of the unemployed. In March the hotel manager decided to replace me with a European assistant and I was given one month's notice.

When I returned to Kiambaa, people were still engaged in the construction of villages. A third hut had been completed and mine was well under way. In two weeks time, we finished the hut and I moved in with my wife and children.

A month later, toward the middle of May, I saw an advertisement in the newspaper. Government, it seems, wanted educated KEM tribesmen to enlist in a training course to prepare them for rehabilitation work among the detainees. Not wanting to do rehabilitation work, I nevertheless decided to answer the ad. My plan was to go through the course and then, if posted in Nairobi, to resign after obtaining a residence permit and seek employment with a commercial firm.

After an intensive interview, I was accepted and posted to Jeanes School in Kabete for training. Three months later, when I'd completed the course, I received an assignment which smashed my well laid plans. Instead of my going to Nairobi, they were sending me to Embu, where I was to work in a juvenile camp designed to rehabilitate delinquents under the age of 16. As a matter of fact, many of these delinquents turned out to be 21 or over and simply looked young.

It was preferable to working in the adult camp, however, and though the pay was very low, I thought I might be able to help the young boys. It was intended that the rehabilitation team instruct the detained youths in elementary classroom subjects, crafts and sports. The classrooms, however, had not been completed by the time I arrived and only the literate youths were receiving instruction so that they might later help to teach their comrades.

Noting my previous experience in clerical work, the camp commandant placed me in his office as a bookkeeper. In addition, I taught two classes a day in advanced English, while the other 14 instructors worked to prepare the literate young men to teach. The rest of the detainees worked in labour gangs during the morning, under close supervision of camp guards, and in the afternoons participated in recreational activities and games under the leadership of the rehabilitation assistants.

Life in the camp, for both detainees and the African staff, was very unpleasant. The camp commandant was a harsh European who had his *askari* administer beatings to the young detainees for any minor infraction of the rules. In addition, the detainees received far too little food considering the heavy work they were forced to do. Rising at 6 a.m., they were lined up for the morning prayer and Bible reading, fed a cup of thin gruel and put to work by 7 o'clock in the manufacture of bricks for the new school buildings or on some other construction or sanitation job within the camp.

Though the warders and *askari* were frequently brutal in their treatment of the detainees, the European rehabilitation officer was a kind and considerate man who earned the respect of everyone in the camp. The young men would always willingly go to him with their problems or when they'd encountered some difficulty with the warders.

Also, a screening team was present and engaged in continuous interrogation of the prisoners. In most cases, confessions were given voluntarily, but sometimes force was used. I remember seeing the camp commandant and chief warder beat the young detainees on several occasions. This, plus the fact that African staff members like myself were prohibited from buying beer at the Asian owned provisions store within the camp and from leaving to visit the nearby town on the weekends without the written permission of the camp commandant, led me to resign from Government service at the end of the year. I gave a months' notice and was terminated on 31 December 1955.

Before leaving Embu, I had to go to the District Commissioner's office and obtain a travel permit. This was entered on one of the pages of my pass book and specified the date, route and destination of my journey. On arrival at Kiambu, I was to report immediately to the Pass Book Control Office and have my Embu residence permit cancelled. To my surprise, however, when I handed the official in Kiambu by book, he brought down on it a rubber stamp reading: "REPATRIATED TO KIAMBU". This meant, in effect, that I was restricted to my village and wasn't to be issued with any movement or travel permits.

Leaving Embu, I had planned to return home for a few days and then go into Nairobi and seek employment. Now, however, I was once again a prisoner in my village. Though all fighting had ceased in the reserves by this time, conditions had become even worse than they were when I left. Forced labour continued and home guards were entering every hut to make sure people had their Confession Certificates. Those found without this document were taken to the guard posts which had been constructed in every Kikuyu village. Treatment at the post was often quite harsh, as Government's thirst for punishing the rebellious Kikuyu tribe had not yet been quenched.

Poverty had increased to such an extent that the International Red Cross came in to distribute milk to the starving peasant children. The shambas had been neglected due to the demands of the communal labour and there was simply not enough food to go around. Only those with Confession Certificates could obtain travel permits or business licenses and thus assist their families with outside cash earnings. I had never confessed anything and was hence both restricted to the village and subject to the abuses of the ever-present home guards.

I thus faced a real dilemma. I had been a loyal member of Mau Mau for over five years now and was in a position to see the damage done to the organization by its weaker members who had confessed and even consented to join the Government side and fight against their former comrades. I hated to think of being classified with these people as a weakling or traitor.

Since the initiation of cleansing ceremonies by Government in 1953, however, more and more people had found themselves obliged or forced to confess. With the mass arrests and detention of over 100,000 Kikuyu men, the forced resettlement of the peasants and the ever weakening position of the forest fighters since mid-1954, came the realization that we had lost the military battle against Government. Thus, the will to resist was steadily decreasing. Death, suffering and starvation can be endured when there is hope of victory; but with defeat a certainty, continued struggle and misery seem useless and death a complete waste.

There was a Confession Center in the location; arriving there I found a long queue of people waiting to enter the office. I knew what these confessions entailed. There were the usual questions concerning the oath, one's activities in Mau Mau, possession of firearms and involvement in killings. To prove himself reliable and honest, a person had to give the names and activities of numerous people with whom he associated in the organization. The statements were then checked, one against the other, and any discrepancies investigated. Thus, if Mr. "X" says that

I kept a panga by my bed and decided that if visited at night by Government forces or settlers, I would die fighting rather than be dragged to the forest edge and used for target practice.

he stole a gun in the company of Mr. "Y", and the latter failed in his confession to mention any such incident, he would be hunted down, arrested and forced through beatings and torture to confess the "truth". It may have happened that "X's" story was untrue; but Government always assumed that the most revealing and damaging statements — particularly those implicating others — could be trusted as accurate. I knew of one such incident where a woman of the village was beaten and had her thighs cut with a razor blade. In order to save her life she finally confessed to a lie about having hidden guns in her hut.

It was not this alone, however, which convinced me of the necessity to confess. My own loyalty, at this point, could only persist at the expense of my family. Just released from prison and three months detention, my father had as yet no income, and so the burden of feeding our family fell squarely on my shoulders. Our livestock had already died of starvation because of the lack of pasture for grazing and, since our shamba had been appropriated for the building of the new village, we had not a single inch of land on which to raise crops. My entire family, which, in addition to my wife and children, consisted of my old grandmother, my father and his three wives, my stepbrother, his wife and three children and my two sisters, who had each acquired one child out of wedlock, faced the real possibility of starvation. It was only my potential earnings which gave them any hope of survival, and this is what decided the issue for me.

To get a job, I first had to obtain a travel permit, which required a Confession Certificate and the revocation of the repatriation entry in my pass book.

With this in mind, I joined a few villagers in the queue and we plotted out confessions. The primary aim of our conspiracy was to avoid implicating others. Among us, we knew the names of several dozen people who had been killed earlier by the security forces and it was agreed that we would give only the names of these people as well as each other's. We were all to have taken the oath on the same day and in the same place and would name as the oath administrator a person recently shot and killed by a home guard. When full agreement was reached, we dispersed, taking up different positions in the queue. The plan worked and when my turn came I fully satisfied my interrogators with a list of over thirty names and all the details of the oath.

With this unpleasant task completed, I obtained the Confession Certificate and a travel permit, allowing me to enter Nairobi for employment. This wasn't easy, however. In addition to having the Confession Certificate and poll tax receipts, one needed to present a good reason for wishing to enter Nairobi. Before the Emergency, I had been issued a license by the Provincial Commissioner to represent a Nairobi insurance firm as its broker in the Central Province. I found this license when going through an old box of papers and decided to use it to gain a pass.

When I went to the D.O.'s office I was amazed to see hundreds of people queued up in front of the building waiting to see the man to get travel permits or take care of other matters. I decided immediately that even by waiting all day my chances of getting into the office would be remote. What I didn't realize, as I stood there trying to decide what to do next, was that by standing on the nicely mowed green grass in front of the building, I was violating one of D.O.'s pet rules. Glancing out of his office window, he saw me on the lawn and angrily ordered me into the office.

He was a man well known throughout the district for his brutality, and so as I made my way through the crowd and into the office I was fully terrified. He had ordered the others to disperse and one acquaintance whispered to me in passing that I was in hot water for having walked on the grass.

Inside the office, standing opposite the desk at which the D.O. was seated, I could see how furious he was over this minor incident. The time had passed, however, when he could have had me shot or beaten and, though very frightened, I pretended to have no fear at all despite the evil looks he was giving me.

Finally, after cursing me in a loud and threatening voice about having stepped on his beautiful lawn, the D.O. demanded to see my poll tax receipts. Very calmly, I produced them one by one, beginning with the earliest and saying: "This lot is for the year 1948, when I started paying. These are the receipts for 1949..." When I'd gone through eight years in this manner I said: "I have only one receipt for 1956 as I've not yet paid for the other. That is why I came to see you, Sir. I thought you could provide me with a pass to enter Nairobi and collect the commissions from an insurance company I represent, so that I could pay the poll tax."

Gradually, the D.O.'s tone had changed and he was somewhat milder on asking to see my pass book and Confession Certificate. Looking them over carefully, he finally called in his clerk and asked him to write out a one-day pass for me. My trick had worked and instead of being dragged into court and fined, as I had expected, I now had the pass in my hand. I politely thanked the D.O. and left the office. Bad luck had turned into good; the hundreds of people waiting to see the D.O. were still milling about and I'm sure very few gained satisfaction on that day.

This was a turning point in my life and coincided with the general trend toward normalcy in the country. Though thousands of men remained in detention camps, and though poverty and communal labour continued in the countryside, fighting had virtually ceased and Government steadily withdrew its restrictive measures. On my one-day Nairobi pass I was lucky to find employment as a typist with the Indian Consulate. Later, after having had several jobs, I was employed by the East African Tobacco Company, where I remained for three years.

It is now 1962 and over two years have passed since the Emergency was officially declared over. My future, as well as that of the country as a whole is still very uncertain. As for myself, I've recently been employed as a typist by the Royal College in Nairobi and have inherited four acres of my father's land in Githunguri. Though now the father of five children, I'm still seriously considering returning to school. If not in Kenya, then perhaps in the United States or Russia. I've learned through bitter experience that without higher education or wealth in the form of land and cattle a man simply can't pull himself securely above the dangers of poverty.

I am not active in politics these days, largely because I don't know where the country is going or what either of our two African political parties really stand for. Mau Mau has been crushed under the heel of British might and now it seems there are no spokesmen for the great aspirations or hopes of my people. We are told merely to forget the past. But I, for one, fail to understand why we should so easily forget the great suffering endured by our people in their struggle for land and freedom.

Don Barnett and Ngugi Kabiro in Nairobi, 1962

THE URBAN GUERRILLA
The Story of Mohamed Mathu

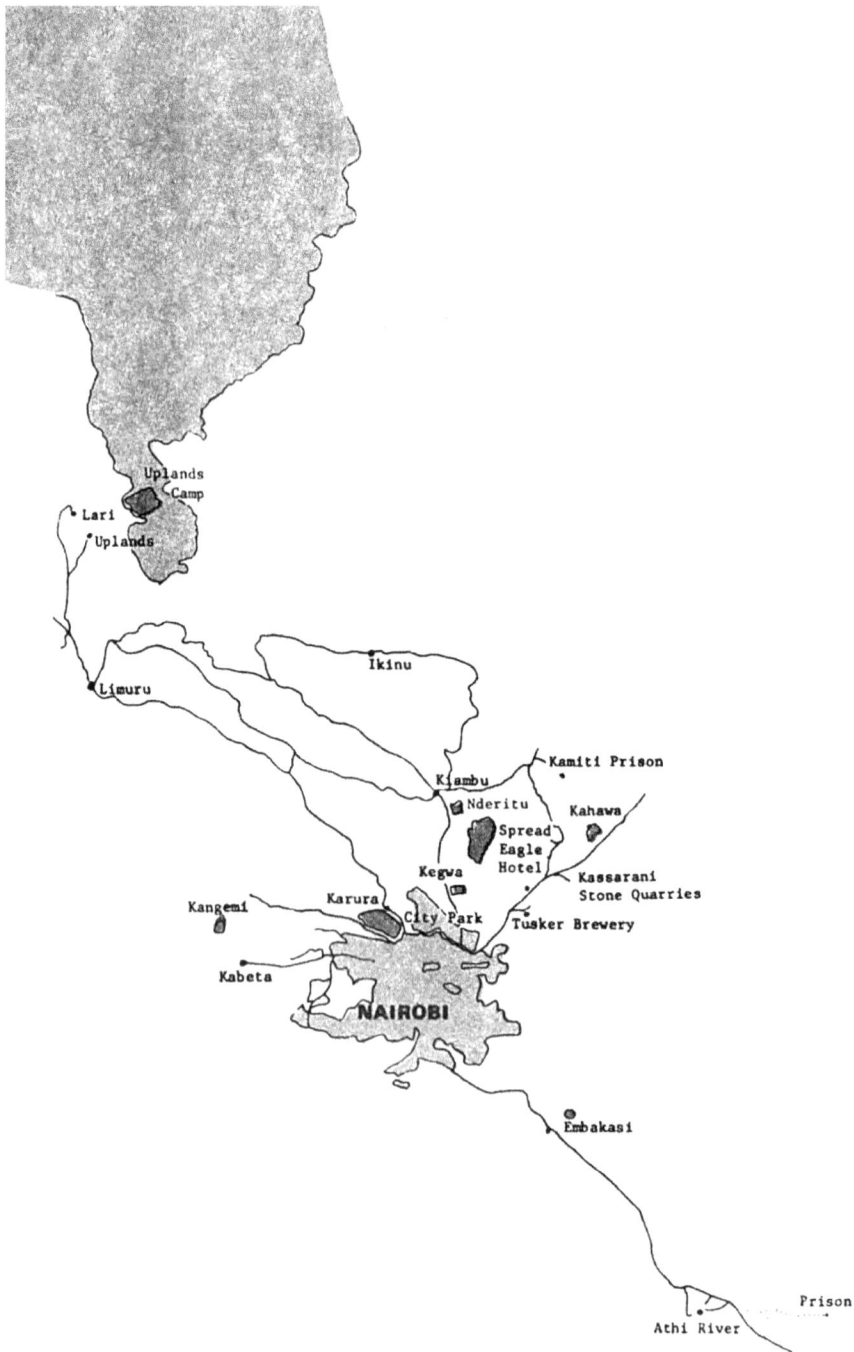

162

Does Mau Mau still exist, asks counsel

DISCUSSES ANTI-OATH CAMPAIGN

that

The sisal industry

IR. KENYATTA CONDEMNS SUBVERSION

THE

MR. ODING. GIVES THANKS TO MAU MAU

IKUYU who were organising or supporting subversiv secret societies were condemned by Kanu's presider Ir. Kenyatta, when he addressed a meeting at Githungu Ciambu on Saturday.

that some of you are go

vice-chairma inga, h. rat

back prepa

U.S. steps up xports to Kenya 20 PER CENT RISE N FIRST QUARTER

KENYA IS TAMIN MAU MAU BRAVE

st Bands' Chiefs o Plan Home

RELEASE DETAINE JAILED F A YEAR

ITH an increase of nearly 20 per cent in its exports to Kenya in the first quarter of this year, the United tes rose from its position as sixth supplier to become third main exporter to the Colony.

The value of the United States imports into Kenya e from £1,146,660 in the first quarter of 1960 to s year — comprising nearly seven per ce

Oath charges

Mau

Pyrethrum growers praised in London

other Nobody will respect don't respect him d.

NOT POLITICAL

emember the Kikuyu pro- that if you hate someone he get hold of your nose and k to it. We must have no tred towards one another. Mau au was a disease which had en eradicated and must never en remembered again.

Four Meru have been charged with administering Mau Mau ed afte oaths in the lower Chure Loca- ntion, tion of Meru. They have been yesterd remanded in custody.

ge comply w

LARGE-SCA BUYING START S

BRITISH Member Parliament, a K entist and a nrnali

THE NEW YORK TIMES, Police to Oust Africans Whites

START is

Introduction

I met David "Mohamed" Mathu for the first time in one of Nairobi's dingy back street hotels. It was late 1961, Kenya was still a British colony, and several thousand "Mau Mau" members and a number of important nationalist leaders remained in detention camps or exile. Our meeting had been arranged by a mutual friend, Ngugi Kabiro.[1]

Mathu was somewhat taller than most Kikuyu, with a gaunt frame and anxious, almost frightened, eyes. His whispered conversation, over-the-shoulder glances and cautious responses reflected long experience as an urban guerrilla and prisoner in numerous detention camps. The anxiety and uncertainty revealed in Mathu's manner had become ubiquitous among Kenya's million or so Kikuyu. Perhaps 100,000 (some say a quarter of a million) had been killed in four years of armed struggle (1952-56); more than that number had been "detained" in British-style concentration camps for as long as nine years and subjected to various forms of torture, humiliation and "rehabilitative" brainwashing. The remaining population in the "reserves" – mainly women, children and old people – had suffered a terrible repression which included rape and torture, forced labor, loss of land and stock, "resettlement" in concentration camp hamlets, collective punishments, restricted movement, curfews and a wave of hunger and starvation which took the lives of many thousands.

Despite fierce white-settler resistance, Kenya's five to six million Africans had recently been granted "Internal Self-Government" and a promise of early independence. For the vast majority of Kikuyu, however, there remained considerable apprehension, confusion and unanswered questions: "Why was their struggle being ignored or condemned by the new African parliamentarians?" "Would independence bring appreciation and compensation for their great sacrifices and losses?" "How would ex-Home Guards and other 'loyalist' traitors be dealt with?" "What would be done about the stolen 'White Highlands' and longstanding Kikuyu land claims?"

....
1 The autobiography of Ngugi Kabiro is given in section 2 of this book, "Man in the Middle".

And what of Jomo Kenyatta, whose strange and often contradictory statements caused many to wonder? Eight years earlier, during the Kapenguria trial, his claim that he knew nothing about "Mau Mau" was viewed by most Kikuyu as a sign of determination not to betray the secrecy vows of the Unity Oath. Now, just released from his "restriction order," Kenyatta was offering guarantees to the settlers and foreign investors, pledging that "The Government of an independent Kenya will not be a 'gangster government' and will not deprive people of their property."[2] (*East African Standard* [EAS], 1 September 1961) At the same time, he and other high ranking KANU (Kenya African National Union) leaders were condemning "...categorically any illegal or subversive movement" (Sunday Post, 20 August 1961) and urging everyone to: "Please forget about the past and remember we are all citizens of Kenya of equal status [sic!]." (*Daily Nation*, 2 October 1961.)

Many became restless. Oathing started up again and the newspapers were full of it. Kariuki Chotara, whom you will meet in the following pages, was once more arrested and charged with being a leader of the Kenya Land Freedom Army (KLFA).[3] Defense Minister Swann, in proscribing it on 8 August 1961, said the KLFA was: "anarchist, bolshevik and terrorist," planning a coup "at some future date," and "... composed of ('500 to 2,000') former Mau Mau who intend to make sure that those who fought during the Emergency reap the sweets of success." (*Daily Nation*, 9 August 1961) Also banned were the Kenya Parliament, the Kenya Land Freedom Party, the Rift Valley Government and the Rift Valley Province Parliament.

Nevertheless, history was to repeat itself. The vast majority of Kikuyu interpreted Kenyatta's condemnation of Mau Mau and the new KLFA, together with his promises to foreign investors and settlers, as a clever deception of the British intended to hasten Kenya's independence – an event which many still hoped would usher in a bright new future,

---

2 The essentials of KANU's Land Policy were summarized as follows: "(1) Security of title to agricultural land will only be given to Kenya citizens, and the principle of 'Absentee Landlords' will not be accepted. (2) Large commercial companies owning agricultural land for the development of tea, coffee and sisal plantations will not be bound by this [sic!]." (Sunday Post, 16 July 1961.)

3 The *East African Standard* reported on August 9, 1961 that: "At Lokitaung, Chotara attacked Jomo Kenyatta and tried to beat him up. He was pulled away by the self-styled 'General' China." The rest of the story, from those who were there, is that the fight started when Kenyatta scornfully asked Chotara, in effect, "Why do you people go on fighting? Don't you know that the longer you fight, the longer they will keep me here?" This helps explain one arrested KLFA member's comment that "If Kenyatta gets in our way, we'll cut him down just the same as any other Kanu or Kadu leader." (*ibid.*)

filled with all the things they had longed and struggled for, especially land, jobs and education for their children. But these hopes were mixed with the fears and scepticism born of past broken promises and bitter years of suffering. Many remembered Kenyatta's Nyeri speech in 1947 when he said: "The freedom tree can only grow when you pour blood on it ... I shall firmly hold the lion's jaws so that it will not bite you. Will you bear its claws?" The Kikuyu masses had certainly born the lion's claws, but unfortunately its jaws were also left free to attack them as KAU (Kenya African Union) leaders, including Kenyatta, ignored pre-Emergency warnings[4] and allowed themselves to be arrested without a struggle, none ever even attempting to escape and join the peasant guerrillas fighting in the forests of Mount Kenya and the Aberdares.

Strangely, as Kenya approached the eve of its independence, it was only a few non-Kikuyu nationalist leaders who dared acknowledge the contribution of "Mau Mau." Oginga Odinga, a Luo, said that "Had it not been for the heroism of the Mau Mau freedom fighters, maybe we could be another South Africa today!" (*EAS*, 4 Aug. 1961) John Keen, a Masai leader, commented that "Mau Mau had been called bad, but when Kenya's *uhuru* was finally won, it would be described as the 'War of Independence'." (*EAS*, 28 August 1961) And Martin Chokwe, Coast Province, and Paul Ngei of Ukambani, made similar statements.

These contradictions and the doubt and confusion they generated were clearly revealed in the manner of Muhamed Mathu, and the basis for them became evident as his story unfolded. After completing two years of high school (much more than most Africans), Mathu gained employment as an apprentice draftsman in 1950. He was working for the Nairobi City Council when the Emergency was declared and held his job right through April 1954, when the British "Operation Anvil" was launched in Nairobi and forced him into full-time guerrilla activity. In the intervening period, Mathu had become active in one of the several guerrilla groups operating in and around the capital city. Disorganized when its top, and much of its middle, leadership was removed at the outset of the struggle, the underground movement entered a period of confusion and decentralization – a period from which it never fully recovered. It was thus unable to take advantage either of its own potential strengths or the enemy's numerous weaknesses. Most of Nairobi's

---

4 It is widely believed among Kikuyu that KAU leaders gained knowledge of the Emergency Declaration some 24 hours before the 20 October 1952 announcement, when most of the top leadership was picked up in pre-dawn raids code-named the "Jock Scott Operation."

86,000 Africans (some 55,000) were Kikuyu and they were employed in virtually every important aspect of the city's life – in domestic service, industry, communications and transport, and as clerks in the lower reaches of the Government and business bureaucracies. Most, as well, were members of Mau Mau. Nairobi itself, unlike the capitals in other African colonies with a seaboard, was situated some 300 miles of sandy road inland from Mombasa on the coast. It had only one small airport (Embakazi International Airport was built during and after the revolution, largely with forced detainee labour), a single water reservoir and very vulnerable power and communications facilities. In addition, almost all Europeans employed at least one Kikuyu servant, cook, garden "boy" or chauffeur ... and there is little doubt that most would have panicked in response to a well-organized and coordinated guerrilla attack in the early stages of the Emergency.

Such an attack, however, was not to come; and by the time it was conceived as a strategic possibility by a somewhat reorganized urban guerrilla "Kenya Parliament,"[5] the colonial-settler forces had regrouped and seized the initiative, which they never again relinquished. The urban guerrilla groups, though able to achieve numerous isolated successes in Nairobi, never really succeeded in overcoming their major weaknesses and realizing their potential strengths – a transformation which, had it been achieved, would most certainly have altered the results of the otherwise abortive Kenya revolution.

Mathu, who became secretary of the Kenya Parliament at the time of its formation, both shared and mirrored the movement's frailties and inadequacies. From the time of his first oath in June 1950, Mathu was plagued by doubts and fears. He tells us that he "... found certain aspects of the oathing ceremony ugly and resented having been tricked into attending it;" also of his "doubts about the future," which "... buzzed noisily around in my head. Guns and ammunition meant violence. What would this bring to me and my people?"

These and other questions and reservations continually arose. They were seated, for the most part, in the organizational and ideological weaknesses of "Mau Mau," as well as in the various contradictions engendered by fifty years of British-settler rule. The underground movement's lack of an educated and revolutionary leadership, knowledgeable about modern guerrilla warfare and the nature of colonialism and impe-

5 The *EAS* of 18 July 1961 contained a copy of revived Land Freedom Army documents and oaths. See Appendix.

rialism, resulted in the absence of an overall politico-military strategy and little or no political education for the militants or masses. Mau Mau ideology was, in addition, burdened with a narrow and negative nationalism and debilitating magical beliefs and superstition. Confusion and conflict arose between local, tribal and national objectives as well as between traditional and scientific ideas, the educated and the illiterate, men and women, personal and collective gain. In such circumstances, revolutionary self-discipline, comportment and integrity are difficult to achieve (or even understand), and opportunism, adventurism and defeatism inevitably assume a large and ultimately commanding role.

In the case of Mathu, these contradictions and shortcomings are manifested in a continuing flow of events. The attack against Asians at a Muslim mosque was clearly the outcome of serious ideological confusion and a "roving rebel band" mentality. His attitude toward the necessity for organizational – and self-discipline is reflected in the comment that he "...thought many of the Mau Mau rules were rather stupid." And that: "Despite the fine I'd been forced to pay...I continued living with the prostitute, drinking beer and smoking in the privacy of my room."

There were also numerous instances of opportunism, as when Mathu buys a rifle for 400 shillings and, figuring that he "... should make something" for himself, "told the elders it cost 600s. and pocketed the difference." Again, there was his flirtation with the Special Branch and the personal advantage he saw in a mock double-agent role. "When the other men left," he tells us, "Seedon gave me 80s. and an informer card bearing his name and phone number ... Obtaining the card was my own idea. I knew I would soon enter the forest and the card could prove useful if I was ever captured by security forces."

Nevertheless, despite these and other contradictions and non-revolutionary practices, Mathu's story reveals at many points a genuine sensitivity and concern for the African and Kikuyu masses. Being intellectually and morally opposed to magical practices and tribal chauvinism, he continually fights against these tendencies – both before his capture and while in detention. This, as we shall see, took considerable courage ... as does Mathu's final comment and warning about Kenya's new African leadership. "Remembering how many of these leaders abandoned us during the revolution, I am suspicious of those who now claim to speak in our name. Are they not abandoning us again in their quest for personal power and wealth? The vast majority of Africans remain very poor. Are the masses of Kenyans simply to become the slaves of a handful of wealthy Black men?"

That was in 1962! – still a year and a half before Kenya would achieve its political "independence." Now, unfortunately, some dozen years later and with the benefit of hindsight, we must note that history has answered Mathu's questions in the affirmative.

A Decision to Struggle

The night of 19 June 1952 was the most remarkable of my life. When I returned from work at about 5 p.m. I was visited in my room in Ziwani African location of Nairobi by two men. One was from my own division in Nyeri, South Tetu. The other was from Othaya Division in this same district of the Central Province. They told me one of my brothers was very sick and wanted to see me as soon as possible.

Before I could ask any questions, Githuku, the man from my division, said they were going to my brother's place on business and would give me a lift in his car. I accepted without question or suspicion and jumped into the waiting car.

We started our journey, passing the main gate of the Royal Airforce Base and continuing along the Fort Hall road to a place near the stone quarries at Kassarani. Here we turned off onto one of the dirt roads. It was just after 7 p.m. and we were about five or six miles from Nairobi when I started to become suspicious. Strange greetings were exchanged between my escorts and people we were passing on the road and a few hundred yards further I saw several men guarding a hidden area a short distance ahead. It dawned on me that instead of going to visit my sick brother I had been tricked into attending an oathing ceremony.

My heart was beating as we got out of the car and went on foot along a narrow path. I had heard on the radio that Kikuyu were being taken into the bush for initiation into the Mau Mau secret society and that those who refused the oath had been killed. I made up my mind not to resist.

After passing several sentries we came to a large, secluded valley. It was just like one of our market centers in the reserves, filled with about 10,000 men and women. It was dusk and I could make out the faces of many people I knew among the larger number of complete strangers.

Within a matter of minutes one of the oath administrators, a man from my own village named Gathiu wa Gichuki, ordered a group of us from the same sub-location to form a circle around one of several banana leaf arches which had been set up in the valley.

Each of the new initiates was to be sworn in separately and when my turn came a thin strip of twisted goat skin was placed around my neck, bracelets of this same skin were put on my wrists and I was given a small, dampened ball of soil to hold against my stomach. Repeating the vows spoken by the oath administrator, I passed under the arch seven times, took seven bites from the chest meat of a ram, sank my teeth seven times into the heart and lungs of a goat, sipped blood seven times from a traditional Kikuyu gourd, inserted small sticks cut from the *mugere* tree into the seven holes of an *ngata* [the bone which joins the neck and spinal column of a goat], and jumped seven times over seven pieces of wild fruit called *ndongu*. This is what I swore:

1. I am taking this oath so as to unite the black men of Kenya, and particularly the Kikuyu people, in the struggle for freedom and the return of our stolen lands.
2. If I meet any member of this society who is in need of assistance or a place to hide, I will help him.
3. If guns or ammunition are brought to me for hiding, I will do so and never reveal the matter to Government or anyone not a member of this society.
4. I will never reveal the existence or secrets of this Society to the white man or his friends or to anyone not of the House of *Gikuyu na Mumbi.*

After repeating each of these vows, I said: "If I violate this sacred pledge, may this oath kill me." The crowd of people surrounding the arch would then chant in unison: "The oath kills he who lies."

When all of us had been initiated, we were given some final words of advice by the oath administrator and told to return to our homes. As I walked back toward Ziwani my head was spinning. I felt confused emotions about what I had just experienced.

Up to this time I had never thought seriously about politics. Born and raised on a small *shamba*, like most Kikuyu children, I started schooling in 1943 at the age of 12. After completing Form 2, I found myself without money to complete my education and went to Nairobi in search of employment. In 1950 I was hired as an apprentice draftsman by the East African Railways and Harbours and 13 months later, having gained some experience, got a similar job at a higher wage with the City Council of Nairobi.

As a young boy I had heard of Harry Thuku, the Kikuyu Central Association and Johnston Kenyatta's visit to England to fight for the return of Kikuyu land. But I just wasn't interested in politics or the activities of the Kenya African Union (KAU). Entering Nairobi I took up a life of petty pleasures, drinking and women. After awhile I moved in with a woman hawker, started to drink heavily and had no thoughts about my own or Kenya's future.

Now, walking home in the darkness from the oath I had just taken, I considered what had been said and done. It was certainly true that the white man had stolen our lands and substituted a degrading kind of slavery for the freedoms we had previously enjoyed. Somehow the European had stripped us of our manhood. For over fifty years he treated us like monkeys just down from the trees and now, they told me, it was time we fought back like men. True! Every word of it true! The white man was the natural enemy of the black and could only be defeated by the force of African unity.

Nevertheless, while the evening awakened in me the sleeping emotions and thoughts of my political and social condition as an African in a white-ruled Kenya, I found certain aspects of the oathing ceremony ugly and resented having been tricked into attending it. Doubt about the future buzzed noisily around in my head. Guns and ammunition meant violence. What would this bring to my and my people?

These were the kind of thoughts and doubts running through my head as I reached my room at about 5 a.m. and lay down for a few hours of much-needed sleep. When I got up and rushed to get to the office by 8 o'clock the confusion was still there, but I made up my mind not to violate the vows I took the night before.

The following evening after returning from work I was visited by my brother and two friends. All three had been members of Mau Mau for some time and they tried to make me understand the nature of the organization and the meaning of the oath. They explained how, in Nairobi, our members were organized on a sub-location, location, division and district basis, with committees on each level electing a few men to represent them on the next highest committee. At the top, said my brother, was the Central Province Committee with members from the various district committees. The CPC and district committees had groups of young fighters whose job it was to eliminate traitors. None of the lower committees had fighting groups and none of the fighters could take action against a man without instructions from the elders of the Central Province or district committees.

We discussed the relation of the Kenya African Union to our organization. They said that the top leaders of KAU knew about and sympathized with our Movement and that we, in turn, were strong supporters of KAU. Both were working to forge an ironclad unity among all Africans, a unity which would enable us to fight successfully for our land and freedom. We would throw off white-settler rule and after winning our independence the land would be ours, salaries would rise and education would be free. Gradually, as we talked into the late hours of the night, my fears fell away one by one.

I learned that sub-location groups met on Saturdays and Sundays and that each group had messengers whose job it was to inform members where and when the meetings were to be held. My brother, who was on the South Tetu Division Committee, said I could assist the organization by using my evenings and weekends trying to recruit new members and collecting entrance fees and dues from persons who had taken the oath. In recruiting members I was not to mention the oath but simply to assess the attitudes and sympathies of potential members toward the Movement.

At this time I was living in Ziwani with a prostitute. I was told that, according to Mau Mau rules, no one was to stay with prostitutes. If I wanted to continue living with this woman I should marry her. They also told me about the rules prohibiting the drinking of European beer and the smoking of European cigarettes.

By the time they left, after many hours of discussion, I was fully convinced that our Movement – known to the Europeans as "Mau Mau" – was just and good and that I would do my best to help in reaching its aims.

Though I will use the term "Mau Mau" it should be understood that this name was popularized by the European press and wasn't used by us when referring in private conversation to our Association. We often spoke of the movement as *Uiguano wa Muingi* or *Uiguano wa Gikuyu na Mumbi*. The meaning of *uiguano* is "unity" and hence the above expressions translate into English as "The Unity of the Community" and "The Unity of Kikuyu and Mumbi." Another term, *muma*, means "the oath" but was often used when referring to the Organization as a whole. The so-called "Mau Mau" oath was most frequently called

"Muma wa Uiguano" or the "Oath of Unity." Finally there was the term "Muiguithania" which means "The Unifier" and was often used when referring to the Movement which sought a united Kikuyu people.

The following morning I went to work as usual and it wasn't until three weeks later, in early July, that I attended my first sub-location meeting. It was held at night and about 20 of us met in Bahati within the single unlit room of a member. The chairman told us that the time had arrived when all Kikuyu must rise in unity and fight for freedom and the return of our lands. We should try to collect money for the purchase of guns and ammunition and should never turn our backs on any opportunity to acquire arms – regardless of the means. Whenever we got any weapons or ammunition we should bring them immediately to him.

The money we collected would also be used to assist unemployed members and to pay legal fees for persons arrested on Mau Mau charges. Later, after the Emergency was declared, the wives and children of men who were arrested or killed were given financial assistance.

The discussion continued along this line until about 10 p.m. when the meeting broke up and I returned to Ziwani. For the next month or two I continued to work with the City Council as a draftsman but spent more and more time trying to recruit new members and collect outstanding entrance fees and dues from members of my sub-location. While moving around the city contacting potential initiates and members I made an effort to assess their feelings toward the Organization and build up their morale and courage. Winning the confidence of friends and acquaintances, I took several people to oathing ceremonies usually held at night in the darkened rooms of members living in African locations such as Kariokor, Shauri Moyo, Bahati, Ziwani and Makongeni.

One Sunday I took two recruits to an oathing ceremony in Shauri Moyo. It began at 2 o'clock in the afternoon and lasted until midnight. Over 200 people were given the oath and when the ceremony was over my two friends and I returned to my Ziwani room. I tried to explain to them the meaning of the oath they had just taken. I said the oath served only to unify our people in the struggle to regain our stolen lands and freedom and that even leading members of KAU were active in the Association. By the time they left most of their fears and doubts had been eliminated.

I attended many meetings during this period, but one held in September I remember vividly. Though I knew it was against Mau Mau regulations I continued to live with the prostitute who was brewing beer. I was told that my offences were to be discussed and only reluctantly attended the meeting. When I confessed, the chairman passed sentence. I was fined 80s. This was a large amount of money to me as I was earning only 210s. a month. At first I refused to pay. On instruction from the chairman I was then stuffed into a gunnysack which was tied and pushed under the bed. After a few minutes, and not knowing what was to follow, I shouted my willingness to pay and was let out of the bag.

I must admit at this point that I thought many of the Mau Mau rules were rather stupid. Despite the fine I'd been forced to pay and the harsher punishment I would face if caught again, I continued living with the prostitute, drinking beer and smoking in the privacy of my room.

I still considered myself, however, a loyal member of Mau Mau and with Government pressures mounting, frequently made my house available for roasting the meat used in oathing ceremonies and for hiding or repairing guns. Many times members gathered in my house to count the money they'd collected or the rounds of ammunition they had stolen or purchased. Again, as I wasn't the only member to violate the "no smoking or drinking" rule, my friends often came by in the evenings for a bottle of beer and conversation.

All those who were enemies of Mau Mau, whether Europeans, Asians or Africans, were called "settlers." This term had come to represent the essence of evil itself to virtually every Kenya African. Nairobi fighters were stepping up their campaign to eliminate these "settlers" and on 7 October 1952 Chief Waruhiu was assassinated just outside Nairobi as he was driving back to Kiambu. As early as 1922 a song was sung by the people prophesying that Chiefs Waruhiu and Koinange would be buried alive for the wrongs they had committed against their Kikuyu brothers. Koinange changed his ways after the return of his son Peter Mbiu from England. He was soon detained and died shortly after his release in 1961.

Waruhiu, on the other hand, remained an enemy and most Kikuyu celebrated his death with three days of beer drinking. They were happy that one of Kenya's "Black Europeans" had left the earth. With few exceptions our imposed chiefs (we had no chiefs before the Europeans came) were simply stooges and tools of the white man and his Government.

Noting our continued growth and strength despite all efforts to crush our Movement, Government declared a State of Emergency on the night of 20 October 1952. In the early hours of the following morning 82 top KAU officials were arrested. Some, like Jomo Kenyatta, were held for trial while others were sent into detention. From this day Kenya was to become an island of death, terror and brutality.

Who was to blame for this? As one who participated I have to admit that Mau Mau initiated the violent taking of lives. The white man, however, for over 50 years had subjected the African to a slow, agonizing death. By paying the African slave wages for his labour, denying him access to secondary and higher education, removing from him the best land in Kenya and treating him with less respect than a dog, the white man of Kenya had created over the years a resentment and hatred amongst Africans which had to explode into violence. The European created the very thing he now condemns.

When an African, regardless of his education or skills, is made to crawl on the ground at the foot of any white man regardless of his abilities, manner or education, how can you expect anything but intense hatred? When being white is enough to make a man think he is superior to *any* African, and when being black is enough to condemn a man to permanent inferiority, how can anything but hatred and violence result? No people, whether black, white or yellow, who are treated as something less than human can resist indefinitely the urge to revolt against such degrading circumstances.

For these reasons I believe that history will condemn the white man rather than the black for the suffering and death which plagued Kenya for over eight years. This is not to say that we Africans made no mistakes or did no wrong. Of course we did. But we would have been in no position to commit these errors if it weren't for the far greater wrongs inflicted upon us by an inhuman British colonialism.

On the afternoon of 21 October as I was returning to the office after lunch with a friend, a group of *askari* rushed up and pushed us into a long stream of Africans who were being directed toward the Caledonia playing field in Nairobi. Reaching this huge open area across the main highway opposite the Coryndon Museum, I was put into a line of men to be screened by African loyalists brought from every location in the Kikuyu reserve. Thousands of us were herded into the field and we all suffered the abusive language and occasional jab in the back by the rifle-carrying *askari*. Luckily none of the screeners from my location in Nyeri knew or suspected anything about my political activities. As they passed

176

along the line they studied each man and then gave their opinions to the European officers accompanying them. Though I was soon released to return to the office, hundreds of others were identified as Mau Mau activists and sent into the detention camps.

As Government daily intensified its anti-Mau Mau activities, brutally imposing the restrictive measures of the Emergency legislation, the European settler felt he had full power to kill any Kikuyu at the slightest whim, wish or suspicion. It was to be an open season on Kikuyu and some European "hunters" were already beginning to put notches on their gun-handles. Guilty or innocent, it made little difference to many who, operating on the premise of collective punishment for collective guilt, believed the only good "Kyuk" was a dead one.

At first none of us knew just what this State of Emergency would entail. As Government brought in troop reinforcements from England and formed their African loyalists into Home Guard units there was much confusion within our Organization. For a month or so, while our leaders in Nairobi tried to figure out the lines of action open to us in the new circumstances, we remained relatively inactive. Perhaps, though I don't know this to be a fact, our leaders were waiting for some hint, advice or subtle directive from Kenyatta or the other detained KAU officials. If so, they waited in vain. All KAU officials – including those tried at Kapenguria – and the vast majority of educated Kikuyu quickly detached themselves from the revolution. I am not saying this to condemn these men as individuals, but whether they were members, supporters or even opponents of Mau Mau it must in all honesty be said that the minds of the Kikuyu people were turned toward violence and revolt by the preachings and political agitation of men such as Kenyatta, Koinange and other KAU leaders. The question we now ask is, "Why did these men abandon us in our hour of greatest need?"

With the arrest and detention of many educated leaders and the failure of other qualified men to step into their shoes, leadership of the Movement fell into the hands of men who lacked the political experience, education and knowledge of warfare necessary for the success of a popular revolution.

While violent methods had been adopted to eliminate traitors, to my knowledge we had no plan for an open clash with Government prior to the Emergency declaration. Our principal aim was to forge an iron-clad unity among Kikuyu, Embu and Meru tribesmen – and all other

177

Africans whose support could be won – so that we might take action as a single body to achieve our political objectives. The most talked-about means of putting pressure on Government was the general strike. We would paralyse the economy of Kenya by a mass refusal to work and a boycott of European and Asian shops and goods. It was also rumored that if all else failed we might rise up one night and kill every European in Kenya. This, however, was seen as a last resort and I don't think any agreement had been reached or plans worked out.

When the Emergency was declared it seems we had neither a plan for revolt nor the leadership to carry through such a plan. For many months we were clearly on the defensive, simply reacting to Government's repressive measures rather than putting into effect our own program of revolt.

Government, on the other hand, with the assistance of its black stooges, informers, Home Guards and other so-called "loyalists," set about attacking Mau Mau with a brutality and disregard for human life which few of us had expected. Restrictive measures, collective forms of punishment and inhuman techniques of extracting confessions and "winning" cooperation were the methods employed. The fear and hatred of the settler toward Africans was unleashed and with military personnel pouring in from Great Britain it was a common belief that the Europeans were trying to exterminate the whole Kikuyu people.

Government round-ups and sweeps of African locations in Nairobi increased. Early one morning at about 3 a.m. security forces surrounded Ziwani and called all of us out of our houses into an open area within the location. Screeners and Home Guards were brought in prepared with lists of KAU officials and persons suspected of holding office within Mau Mau. It was generally assumed that all of us were members or supporters of Mau Mau but Government concentrated its efforts in an attempt to round up leaders or active fighters in the Organization.

As in the many sweeps which were to follow, none of the screeners knew anything about my activities and seeing that I was a City Council employee and that my documents were in order released me without much trouble. It was about 7 a.m. when the security forces left. I had just enough time, if I hurried, to dress, have a cup of tea, and catch a bus for work.

One afternoon in December at about 5 p.m. five men came to visit me in Ziwani. They spoke about an *askari* in Kariokor who was badly mistreating Kikuyu and asked if I would join them in teaching him a lesson, while at the same time removing his pistol. I agreed and we set out singly toward Kariokor. Spotting the *askari* checking someone's identity papers, we surrounded him and moved in from different directions. The man approaching from the rear jumped on the *askari*'s back and grabbed him around the neck. The rest of us rushed forward and wrestled the *askari* to the ground, landing a few blows in the process, then grabbing his gun and running off in different directions. We met back at Ziwani and later that night took the pistol and sold it for 200s. to the chairman of the Nyeri District Committee.

I must mention, at this point, that in Nairobi our Movement had attracted many men who had earlier been driven by unemployment and hunger into a life of crime. These men were employed in eliminating traitors and were very active in stealing guns, ammunition, other necessary supplies and money. They would not, however, perform these services for nothing. They always insisted on being paid for the goods they managed to acquire. This selfish desire to make personal gains out of the revolution did much, as I now look back, to damage and perhaps even destroy what began as a just struggle against British colonial rule. Too often the high principles of the revolution were thrown aside for personal wealth, power or safety.

When I took my share of the money we made on the pistol, I wrongly thought: "Why shouldn't I make a little money for my efforts?" I knew that even some of the elders on the Central Committee were putting money from the dues we paid (each member paid a monthly "poll tax" of 20s.) into the bank for their private use.

It should not be thought, however, that this strain of narrow self-interest infected everyone. I believe the vast majority of Kikuyu men, women and children faced death and suffering bravely and thousands of young fighters entered the forests shouting Freedom and Land and thinking only of the collective good of our people.

Throughout the early months of 1953 I continued my job with the City Council and my activities in Mau Mau. I attended meetings and oathing ceremonies, recruited members and collected dues. I also allowed my house to be used for a variety of purposes including the hiding, cleaning and manufacture of guns and as a place where hunted men, or women whose husbands had been killed or arrested, might spend a night or two before moving on.

It was during this period that cards containing a person's name and rank within the Organization were issued to every member. These cards were carefully hidden behind other documents in a man's Government identification and employment booklet.

One night in May I was visited by Wambugu Gacoya, a close friend from my division. Wambugu, a rather short, slight man, was very talkative and liked to think of himself as being more clever than he actually was. He was one of the men who spoke to me that night after I'd taken the oath and, as a friend, had a strong influence on my activities within the Organization. We talked about practical matters and Wambugu asked me if I wanted to be Secretary for the Muhito Location Committee. He had recommended me for the job because of the good work I was doing for the Organization and I could begin immediately. I was pleased to hear this and gladly accepted.

My main task on the location committee was to fill in cards for new recruits who were about to enter the forest. When meeting fighters from different areas this card would identify the man as a comrade and remove suspicion of his being a Government spy. I also assisted in distributing the necessary equipment to newly formed fighting groups. Late at night, in an area of Bahati location called Far-Bahati, shoes, raincoats, shirts, pants and jackets were allocated to recruits before they were escorted to our arms depot at Kassarani. About five miles from Nairobi near the rock quarries and the Spread Eagle Hotel on the Fort Hall road these recruits were issued guns, *pangas* or *simis* and were instructed for a day or two on the use of firearms.

Several times I helped escort these men to Kassarani. After turning them over to our permanent guard, Muchina, for instruction I would return to Nairobi in the early hours of the morning. The new fighting groups, usually numbering from 100 to 200 men, would then be escorted in small groups, first to Thika, then to Fort Hall and finally into the Aberdare or Mount Kenya forests.

In June 1953 I was deeply saddened by the news that one of my brothers, Kiromo, had been killed. He was fighting in the forests but was captured when he returned home one day to see his wife and children and our parents. After his arrest the Home Guards, instead of taking Kiromo back to their post, shot him in cold blood.

While still pondering my elder brother's death, less than a month later, I learned that Mwenja, one of my younger brothers, had also been killed. He had just been recruited into an Aberdare fighting group and was shot while making his way into the forest. To my desire for land and freedom was now added a strong urge to avenge the death of my brothers.

In September 1953 after thousands of men had entered the forests and formed themselves into fighting units, the Central Province Committee in Nairobi decided to change its name to the Kenya Parliament. The center of the battle had shifted to the forests of Mount Kenya and the Aberdares and with regular communications difficult to maintain and a new leadership emerging in the forest, the committee of elders in Nairobi took on a new role in the revolution. The Kenya Parliament concerned itself primarily with leading the activities of Mau Mau in Nairobi and supplying the forest fighters with recruits, money, arms and other necessary materials.

Of the 50,000 Kikuyu living in Nairobi at this time only about 300 of us were actively engaged as fighters authorized to possess arms and acting on instruction from the Kenya Parliament. After several informal meetings held by the leaders of the fighting group, it was decided to organize a Kenya Land Freedom Army (LFA) which would combine all Nairobi fighters under a single command acting on orders of the Kenya Parliament.

Wambugu, by this time a general, was to act as a link between the Land Freedom Army and the Kenya Parliament. He came to visit me in Bondeni Location where I had moved a short time earlier. He asked me to be Secretary of the LFA saying that as an honest, educated young man I could then be of much greater service to the Organization.

Three weeks later, at the end of September, Wambugu called me to attend a meeting of the LFA. It was held in a vacant Asian house in Far-Bahati. We made our way to the meeting at night, having to crawl under the barbed-wire fence surrounding the area. Near the house I saw many armed *askari*. The first to see us gave a signal. He clicked his tongue three times against the roof of his mouth and gave three short whistles. Responding in a similar way, we identified ourselves as comrades and the sentry came forward to lead us into the house.

Inside were about 15 leaders of the LFA who had called this first formal meeting to establish the rules and regulations of the Army and to properly confirm its founding. The meeting was called to order by Commanding General Mwangi Enok. I sat down in the rear with my notebook, prepared to record the minutes. I was too busy writing to participate in the discussions but after much talk and the passing of

13 rules, I was called forward and introduced to the men as their new Secretary. Mwangi Enok asked me to read the minutes I had recorded. Following are some of the more important rules we passed:

1. No one was to be in possession of arms or ammunition without the knowledge and approval of the LFA Committee in Nairobi.
2. No fighter was to carry his weapon unless on a specific mission; otherwise, weapons were to be kept well hidden.
3. If any fighter was arrested while he still had ammunition in his gun, he would not be given legal assistance by the Committee.
4. No one was to take his weapon and join another fighting group without the knowledge and permission of the Committee.
5. No fighter was ever to intimidate or threaten with arms any other member of the LFA.
6. Any fighter injured in battle and unable to be moved to safety must be shot and not left alive for capture and interrogation by Government.
7. No one was to drink European-manufactured beer unless obliged to while on official business, such as attempting to bribe an *askari*, etc.
8. No one was to smoke European-manufactured cigarettes, though the smoking of *kiraiko* and *bhangi* was permitted.
9. No one was to ride in European-owned buses.
10. No one was to disclose any information concerning the LFA to any person not a member of the group, even if they were members of Mau Mau or fighters attached to different groups.

The punishment for violating these rules was simple. For the first offence, a man would be warned. Second offenders would be killed. It was felt that only through the threat of this severe punishment could the members of the Committee be assured that its rules would be obeyed.

We had no formal court system in Nairobi, though any committee, from the sub-location level to the Kenya Parliament, could sit in judgement of a man accused of having violated a rule. As in my case, minor offenders otherwise considered to be good men were usually fined and sometimes caned. Persons who committed serious crimes such as giving information to Government, or who were known to be regularly violating well established rules (such as riding on European-owned buses or drinking beer) rarely got a hearing. The case was discussed by a district committee or the Kenya Parliament elders and fighters were instructed to execute the guilty person.

After the official business was completed discussion about the rules continued. One man asked if it were all right for a fighter to marry. And after some discussion it was decided that this was a personal matter and shouldn't be covered by LFA rules.

It was during this informal talk that one of our sentries was pushed into the house by some of his comrades. He had abandoned his post and gone to the nearby home of a woman-friend. The others tracked him down and now wanted to punish him. We calmed the man down and discussed the case at some length, finally deciding that since it was his first offence we would let him off lightly. He was demoted in rank from a colonel to a captain.

I hadn't attended any of the leaders' informal meetings and didn't know how these ranks were originally decided upon. The officers present at this meeting aside from Mwangi Enok and Wambugu were Brigadier General Gitonga Gathanju and four colonels: Muturi Gacoya (Wambugu's brother), Mwangi Toto, Kagema Kiniaru and Kariuki Chotara.

It was about 4 a.m. when the meeting finally broke up. Before leaving the house Gitonga Gathanju instructed all of us including the guards to grease, wrap and bury our arms in Far-Bahati field, which was to be our permanent arms hide. I walked out with Wambugu who spent the rest of the night with me in Bondeni.

One day in early October 1953 I was told by Wambugu to visit a certain Asian print shop on Grogan Road. An African employee would give me some blank I.D. cards, writing paper with a "Kenya Land Freedom Army" letterhead, envelopes, stamps and a rubber stamp with our name on it. I got these things and after filling in the name and rank of each LFA fighter on an I.D. card, distributed them to over a hundred men in Far-Bahati.

Later that month Mwangi Enok and Wambugu came to Bondeni and asked me to help them write a letter to the *East African Standard*. They wanted Government to believe that Mau Mau was quickly spreading to the other Kenya tribes. We wrote the following letter: "To all African comrades: General Ogutu, our Luo comrade, has been appointed to contact the leaders of all non-Kikuyu tribes such as the Kamba, Baluhya, Masai and his own Luo tribe and assess the strength of their fighting forces. Ogutu is now in Nairobi discussing the details of his mission with the Kenya Parliament."

There was no General Ogutu, of course, and the only non-Kikuyu support we had came from a small segment of Wakamba and the Narok Masai. Our policy and the attitude of some members helped to isolate us from the other Kenya tribes. First there was the oath itself which was essentially Kikuyu and not liked by people of other tribes. Many of us felt that a more general and flexible oath, adapted to suit all Kenya Africans, was what we needed. A second reason for our isolation was the belief held by some Kikuyu leaders that this was our struggle and that the rewards of victory, such as high positions in the future government and military, should not be shared with men of other tribes. I didn't share this attitude and now believe it was a major factor contributing to our eventual defeat. Nevertheless, I could not see the error of our ways as clearly then as now and I continued working as secretary of the LFA and doing my best to propagate the ideas of the revolution. I wrote out many of the songs which were being sung in the forests and even created a few new ones about our struggle in Nairobi. Here is a song I wrote about one of the Bahati sweeps:

1. On January 7th we were surrounded at Bahati
   By the white community.

   (Chorus)

   We will never be silent until we get land to cultivate
   And Freedom in this country of ours, Kenya.

2. Home Guards were the first to go and close the gates
   And Johnnies entered while the police surrounded the location.

   (Chorus)

3. When we were surrounded we were ordered out of our houses
   And told to pack up our belongings as we were to be detained.

   (Chorus)

4. We packed our things and were taken to an opening just outside
   the location
   Where many Kikuyu and other tribesmen were selected for
   detention.

   (Chorus)

5. Some of those chosen were sent to Manyani,
   Others to MacKinnon Road, the region of sandy soil.

   (Chorus)

6. You, traitors! You dislike your children, caring only for your stomachs;
You are the enemies of our people.

(Chorus)

We will never be silent until we get land to cultivate
And Freedom in this country of ours, Kenya.

During this period, the main task of the LFA in Nairobi was to acquire arms, money and other supplies – through either theft or purchase – and to eliminate traitors and enforce the rules of our organization. On the whole, I would say we had the sympathy and support of the vast majority of Nairobi Africans.

Men from Nairobi were continually being recruited and sent into the forest. Often we received a report that Waruingi, who fought in and around Kiambu, or one of the leaders of the Aberdares or Mount Kenya fighters needed a certain number of men. This information was sent to the Kenya Parliament which would have its representatives from the district committees ask each location to contribute a certain number of young men for the forest.

I continued to help escort these new fighters to Kassarani, and as time went on we had to take ever greater precautions against Government agents slipping in amongst the recruits. In addition to supplying no weapons until we reached the Kassarani depot, none of the recruits were told where they were heading and they were escorted by heavily armed guards all the way to the forest edge guaranteeing that none should turn back. At Kassarani all Government documents (work cards, poll tax receipts, etc.) possessed by the recruits were taken and burned. This further ensured that the men would remain in the forest, for if they came out each knew he would soon be caught without the proper documents and immediately detained if not shot by Government.

In November another meeting was held in Far-Bahati. I remember discussing the procedure to be followed if a man were captured and interrogated by Special Branch. We decided that each man should prepare for himself a simple, harmless and misleading confession in the event of his arrest. He was to say (1) that he was forcibly administered the Mau Mau oath in (2) an area strange to him, such as the Masai reserve, and that (3) he didn't know the oath administrator or any other persons present at the ceremony. It was necessary at this time for any arrested Kikuyu to admit having taken at least the first oath. Government assumed that all

LIFE HISTORIES FROM THE REVOLUTION

Kikuyu had taken the oath and men were known to have been summarily shot for refusing to admit this. Our main concern was to guard against a comrade implicating and endangering others through his own confession. We also discussed what to do if a comrade was captured by Government and then escaped or was released. We agreed that such a man would have to be carefully screened and kept under close observation for a time before being allowed to take up his old duties within the Organization. Every precaution had to be taken against those who might have gained their release by promising to act as Government agents and informers.

A resolution was also passed that members could drink European beer in situations where refusing would arouse the suspicion of *askari* or other Government servants. Our rule against drinking beer was well known and if a man refused a bottle offered by an *askari* he would immediately be thought a member of Mau Mau.

There were certain members of the Kenya Parliament with whom we maintained contact and after the meeting I wrote a report on all important matters discussed and gave it to Wambugu for review and approval by the elders.

Guns and ammunition were difficult to get in large enough quantities and this was one of the main tasks of the Nairobi fighters. Though usually stolen from Europeans or purchased from a few Asian dealers, it was not unusual for us to buy weapons from Home Guards, Tribal Police or other *askari*. I remember one occasion in December when I learned of a Nandi KAR man who had a .303 rifle he wanted to sell. Through Wambugu I got permission from the elders and contacted the Nandi. He wanted 1,000s. for the rifle but finally, as he couldn't easily return it, he accepted 400s. Figuring I should make something for myself, I told the elders it cost 600s. and pocketed the difference.

In January 1954 a man calling himself General Ndiritu Kirigu arrived in Nairobi with 30 fighters. He had just come from the forest, he told us, and was badly in need of money and supplies. He told many tales about Dedan Kimathi, Stanley Mathenge and Generals China and Tanganyika, and about the fight in the forests. Thinking him a good man we decided to help Ndiritu, giving him two rifles, three shotguns, clothing and some medical supplies. In addition, as he was a Nyeri man, the Nyeri District Committee voted to give him 5,000s.

It was only later that we discovered Ndiritu had fled from the forest and was acting on his own like a common criminal. This was not an exceptional case and the term *"komerera"* was used in describing men like Ndiritu who were simply hiding from Government in the reserves or forests. These men were feared and disliked. Since they frequently stole animals and other food from the peasants and rarely did anything but run and hide from the security forces they gained a reputation as cowards.

Early in February Ndiritu was shot through the thigh while going to his hideout in Karura Forest, which adjoins the wooded area of City Park. His other permanent camp was in the bush near the Kenya Girls' High School in Kilileshwa. He was taken to the quarters of a comrade who worked as a servant for a European in Kilimani. Here, under our care, he slowly recovered.

Throughout this period I had retained my job with the City Council and continued to live in Bondeni. This was a location lived in mainly by Government loyalists and very few Kikuyu. It was relatively safe and my house was increasingly used to clean and hide guns. We did this right under the noses of neighboring Home Guards who assumed this type of thing only happened in Kikuyu locations like Bahati and Kariokor.

My work as a draftsman continually deteriorated as my activities within Mau Mau forced me to keep irregular hours and miss many days at the office. My relations with my European and Asian superiors were not good and I began to feel that my days with the City Council were numbered.

For about six months now I had been keeping company with a young girl from a neighboring sub-location in Nyeri. She was in Nairobi living with her brother at Kariokor. Toward the end of March we decided to get married. A marriage ceremony of either the traditional or civil type, however, was very impractical under the circumstances then prevailing in Nairobi. Finally, after I'd convinced her brother of my good intentions, Helena moved in with me at Bondeni. She was my wife and we would take care of the formalities later. Shortly thereafter, on 1 April, I was given notice by the City Council. I would be unemployed at the end of the month.

Government had for some time now tried to cut the connection between Nairobi and the forests. They knew that Nairobi was the main source of arms, recruits and other supplies for the fighters in the Aberdares and Mount Kenya but found it difficult to stop the flow. On 22 April Government forces launched Operation Anvil, an all-out attempt to crush our organization in Nairobi and isolate the city from the rest of Kenya.

The operation began very early in the morning with security forces surrounding the major Kikuyu locations of Bahati, Makongeni, Ziwani, Pumwani and Kariokor. At about 3 a.m. residents were called out of their homes by loudspeakers and told to prepare for a small *safari*. Most of the locations were surrounded by barbed wire fences leaving only a small gateway through which to enter or leave. With this entrance guarded, those caught inside the locations had little chance of escape. Through our agents working in Government offices or posing as Home Guards or *askari* we generally got advance warning of a major Government action. There had been rumbles about a large Government sweep several days before Anvil and most of our activists managed to sleep outside the locations on the night of the 21st. Those rounded up were mainly passive supporters; others were completely "innocent" or even Government sympathizers.

Everyone was screened and we learned that Government had several informers planted in our Organization. Different coloured cards were used; those given green or yellow cards were eventually released while those given red cards were sent into fields surrounded by barbed wire fences and then taken to waiting trains for transfer to Manyani or MacKinnon Road Detention camps. The operation continued in Nairobi for three days and I would say that around 30,000 Kikuyu, Embu and Meru were sent into detention.

After Anvil all remaining Kikuyu were forced to move to Bahati and Makadara where they could be kept under close supervision. Only those Kikuyu living in the railway workers' quarters or staying on the premises of Europeans as house servants were exempted from this ruling.

I had not yet left the City Council and, living at Bondeni, wasn't bothered during Anvil. A short time later Bondeni was surrounded and *askari* entered each house giving us forms to fill out. We were told to put down our name, location of origin, occupation and everything we knew about Mau Mau including our own activities within the Organization. They also told us to name anyone we suspected of being a Mau Mau "terrorist."

I put down that I'd earlier been forced to take the oath but had since had no connection with Mau Mau . . . that I didn't know any of the people at the oathing ceremony except the administrator. I gave his name knowing he had since been killed.

I locked myself in my room as ordered by the *askari* and when they came back I opened the door and put the form into the slit of a small wooden box. They told me to pack my things. Being a Kikuyu I would have to move to Bahati. They gave me the key to room number T2 and I moved in that same day.

About a week later I let Brigadier General Kagema Kiniaru and his wife move in with Helena and me. I got to know Kagema when he lived with my eldest brother at Kassarani in 1952. In September that year Kagema was charged with being involved in the murder of a settler named Wright. To save himself he testified on behalf of the Government prosecutor and a short time later was invited by Special Branch to work as an informer. He told the Organization about the Special Branch offer and was instructed to accept. It was very useful to have men like Kagema (already a leader in the Movement at the time I became a member) infiltrate key branches of Government. The Emergency had just been declared and we needed all the information we could get about Government plans and intentions.

I liked Kagema and thought he was a very clever person. A short stocky man, he was good natured and always with an interesting or funny story to tell. I knew about the informer card he carried and was not really surprised when he had a European visitor late one night at Bahati. I was awakened by knocking at the door and saw the European enter holding some watches. He talked to Kagema about them and then came over and asked me if I'd ever seen them before. Apparently they were stolen and later recovered by the CID (Criminal Investigation Division). I said I'd never laid eyes on the watches before and showed him my own. At this point Kagema stepped outside with the man and I went back to sleep, having drunk too much beer earlier in the evening. In the morning Kagema told me the man was from Special Branch and came to check on a certain Mkamba in the location. The man was found in possession of stolen goods and arrested.

Being now unemployed I decided to devote all my time and energy to the Movement. In addition to keeping all the records of the LFA I joined the fighters whenever they needed help in a raid or in eliminating traitors. In May a meeting was held at Far-Bahati. Among other things the question of Nairobi Muslims was discussed. It was felt by some of the men that these people were using their evil magic to help Government destroy our Movement. I remained silent, neither believing in magic nor feeling free to criticize the others. It was finally decided that 20 of us should raid one of the large mosques the next night.

Armed with three Sten guns, five rifles and the pistol, which I carried, we approached the Eastleigh Mosque in groups of two or three and took up positions outside the low wall around the front courtyard. It was about 8 p.m. and a number of Muslims milled about, some talking, others engaged in prayer. Gitonga Gathanju gave the signal to open fire. Caught in our cross-fire the Muslims in the courtyard panicked and others rushed out of the mosque to see what was happening.

Knowing the security forces would soon be there we kept up our fire for only a minute or two then dispersed and made our way back to Bahati. There we quickly buried our arms and returned to normal activities. Next morning the newspapers headlined the attack, reporting that eight people had been killed and many more injured.

About a week later we attempted a similar raid on the Pumwani African Mosque. This time, however, armed with only a Sten gun and pistol, we were unsuccessful. The Sten failed to fire and we pulled back before doing any damage. Some believed that the Muslims used magic to cause our guns not to fire.

It was a wet rainy night and though we were unaware of it, European police had followed our tracks to Bahati. They surrounded the area and brought in Geiger counters to search for weapons. Though we had already left the location the enemy discovered our Far-Bahati arms hide and recovered 11 revolvers, two homemade guns, two hammers and several *pangas*. A picture of these weapons appeared on the front page of the Standard the following morning.

Shortly after this incident the Kenya Parliament decided that all fighters should go through a purification ceremony. They believed the misfortunes we were having, including the loss of men in battle, were being caused by failure to remove the evils contaminating us.

We were to go to the Eastleigh garbage dump where, at 8 p.m. on Saturday night, a woman seer would purify us. I walked to Eastleigh with Mwangi Toto, Kariuki Chotara and a few others. On arrival I saw that over 100 of our fighters had assembled for the ceremony. Each of us was instructed by the seer to cover himself with the blanket he had been asked to bring. The women passed amongst us sprinkling the contents from the stomach of a slaughtered goat on every man. She then picked up a calabash filled with the goat's blood and moved about mumbling certain traditional Kikuyu sayings which I couldn't quite make out.

*Each of us was instructed by the seer to cover himself with the
blanket. . . she then picked up a calabash filled with goat's blood
and moved about mumbling certain traditional Kikuyu sayings.*

At this point, just as the seer entered a nearby caretaker's hut for
more paraphernalia, I heard several shots ring out in the darkness. We
had been spotted by a small enemy patrol and they were firing in our
direction, though still some distance away. I threw off my blanket and
ran quickly to the Nairobi River which I crossed, coming up on the
other side and entering Bahati. Spending the rest of the night with a
friend, I learned the following morning that none of our fighters had
been captured or injured. The old seer, however, was arrested and sent
to Kamiti Women's Prison where, as Helena later informed me, she
continued with her magical practices.

Not long after this incident Kagema and I decided to visit Ndiritu,
who was staying with a Mau Mau member in the staff quarters of Mathari
Mental Hospital. Just as we entered the compound I noticed a group of
askari coming toward the quarters. It was obviously going to be a sweep.
I quickly moved toward one of the exits trying to escape the net. The
place was surrounded already, however, and I walked right into the arms
of some *askari*. Not knowing what happened to Kagema I was taken with
some others to Mathari police station and thrown in a cell. Soon I was

taken out and driven to Special Branch Headquarters, Nairobi. Here, in a cluster of wooden buildings near the City Hall, I was subjected to the usual abuses of the *askari*. I spotted Kagema in the crowd but was led with two other men into a small room. We were ordered to take off all our clothes and then inspected closely by a European officer. Apparently they were looking for Ndiritu, as the man carefully examined my thigh in the place where Ndiritu had been injured.

Told to put on my clothes, I was taken into another office where I saw Kagema smoking and talking to a European officer. The man was saying that when released Kagema should tell his Mau Mau comrades that he'd bribed an *askari* at Kileleshwa and gotten out that way. I listened as Kagema spun a tall tale about how he and I had gone to Mathari to gain information about Ndiritu and Mwangi Toto for Special Branch. It was all a pack of lies but when the Europeans turned to me for confirmation of the story I nodded my head in approval. A few minutes later we were released and went back to Bahati. I could see how useful it was to pose as an informer and was impressed by the clever way Kagema had convinced the Europeans through his card and lies that he was a loyal servant of Government. He said he'd told them I was his assistant and I was thankful, knowing full well that he'd saved me a lot of trouble and, with no employment card, from almost certain detention.

It was still in May when Ndiritu, who had recovered from his injury but failed to leave Nairobi for the forest, committed a grave mistake. He and some of his men raided our Kassarani depot and forced Muchino to give them arms and ammunition. When we learned of this a meeting was held and it was decided that Ndiritu would have to pay with his life. He was captured about a month later, taken into Karura Forest and executed with a hammer. His body was buried on the bank of the Ruiruaka River which runs through the forest. I took part in none of this, but felt little sympathy for the man.

Ndiritu's raid, plus our losses at Far-Bahati, had left us very short of weapons and ammunition. Prompted by the elders we decided to let Mwangi Toto, Kariuki Chotara and Mwangi Kirigi take some of the men into Kiambu with most of our remaining weapons. They were to raid police and Home Guard posts in an effort to replenish our depleted arms supply.

In late June 1954 Wambugu Gacoya was arrested. As I walked down Hardinge Street with Kagema a few days later he asked me to wait outside

Gailey & Roberts while he went in to see a European friend with whom he'd served in the Second World War. In about 15 minutes Kagema came out and said his friend told him that Wambugu had confessed and given Special Branch the names of almost all our Nairobi leaders – including his and mine. Kagema told the European that he and I were working for Special Branch and that Wambugu's mentioning our names just proved he had no idea about our real activities. We left quickly as I felt the situation was extremely dangerous.

After warning the elders about Wambugu's confession I decided to stay in hiding. For the next week I stayed with friends, only returning to T2 Bahati for a few hours at night. I learned that Mwangi Toto was at the Kigwa coffee plantation in Kiambu and had made up my mind to join him there.

When I told my plan to one of the elders he said a joint meeting of the Kenya Parliament and Land Freedom Army was to take place in a few days to decide on future activities and that I should not leave the city yet. This meeting was held during the first week of July and was attended by over 30 leaders. In the darkness of the Kasarani stone quarries it was decided that the LFA fighters should take all the remaining supplies and enter the forests around the city to fight. After Anvil there had been several other major enemy operations in Nairobi and it was now difficult to operate in the city. Successes were hard to achieve and with Government pressure mounting, the flow of arms and ammunition into the Movement had steadily decreased. In addition, with Government having the names of our leaders, staying in the city was becoming more and more dangerous.

Just after we'd decided to send for Mwangi Toto to help us organize ourselves into a forest army, the meeting was interrupted by three of Ndiritu's men. They were very angry and it seemed they wanted to avenge the death of their leader. We tried to persuade them of Ndiritu's guilt and to abandon any plans they might have for getting even with his executioners. Not satisfied with our arguments they insisted on taking one of our leaders aside for questioning. When we refused the only armed man among them drew his pistol and started firing. Kagema was hit by a stray bullet and though we fired a few shots after them the three men fled into the darkness and escaped.

The meeting broke up after this incident and I stayed behind to see what I could do for Kagema. He had been shot through the groin and couldn't walk. I dragged him to a safe place and asked him what he thought I should do.

"My best chance," he said, "is for you to go see my European friend. His name is Major Seedon and you can find him at Gailey & Roberts offices on Hardinge Street. Tell him we were trying to get information for Special Branch about Mwangi Toto and Ndiritu and that I was shot by one of Ndiritu's men near Kassarani. Ask him to come pick me up as I've been badly injured."

It was quite late and I set off on foot toward the city. When I arrived the sun was already up. After a few bites of breakfast I went to see Major Seedon. I asked one of the employees in the building where I could find the man saying that Kagema Kiniaru had sent me to see him. The office said that Seedon was an important man and that I'd have to wait while he delivered my message.

In a few minutes I was ushered into Seedon's office. "Come in, Mr. Mathu, and have a seat." I didn't know that he knew me by name or, as I soon discovered, that he was a senior Special Branch officer. He asked me about Kagema and what we had been doing. I quickly decided not to mention Kagema's bullet wound. Seedon would ask more questions and I didn't want to give him any details about what had happened. "Kagema is fine," I said. "He's at Kassarani near the Spread Eagle Hotel, where we've been trying to get information about Mwangi Toto's gang. He sent me to ask you for some spending money and a card to keep me from being arrested by security forces in the area."

Seedon began asking questions about what we had learned at Kassarani and I said that Mwangi Toto had been at Kassarani a few days earlier but had since left with his gang for Naivasha. He seemed pleased with my report, calling in three other Europeans whom I took to be fellow Special Branch men and telling them what I'd said. He also told them about me saying I was a good man and a friend of Kagema.

When the other men left Seedon gave me 80s. and an informer card bearing his name and phone number. I thanked him, said goodbye and left the office. Obtaining the card was my own idea. Knowing I would soon enter the forest the card could prove useful if I was ever captured by security forces.

I walked down to River Road to make arrangements for Kagema. Two plain clothes Asian CID men stopped me in one of the shops and, finding I was without an employment card, arrested me. When I produced my card from Seedon, however, they phoned him, verifying my story and telling me to go on my way. I went immediately to a comrade who owned a truck and together we drove to Kassarani. We picked up Kagema and took him to the quarters of a cook in Kilimani. I went to see a medical assistant friend of mine at King George VI Hospital to arrange for treatment and medication. When I returned to tell Kagema, I learned that he'd left a few hours earlier. He called a taxi from the house and left without saying a word to the cook.

"Kagema will go directly to Seedon," I thought. "And he might say something to contradict my story." I fitted the card from Seedon between my other documents and decided to have nothing more to do with Special Branch. My fears were confirmed in the next few days. While in hiding I heard rumors that Kagema had been arrested and sent to a prison hospital.

Before entering the forest I had to make arrangements for Helena as it wasn't safe for her to remain at Bahati. I contacted two African constables who had taken the second Mau Mau oath and were trusted members of the Movement. It was agreed that one of them would take Helena to the Mathari police station quarters where, posing as the sister of a constable, she would be safe.

I then went to Kassarani with our truck driver to bring some supplies into Nairobi and when I returned I waited in the Bahati house of a friend. At about midnight I went to T2 to tell Helena of my plans and the accommodations I'd arranged for her. Within a few minutes of entering my house, however, there was a knock at the door. The place was surrounded by security forces and we were trapped inside. Later I learned that my "friend" had reported my presence to the Home Guards at the chief's post in the location.

After thoroughly searching me and the house the *askari* led me to the chief's camp. Though they had found nothing in their search and my documents – except for the employment card – were in perfect order, it seemed they had some information about me, perhaps from Kagema. Helena was left in T2. I hadn't even had a chance to tell her of the arrangement I'd made and felt I had to escape.

They had taken all my documents and I made a deal with one of the prisoners assigned to clean up the chief's quarters. I offered him 10s. to find my papers and return them to me. Luckily the plan worked and when the man brought my documents I hid them in the bathroom, later slipping them to my wife when she came by to pay me a visit.

The following evening the D.O. and three *askari* drove me over to the Shauri Moyo Home Guard post. The *askari* stripped me of my watch and clothing – leaving me with only a pair of undershorts – and began to interrogate me. I refused to answer any of their questions and was severely beaten and kicked. After an hour or so, with my face badly cut and bleeding, I pretended to be unconscious and was dragged into the kitchen area of a house within the post. Thinking I was badly hurt and unable to move, they left me there on the floor leaning against a bag of charcoal.

Late that night the *askari* posted to guard me fell asleep. I bided my time until about 4 a.m. and then, in the dead silence of the early morning darkness, I crept slowly past the guard and toward the fence. Moving on my stomach all the way, I crawled under the barbed wire and made my way quickly to the nearby house of a friend. He gave me food and drink and after I'd cleaned up he let me have one of his suits and a pair of shoes. The morning sun was up by the time I'd gotten dressed and asked my friend to deliver a message to Helena. I wanted her to come see me at Shauri Moyo and she arrived a few hours later. We spent that night together and I explained the plans I'd made for both of us. The following morning as she was returning to T2 Bahati to collect her belongings, she was arrested. On hearing this I went straight to my two constable friends. I asked them to go to the chief's camp at Bahati and say they'd been sent by Special Branch to bring David Mathu's wife in for screening. If there were any questions they could say that I'd been recaptured and that Special Branch wanted to interrogate Helena and me together.

With all the confusion that existed in the security forces at this time – the various branches, such as Tribal Police, Home Guards, Special Branch, CID, military personnel, etc., were not well coordinated – it was not difficult for the African constables to walk out with Helena. The chief placed her in their custody and they took her directly to Mathari police post where she remained safely with their wives for almost two months.

Next day a friend, Icharia Waiti, came to see me at Shauri Moyo. He had two pistols and invited me to take one and go with him to Kariokor location. That afternoon and evening we talked, drank Kikuyu beer and made plans to leave Nairobi and join Mwangi Toto. The following morning I went to see Helena at a pre-arranged spot and gave her the 80 shillings I'd received from Seedon. She was feeling alright though still a bit shaken by her experience with the police. We talked for awhile and then parted.

Returning to Kariokor, I went with Icharia to collect three pistols and some ammunition he'd hidden and we then set off to find Mwango Toto. Night had already fallen. We made our way through the bush bordering the Nairobi-Fort Hall road. About three miles from the city, we passed through the Karura Forest and moved on to the huge Kigwa plantation. Luckily, while moving through the dense coffee groves, we ran into one of Mwangi's sentries. After returning his signal we were escorted to the camp. Mwangi had about 40 men with him and was glad to see us.

I turned over the guns we brought and took back the record books which Mwangi had taken with him to Kiambu. I told him about my experiences in the city since he'd left and explained about Kagema and of the informer card I'd gotten from Seedon. He agreed that I should keep it with me, so while my other documents were being burnt I sewed the card into the collar of my leather jacket.

I had known Mwangi Toto since mid-1953 when I became active in the underground Movement. He had a good sense of humour and never acted superior or demanded any special privileges for himself, eating and living just like the rest of us. Though I came to realize later how jealously he guarded his position as leader of the group, he was a brave fighter and well-liked by the men under his command. Mwangi had entered the forest to fight, not just to hide from the security forces like Ndiritu and other *komereras*. While he had little formal education, Mwangi was not too concerned with religious or magical practices and usually kept the political objectives of the revolution clearly in mind.

After hearing about the group's activities in Kiambu and entering some information in the records, I ate and sat around talking with the fighters. Finally I decided to turn in, very tired from the day's journey and excitement

'ARMY PLANS' LIST PUNISHMENTS

THE following is a translation of the alleged "army plans" in the Kenya Parliament:

Every person should obey the party in which he is, and should respect the day fixed for meeting;

There is no permission to leak out the news of the party in which you are if it has not been agreed, and what has been agreed upon may be revealed;

No one is allowed by the Kenya Parliament to have his own separate party which is not known by the Government of the Africans, if he is known that he has his own separate party, this rule will convict him.

There is no permission for a leader to keep a prostitute or seduce somebody's wife so as to make her a prostitute. If he is known to have done that, there is judgement reserved for it.

No one should keep for himself weapons while he is a member of the party, keeping a weapon as his own. If he is known, judgement is reserved for him:

There is no permission for the leaders to quarrel, if they have disputes among themselves, they should let the leader know the reason of their dispute;

There is no permission for the weapons to be kept by more than three persons, they should be kept as follows — by the general, by his assistant, by the commandant,

There is no permission for any party member to take beer or spirit unless it is opened for consumption by the African Government. If anybody consumes it, the fine is 200/- or alternatively 30 strokes;

There is no permission to receive anybody unless he has passed through the party scouts;

There is no permission to receive someone who has passed through pipe-line, if such a person is found, he should be sent to the army scouts.

The Urban Guerrillas

My immediate feeling upon rejoining my friends was one of excited happiness. I would be the group's secretary and could now openly and actively struggle for our land and freedom. I don't think I really believed we could defeat the British, but I did think we could force the colonial government to yield to our political demands. By fighting we could draw the attention of the outside world to our plight, to the slave-like conditions under which our people were made to live. Poorly trained and equipped, our only answer to British power and repression was terrorism and the destruction of European property and security.

That night I slept with the others under a clump of coffee trees. I put my raincoat on the ground and covered myself with one thin blanket. I spent the rest of the night shivering and tossing on my new earthen bed.

We remained at Kigwa for three days then moved on to another hideout on the Ndiritu farm near Kiambu police station. We spent the next four days planning a raid on Kamiti Prison. Three of us, Mwangi Toto, Kariuki Chotara and myself, did most of the planning and then presented our ideas to the others for discussion.

Mwangi explained that we were running short of ammunition and for this reason had decided to raid Kamiti. He would lead ten men armed with our two Stens and eight rifles. They would leave the camp that night soon after dark. Chotara and I would remain behind with the others.

I knew Kariuki as a boy but when we met in Nairobi after I joined the Movement it was the first time we'd seen one another since 1943. In his mid-twenties, Kariuki still looked like a boy of 15 or 16, his short slender build adding to this impression of youth. We once again became good friends and I admired his courage in fighting and his strong feelings toward our people. He was gentle and warm toward his comrades and the uneducated masses but could be hard and fierce in battle against the enemy. I think it was his honesty of purpose and humility that I liked best; he was fighting for the people and felt a pride and dignity in doing so.

Late that night the ambush was set. The askari *walked
right into it and were quietly cut down with* pangas.

That night as we spoke while awaiting Mwangi's return, Kariuki
talked of the Kenya which lay ahead for the Africans, of a life of dignity,
respect and material comfort. We would drive the white man out and
then become leaders in the army of an independent Kenya.

It was around midnight when I heard the call of the *Kanyuajui* bird
piercing the silence of the night. Three times, then silence, followed by
three more calls. It was Mwangi and the others signaling our sentries.
Life in the forest demanded a set of signals and each group usually had its
own distinctive bird or animal calls. When on the move at night through
the forest or bush we identified ourselves by the use of two names, *Kilima*
("mountain" in Swahili) and *Gituku* ("skin cap" in Kikuyu). Anyone
failing to respond to one or another of these names by answering with
the alternate term was taken as an enemy.

Soon Mwangi entered the hideout. I noticed as he sat down to tell
us what happened that all ten men had returned safely. "The raid," he
said "was unsuccessful. We reached the prison at 9 p.m. and only a few
askari were guarding the entrance. I decided to attack the main gate but

when we opened fire after creeping to within 20 feet of the gate, we met stiff resistance. The prison was heavily guarded and I was convinced it would be suicide to rush the gate; so I ordered the men to cease fire and withdraw."

Two days later we made our way into the Uplands Forest of Limuru. We were now 45 fighters and our food supply was very low. On reaching the camp where two small shelters had previously been built, 20 of the men were sent to raid the stock of a Home Guard who would be spending his night at the post. They returned several hours later with 16 sheep which we slaughtered, roasted and ate to our fill.

In the morning we sent 30 fighters to guard the approach to our camp near the forest edge. At about 9 o'clock security forces were spotted heading our way, a small group of Tribal Police and Home Guards. When they came within range we opened fire, forcing them to retreat. Coming back with reinforcements, they were once more driven off. On their third

"Karanja Kirai was our strongest believer in Kikuyu religion and magic . . . he insisted on performing traditional practices which I considered useless."

attempt at about noon, however, security forces arrived in large numbers and drove our fighters back toward the camp. We had packed all our belongings except for some utensils and moved to the far edge of the forest, planning to circle the enemy and leave the area. The enemy forces split up into small units to hunt for us and the rest of the afternoon we stayed hidden in the forest. There were two or three small skirmishes, but when darkness came the enemy withdrew.

We knew that by morning we would be surrounded and that Government would probably call in planes to bomb the forest. So we couldn't rest. Moving silently we made our way hurriedly toward the coffee fields near the Brackenhurst Hotel. It was a 20-mile walk taking about eight hours. We arrived in the darkness of early morning and I was asleep before the sun rose.

The following day one of our new recruits told us that two *askari* were posted at night to guard the European school near the hotel. They each had a rifle and ammunition which we could easily acquire. Mwangi, Kariuki and I discussed the matter and decided to send seven men armed only with pangas to ambush the *askari*. Late that night the ambush was set. The *askari* walked right into it and were quietly cut down with *pangas*. We gained two .303 rifles and 120 rounds of ammunition.

One of the fighters who took part in the ambush, Karanja Kirai, insisted that we all undergo a ritual purification. A sheep was slaughtered and the stomach contents were rubbed on our feet and weapons in order (it was believed) to cleanse us of the evil we had contacted and protect us from the curses of the dying *askari*.

Karanja Kirai was our strongest believer in Kikuyu religion and magic. He was a simple, uneducated man and liked by all the others. I didn't like it, however, when he insisted on performing traditional practices which I thought were useless. Each morning and night he would lead us in prayers. Facing Mount Kenya with some of the men holding soil in their right hands, we would listen as Karanja spoke the prayer. Though they varied from day to day, the prayers always expressed our need for Ngai's help and went something like this:

> "Oh God of Mount Kenya, help us fight our enemy and don't let him take us by surprise. Help us win the struggle against the European by giving our fighters guns and ammunition. Please, oh God, protect Jomo Kenyatta and our other great leaders from the evils of the white man."

To end the prayer we would all say: "*Thaaithataya Ngai, thai*", which means "Praise God. Peace be with us."

Karanja also insisted that we shake our blankets each night before going to sleep and in the morning as soon as we awoke. After shaking the blanket each man was to spit on it to remove the evil spirits. I never did this, thinking it a bit silly, and was sometimes ridiculed by the others who thought it was I who was stupid. They would jokingly accuse me of being "just like the rest of the *tieties.*"

Karanja could never convince Mwangi that we needed a permanent seer but he did persuade us to visit one who lived in his sub-location of Kiambu. While the others were in the old woman's hut I remained outside, thinking it safer and being unconcerned about what the seer had to say.

When the men came out after about an hour Mwangi told me what the woman said. We were not to have any contact with women while carrying our weapons, and when we killed someone in battle we were to go to the nearest river, wash ourselves and if possible be cleansed by a seer. Before being used again all our weapons were to be rubbed with the stomach contents of a sheep.

At Ndiritu farm a few days later I learned that arrangements had been made to give the second oath to some Kikuyu living nearby. An oath administrator named Gakuru was living among the workers on the labour line of the farm and would be in charge of the ceremony.

Gakuru came to the hut where the oath was to be administered bringing several strips of roasted goat's meat. It was late at night. Inside the darkened hut lit only by a small paraffin candle several people had gathered. Three men and six women, including two Wakamba, were to take the oath.

It began with the women who were called in and asked by Gakuru to remove all their clothing except the short underskirt. They formed a circle around Gakuru who laid a long strip of meat across their shoulders so as to join them. He then uttered a series of vows similar to those of the first oath, which the women repeated. The only new vows I could hear while sitting in the corner of the hut were that the initiate should assist the fighters with food and lodging when called upon and that they should always warn the fighters when the security forces approached.

With the vows completed Gakuru handed each woman a small piece of meat and asked her to insert it momentarily in her vagina. Then, taking a small bite of the meat they held in their right hands, the women swore: "If I reveal the secrets of the Mau Mau fighters or inform Government of their presence or activities, may this oath kill me." The women were then told to put on their clothes and wait outside.

The three men were called in and after removing all their clothes were joined, like the women, with a long strip of meat. Another piece about two feet long was handed to each man. They were to insert their penis into the hole cut in one end and hold the other in their right hand. The vows were the same as those taken by the women except that after each one the men would take a bite of the meat and swear that if they violated the vow the oath should destroy them. When the men had dressed and left the hut I was asked by Mwangi to give the initiates their final instructions and advice. I was upset by the ceremony, which was my first contact with the second oath, and had little heart for the task. Nevertheless, I couldn't refuse.

The initiates were called back into the hut and I said: "This oath is given only to those in a position to help the fighters. You can help us with food and by warning us when the enemy approaches. You should have no worries about the oath you've just taken. It is not something bad, but rather makes you better people who can now join us in the struggle for land and freedom."

As I spoke these words my heart was heavy. I couldn't really believe that this was a good thing; nor would it make these people want to help us if they didn't already.

At Kigwa Estate in late August I got permission from Mwangi Toto to visit my wife. I shaved, got a haircut from a nearby barber, polished my shoes, dressed as a typical Nairobi office worker and boarded the bus to Mathari police station. At the gate was an *askari* who wanted to see my papers and seemed suspicious. Luckily he was as stupid as he was curious. I handed him ten Clipper cigarettes and said I worked as a plumber for the City Council and had left my papers in my overalls. I was there to visit a friend. He was satisfied and he opened the gate so I could enter.

I talked with Helena and gave her the 50s. I'd brought. Then I went to see some relatives who lived not far from the station. I spent that night and the next with my wife in the *askari*'s quarters and then returned to Kigwa. When I arrived at the camp I learned that the men had gone to raid Ikinu Home Guard post in Limuru. They left a comrade behind to wait for me and he said they were planning to go to Ndiritu farm after the raid and that we should meet them there.

At Ndiritu Mwangi told me about the raid and I entered it in my books. They had successfully attacked the post, gaining two shot guns and a pistol and killing or wounding a number of Home Guards. I was saddened to learn, however, that my good friend Icharia Waiti, the man I had entered the forest with, was killed trying to break into the house of a Home Guard.

I asked Njoroge Kihara, who kept the record books in my absence, if he had entered anything. He said no, then told me the following story. He and some other fighters went on patrol in the Limuru area and ran across a Kipsigis night watchman guarding the home of a European settler. "We killed him," said Kihara, "and removed his heart, liver and a calabash of blood. Then we took an oath with these things, swearing not to reveal what we'd done." He went on to give some of the details, but I was too upset to listen very carefully. I didn't enter the incident in my record books.

That night I lay back and instead of sleeping spent many hours pondering Kihara's story. I hated what they did and wouldn't have allowed it if I'd been present, but to criticize them would be dangerous. I had entered the forest to fight for land and freedom against the European oppressors, not to kill Africans and practice useless oaths and magic. Our real enemy and goals, I feared, was being lost sight of.

A thunderstorm broke and the rain began pounding down on my raincoat and seeping slowly along the ground under my blanket. My head was still spinning with a terrible sense of confusion when I dropped off into an uneasy sleep.

After spending about a week at Ndiritu farm we moved back to Uplands Forest and made our camp in a densely covered area near a silent flowing stream. We had begun our 20-mile safari soon after night-fall and arrived while it was still dark.

The following morning we slept late and at noon prepared some sheep we stole the night before from a Home Guard's farm. When we'd finished eating at about 3 p.m. I was called aside by Karanja Kirai and a few others. They took me a short distance from the camp and then, looking very serious and with murder in their eyes, started accusing me of being a traitor. Karanja, leader of the small group, began by saying: "You're a Government informer and traitor, David Mathu, and we are going to kill you. Many brave fighters have been captured or killed because of the information you have given Special Branch. Do you have anything to say for yourself?"

"I am completely innocent," I shouted, "and have done none of the things you accuse me of." They formed a tight circle around me and as I pleaded my case some made threatening moves with their *simis* and *pangas*. One man called Dururu strongly supported what Karanja said. Acting as if he wanted to kill me straight away, he lunged forward with a pocket knife and cut a three-inch gash on my right shoulder. "You're just like the other *tieties* [referring to the hated Black "Europeans" who always wore ties and dressed like their masters] and should be killed," he shouted. "Do as you like," I said, "but you know I'm innocent!"

At this point, with sweat pouring from my brow, Karanja stepped forward and laughed, saying, "Don't fear for your life David, we've only been preparing you for the Kindu oath." Feeling great relief mixed with resentment, I dropped to the ground and joined the others in a hearty laugh, relieving the tensions which had mounted.

Karanja then told me to remove my clothes and shoes. He pulled two rounds of ammunition out of his pocket and rolled two balls of dampened soil between his hands. He ordered me to put my hands behind my neck and bend forward from the waist. A bullet and ball of soil were put in each of my hands and then they bound my wrists with reed.

In this position, standing naked under the high trees in the narrow rays of the afternoon sun, I took the Kindu oath. I repeated the following vows spoken by Karanja while the other men slapped my back and buttocks with the flat sides of their *simis*, an action intended to strengthen the courage the oath was supposed to instill in me.

> I will never reveal that I have taken this Kindu oath to anyone not a member of our group.
>
> I will never disclose the secrets of the fighters to Government, and if I do you should kill me.
>
> I will never desert the Land Freedom Army or leave for any reason without informing our leaders and getting permission.
>
> I will never violate the rules or regulations of the Land Freedom Army.
>
> If you kill me because I have betrayed you, I shall not curse you over my blood.
>
> I will never take the "Moscow" oath. [An anti-Mau Mau oath invented by Government and administered to spies and informers. The oath began with music and the term "Moscow" is a distortion of "Musical."]

I will never refer to guns and ammunition in the usual ways but always as *"kindu"* ("thing") and *"mbembe"* ("maize kernels").

I will never reveal or expose my *kindu* or *mbembe* to anyone not himself a fighter.

If I am sent to kill someone I will never refuse or allow myself to sympathize with the victim.

I shall remain a servant of Jomo Kenyatta, respect the leadership of Mbiu Koinange and remember our old comrade Jesse Kariuki until the day we win our independence.

I will never serve any but an all-African Government.

When the vows were over they sprinkled some crushed aspirin on my wound. After having put on my clothes, I returned to the camp. Two other fighters were then given this same Kindu oath.

They formed a tight circle around me and . . . made threatening moves with their simis and pangas. . . he lunged forward with a pocket knife and cut a three-inch gash in my right shoulder.

Early September found us back at Ndiritu farm where we were joined by one of our old members, Waithaka Mutungi. He had been captured and only recently escaped from the Lukenya Prison. He told us of the horrible conditions there and said it would not be difficult for us to attack. There were not many guards and if successful we could release the prisoners and get a large amount of arms and ammunition. We discussed the matter and Mwangi decided to send one of our scouts to the prison with Waithaka to investigate. They returned three days later and our scout confirmed Waithaka's story. The camp was poorly guarded and had not been reinforced since Waithaka's escape.

Mwangi, Kariuki and myself, together with Waithaka, set about planning the attack. We would send in 20 well-armed fighters, out of our total force of around 50, and plan to attack the prison between 8 and 9 p.m. when a raid would be least expected. The prison was about 20 miles from Ndiritu, some five miles south of Athi River detention camp. We discussed the route we should take and decided to make two stops for food; one at the Tusker brewery four miles from Nairobi, and the other at a place near Embakasi airport.

Wanting to repair some guns and finish two homemade rifles, Mwangi Toto accompanied by Kariuki and two others went to one of the abandoned huts on the farm's labour line a couple of hundred yards from our camp. It was around midday when we heard shots coming from the direction of the labour line. Enemy forces had spotted Mwangi and the others and had them pinned down in the hut.

We decided to leave the area immediately but after moving a hundred yards or so we came upon an old man who had a *shamba* nearby. He told us we were surrounded and pointed to a small clump of trees a short distance away saying it was the only way to escape. We moved quickly but by the time we reached the trees the security forces had already closed the gap. Our only chance at this point was to try and break through the Government encirclement. We crept to within 20 yards of the line of Tribal Police and Home Guards, then opened fire and started to move forward. When the enemy held their positions and returned our fire, we retreated a few yards. As the Government forces on our flanks and rear moved in for the kill, we decided to use our only hand grenade. It exploded a few feet in front of the enemy cordon barring our path. Running out through the hole we'd created, we were several hundred yards away before the dust from the grenade had settled.

Kariuki was gentle and warm toward his comrades and the uneducated masses but could be hard and fierce in battle against the enemy . . . he was fighting for the people and felt a pride and dignity in doing so . . .

Moving at top speed for over two miles, and thinking we were just about out of danger, we ran straight into a small group of Tribal Police heading toward Ndiritu. We exchanged fire but the Tribal Police withdrew when they saw they were outnumbered. It was now about 3 p.m. and after a few more encounters with Government patrols, night finally fell and we made our way safely in the darkness toward the Fort Hall road.

Crossing the highway a few miles on the Nairobi side of Kassarani, we entered the Tusker labour line. Most of these workers were either members of the Movement or sympathizers. We were taken in and given food and drink. By sunup we had built a temporary camp in the forested area near the plant.

Late that morning I was sent with a comrade to Nairobi in order to get supplies and money. We entered Muthaiga and went directly to the quarters of a member who worked as a cook for a European. I wrote a message to one of the Kenya Parliament elders telling him what we needed and had it delivered by a friend of the cook. We spent the night in a thicket of trees on Muthaiga golf course.

Next morning we returned to the cook's quarters. Talking and drinking Kikuyu beer we awaited a reply to my message. Late that afternoon our messenger returned bringing us 500s. but no supplies. In the early hours of the morning after another night on the golf course, we walked back to Tuskers.

One of the brewery workers was sent to the local shops to buy us several shirts, cigarettes, and some meat, maize-meal and potatoes. With Mwangi and Kariuki gone, a man called Kariuki the Black (so named because of his very dark skin) took over leadership of the group with me as his assistant.

That night we moved on to Embakasi where a large airport was being built with the forced labour of detainees. We hid in the bush during the day and at night Kariuki went to see a friend who worked at Embakasi railway station. The man gave us some food and we began the night's safari. At about 10 p.m. we reached a hill overlooking the prison about two miles away. Here we stopped, sending our scouts ahead to make a reconnaissance of the area, and settling down to spend the night.

. . .we entered the labour line. Most of these workers were either members of the Movement or sympathizers. We were taken and given food and drink.

*Our only chance at this point was to try to break through the
Government encirclement . . . we decided to use our only hand grenade.*

Next day, Friday the 17th of September, we remained in hiding
and at about 8 p.m. began our move toward the prison. It was a large,
rectangular structure surrounded by barbed wire and a deep moat and
protected by several watchtowers. There was only one entrance and to
get to it we had to pass through a cluster of huts occupied by Wakamba
tribesmen. As anticipated, they were drinking and talking and paid no
attention as we walked by. They probably took us for Wakamba coming
to visit relatives. It was good there were only 20 of us. If we'd brought the
other men it almost certainly wouldn't have worked.

Just past the Wakamba huts one of our men noticed he had dropped
a handkerchief containing over 30 rounds of ammunition. We stopped
for a moment to try and find them but failed and then hurried on our
way. Coming to within 15 yards of the entrance we lay down and pointed
our guns toward the gate. Kariuki gave the signal. He whispered "fire" to
alert the men then shouted "fire!" Githongo blew the bugle and another

211

man sent up a red and blue flare as we opened fire on the guards. They returned our fire but we ran toward the gate, shooting and shouting "kill and capture."

In seconds we reached the entrance and finding one of the guards dead and the other wounded we started hacking down the wooden gate with pangas and long heavy poles. Once inside we met surprisingly little resistance. Most of the tower guards were too frightened to stand up and fire, merely taking cover in their high shelters. The *askari* in the barracks locked their doors while those in the compound area ran for cover. The European prison commander ran and shut himself in his house a short distance away. He would probably send out a radio message about the raid. I hoped his *askari* didn't realize we were only a handful of men and recover their lost courage.

I was one of the first men through the gate and headed straight toward what I thought was the arms store. A few of us smashed down the door and went inside. To our disappointment we found only three rifles, two shot guns, a revolver and about 300 rounds of ammunition. Waithaka was not to be seen in the melee and in the action that followed none of us discovered the major armoury located in another compound.

Hearing the shouts of the prisoners we broke down the doors of the corrugated iron barracks and told them to grab their blankets and take off their prison uniforms. When the 200 prisoners were freed we decided it was time for us to leave. We'd taken the the prison by surprise and I'm sure our strength was vastly overestimated.

Outside we told the prisoners they were free to leave and go either to Nairobi or into the forests to join the other fighters. The bush around Nairobi was too sparse to safely contain a fighting group of more than 60 or 70 men.

About 300 yards from the prison I noticed that one of our men was missing. Glancing around I spotted Githongo lying on the ground a short distance away. Standing to sound the bugle, he had exposed himself to the fire of the guards. I found he had been shot in the thigh. The bone was badly fractured. Kariuki was with me and we called over four men from the injured comrade's district. We quickly discussed the matter. We knew that within minutes the security forces would be swarming all over the place. Githongo couldn't move and we couldn't afford to carry him and thus endanger the whole group. The terrain around Athi River was flat and coverless. If we were to escape we had to move fast.

The Fort Hall men sadly decided that since Githongo could not be carried to safety or left to be captured and interrogated by Government, he would have to be shot. Githongo was then consulted and told about our decision. "Do what you think best for the group," he said, "and leave quickly."

One of Githongo's Fort Hall comrades then put a revolver bullet into his friend's head killing him instantly. We quickly removed his watch, jacket, trousers and shoes and rushed to catch up with the others.

Some of the prisoners came back with us toward Nairobi while most disappeared in the darkness in groups of two or three. Near Embakasi airport we came across three British soldiers who had fallen asleep while on guard duty. We were tempted to kill them but didn't want to alert the enemy forces in the nearby camp.

It was 6 a.m. when we finally reached Tusker brewery. A messenger had been sent ahead so our comrades knew we were coming. Crossing the road we entered Karura forest and made our way to a temporary camp. Kariuki and I decided to go to Nairobi. We wanted to tell the Kenya Parliament about our successful raid and to see the morning newspaper.

Before we left, one of the prisoners who had stayed with us now asked if he might join the group. A few of us thought it was all right, but Kariuki rejected the idea because the man was a Luo. "This is a Kikuyu struggle," he said, as most of the others nodded their heads in approval, "and we don't want any Luo to have claims on us after the victory is won." I felt this was a very narrow view. It was an "African" as well as a "Kikuyu" struggle we were engaged in; why weaken ourselves by rejecting the help of other tribes? Looking back I think this type of thing did much to destroy our chances of success.

Going to the cook's quarters in Muthaiga, Kariuki and I sent a message to one of the elders asking him to bring us the morning newspapers. In about two hours three members of the Kenya Parliament arrived to congratulate us on the raid. They brought some cigarettes, 300s. and the papers. It was Saturday and the *Standard* had not yet gotten news of the raid. Another paper, however, carried headlines of the "LUKENYA PRISON RAID" and we discovered that our gang of 21 men had been reported as a "body of over 100 well-armed gangsters."

After a long discussion about our attack and other matters, the elders left and Kariuki and I slept the rest of the afternoon. That night he went to rejoin the others and I remained for the next two nights with

Helena at the Mathari police post quarters. Monday morning while heading back to Karura, I read a detailed account of our raid in the *Standard*. An inquiry was being made by Government and I was surprised to learn that; "Security forces in the search, which numbered nearly 1,000 on Saturday, were reduced to 400 yesterday . . . and included two companies of the Royal Northumberland Fusiliers, three troops of police armored cars and a large number of Kikuyu Home Guards. Tracker dogs were used and spotter planes from the KPR Air Wing flew over the area."

The article went on to say that, "The attack itself was obviously carefully planned. It began at about 8:45 on Friday night and was all over in about 20 minutes. The gangsters crept silently upon the camp, which is in an open plain with a 100-foot high ridge about 500 yards away. The attack was launched suddenly, signaled by bugle calls and the firing of a Very-Red light into the sky. Terrorists charged, shouting, and poured a fusillade of shots into the corrugated aluminium huts and at the sentries, one of whom was killed as he stood outside the Guard Room."

At Karura I rejoined the men and we set off that night toward Ndiritu. To commemorate the raid I wrote a song. It was sung proudly by the fighters during the next few days:

While fighting in the forests, encamped in the coffee fields,
We young fighters planned our raid on Lukenya Prison.

When the discussion was over and we had all agreed,
Our scouts were sent to investigate.

They went and returned, giving us a report;
We should prepare ourselves for the attack.

We began our journey, we young fighters, toward Lukenya;
Keeping well-hidden all the way.

When we arrived our fighters lay down;
We opened fire and killed two guards.

The Black people imprisoned were crying for help
Saying, "Oh, our people, open the doors for us."

After fighting and releasing the prisoners, we prayed to *Ngai*
So that he might assist us to escape safely.

All Black people of Nairobi were happy
Congratulating us for our brave deed.

. . . we broke down the doors of the corrugated iron barracks and told them to grab their blankets and take off their prison uniforms.

Soon after our return to Ndiritu we were pleased by the reappearance of Mwangi Toto and Kariuki Chotara. Trapped in the hut, with one of our men already killed, three of them surrendered. Kariuki managed to escape before they could get him to Kiambu police station and Mwangi broke out of the post a few days later. The third man, Dick Mwangi, was killed when he refused to cooperate with interrogators.

On the evening of our third day at Ndiritu a large patrol of Home Guards was spotted moving along the dirt paths which criss-crossed the plantation. They had seen one of our sentries who, thinking quickly, said he was from the nearby Guard post (we often had sentries wear Home Guard armbands for just such an occasion). He asked them to follow him as he thought there were Mau Mau in the area. He led them toward our position and when they came within range we had prepared our ambush. We opened fire, killing six, wounding several others and gaining four shotguns and a few spears.

We knew the shooting would attract security forces so we left in a hurry. Crossing the Kiambu-Nairobi road we made our way through the bush in a south-easterly direction, approaching Nairobi from the east. Near Kangemi, a village occupied by landless Kikuyu a couple of miles from the city, we set up camp for the night. Most of the villagers sympathized with the Movement and provided us with food and drink.

We were told that General Waruingi was in the area and just after we'd finished eating he came to see us with 25 fighters. We spoke for several hours and I asked Waruingi about his activities in Kiambu, saying I wanted to record them in my record book and show it to the Kenya Parliament. He told us of raids he had carried out against Home Guard and police posts and we, in turn, explained our raid on Lukenya and other activities.

It was late when Waruingi left to return to his own hideout. We arose early in the morning so as to reach Kileleshwa before sunup. There we set up temporary camp near a small stream in the thicket not far from the police station.

On the morning of the third day a man and his son accidently passed fairly close to our hideout. They were stopped by one of our sentries and brought into the camp. The man worked for a nearby nursery and had a card, like the one I carried, indicating that he was attached to Special Branch as an informer. Most of the men wanted to kill him but I argued that perhaps he was innocent.

I got permission to talk to the man alone and we walked a short distance away. He explained how he'd taken the card from Special Branch in order to move around Nairobi in safety. Without it, being a Kikuyu, he would have been killed or detained long ago. "I'm a Kikuyu like yourselves," he said, "and have never done anything against the Movement of our people. This card proves nothing for I am a true son of Gikuyu."

I sympathized with the man and believed him innocent. I also thought about the young boy at his side. How must a son feel when his father is killed before his eyes. Returning to the others I found them still set on killing him, even after they heard what I had to say. Finally, I suggested that since he might be innocent we could keep him with us till nightfall, when we planned to leave Nairobi anyway. One of our men moved aggressively toward the man and I stepped between them saying, "I think the poor man is innocent! If you kill him, you'll have to kill me too!" Luckily, most of the men had been won over by my arguments and Mwangi decided the issue by saying we would keep him with us until we left. I was very relieved.

Our next stop was Muthangari, a couple of miles from Kileleshwa police station. We arrived shortly after dark and when we finished eating I discovered that four girls had been brought into the hideout from a nearby village. They spent the night with four fighters and returned to their homes the next morning. This was the first time any of our men did something like this and I didn't like it. It wasn't that I believed in the traditional taboo against fighters having sex; but this just wasn't the time or place for it. Having the girls in the camp also put their lives in danger.

Before sunup we were back at Kangemi where we again met Waru-ingi. He and his men spent the day with us and at night Waruingi asked if he could share our hideout with his men. We discussed the matter but decided it would be safer if he camped elsewhere. If attacked by Government there was no sense endangering both groups. Waruingi agreed and left with his men.

Next day found us in Mukuru, an area just beyond the African locations south of the city. We had made up our minds to re-enter Nairobi and eliminate some notorious "tieties." These traitors were particularly brutal to the people in Bahati. After work they would put on Home Guard armbands and enter the location, forcing themselves upon women, beating and even shooting innocent people and robbing the inhabitants of money and valuables. Afraid of fighters like ourselves, these cowards amused and enriched themselves at the expense of old and disabled men, women and children.

It was decided that ten of us would enter Bahati at night with a couple of the men dressed as "Black Europeans." The latter went to a loyalist bar and started buying drinks for the traitors. When the bar closed they invited them to their house in the location for a few beers. Once in the trap they were killed. Karanja Kirai poured a libation of beer on the ground for the ancestral spirits, pleading for their approval and assistance in the struggle.

A few days later at Mukuru we were contacted by a man called Captain Nyaga. He learned of our whereabouts from a sweeper and wanted to talk with the leaders of the group. Nyaga was a friendly, talkative man. He told us many stories about Kimathi, Mathenge and the fight in the Aberdare forests. When we asked why he'd come to Nairobi he said his men, then waiting near Kahawa, were urgently in need of arms, ammunition and other supplies and he thought we might help him.

We trusted Nyaga and since he planned to return to the Aberdares immediately it was decided we would give him seven shot guns, some ammunition and clothing and 200s.

We provided Nyaga with a 30-man escort as far as Kahawa. Here, joined by his 60 fighters, he headed off toward the forests. It was only later, when I shared a cell with Nyaga at Kileleshwa police station just before he was hung, that I learned how he and his men had been

....when the askari *were almost upon us we opened fire.
Armed only with pistols, they turned and ran."*

Mwangi Toto . . . struggled forward a few yards and died in my arms.

ambushed and most of them captured. They had only gotten a mile or so from where our escort left them.

The four of us who remained behind hid in a large sisal plantation called Mukuru Estate. Mwangi knew one of the farm labourers, who gave us food and drink. That night our 30 fighters returned from Kahawa and we slept in the fields, hidden only by the short sisal plants.

We told the farm worker to come see us in the morning and at about 10 a.m. we spotted a man walking toward us. Mwangi, thinking it was his friend, stood up and walked out to greet him. It was a stranger, however, and seeing Mwangi holding a pistol, the man turned and ran. He was too far away to shoot and it would have been unwise anyway. Though the man might report us to the security forces, we had to take the chance that he wouldn't. In broad daylight we couldn't risk leaving the plantation. The area was flat and barren with little cover or natural protection. This close to Nairobi it would have been suicide to leave the sisal.

"Perhaps I could get a few of them before they finished me. As I grappled with the black man (who should have been my brother) a European moved up from behind and wrestled me down. . ."

At about 3 in the afternoon we heard shots fired some distance away in the plantation. A guard spotted two Europeans and several African *askari* moving through the sisal looking for us. The *askari* were firing wildly into the field hoping we would expose our position. Though they hadn't seen us, they were walking almost directly toward our position. The Europeans stayed back about 200 yards away and when the *askari* were almost upon us we opened fire. Armed only with pistols they turned and ran. We followed closely in their tracks. Not that we intended to chase them; it just happened that they fled along the path of escape we earlier decided upon.

Coming out on the road we noticed a Land-Rover which the police came in. We set it on fire then crossed into the bush paralleling the road. After running about five miles we came to another sisal plantation, the Koyole Estate. Thinking we'd lost our pursuers, Mwangi decided we should stop and rest. Guards were posted and we shared a bottle of Nubian gin one of the men brought from Tuskers. Mwangi and I then dropped off to sleep. Unfortunately, so did several of the guards.

The security forces who had followed our tracks were surrounding our position. About half an hour later, as we lay sleeping, an enemy force of around 200 men opened fire. Not knowing exactly where we were, they had formed a wide circle around us and when the shooting started, shaking us into a sudden awareness of our precarious situation, we dispersed in small groups, returning the Government fire as we went. Mwangi Toto was hit and killed before he even had time to figure out what was happening. He struggled forward a few yards and died in my arms.

The area offered us little cover, so with a few others I headed toward a nearby dam, hoping to hide in the rushes surrounding it in the swampy water. Enemy forces were only 20 or 30 yards away. I ran a zigzag pattern down the sloping hill and miraculously escaped the bullets I could hear zinging past me.

I neared the dam and entered the waist-high grasses. I noticed one comrade lying in the murky waters. Thinking I might yet escape and not wanting to ruin my record books, I set them down on a small dry area then plunged forward into the swamp for cover.

The main battle was still being fought in the fields and I could hear bursts of Stens and rifles as I crawled on my stomach through the rushes. Holding my pistol above the water, I entered to a point where only the upper part of my head was visible. "There is still a chance", I thought.

The shooting let up and I could hear European officers shouting out commands to their men who were surrounding the dam and moving in for the kill. Amidst sporadic bursts of gunfire I lay death-like in the swampy water. I knew there was little hope now. One comrade hidden a few feet away signaled, asking if he should use his rifle. "No," I whispered, "don't shoot! You'll only expose our position and they'll throw in grenades." Sinking my pistol deep in the mud beneath me, I realized my only chance was the slim possibility of escaping detection.

The splash of boots in the water seemed only a few feet away and as I lowered my head into the water I could hear heavy breathing directly above me. The *askari* didn't move for a moment or two then, starting off in a different direction, he stepped right on my leg.

Shocked, he jumped back. I lunged forward trying to grab his rifle. Perhaps I could get a few of them before they finished me. As I grappled with the black man (who should have been my brother) a European moved up from behind and wrestled me down. The constable, still dazed and standing only a few yards away, raised his rifle and fired. The bullet grazed my forehead just above the left eye and I dropped unconscious into the water.

I was dragged out of the swamp by the European who ordered the *askari* not to shoot again. My head was bleeding badly as they half carried, half dragged me to a Land-Rover. When first pulled out of the water I had been searched and they discovered the 22 bullets tied in my handkerchief. For some reason they put the bullets back in my jacket pocket and as I stumbled to the car I managed to drop most of them one by one onto the ground. I still had three left when they pushed me into the car and I slid these behind the seat.

It was 12 October 1954 and I had fought my last battle. Some of the men, I learned later, had managed to escape. But six of my comrades had been killed and three of us captured. Karanja's appeal to the ancestors hadn't helped. To this day I don't regret having fought with my people in what was a just struggle. We made many mistakes. I was aware of some at the time and others I only discovered later. I hope we can all learn from these mistakes and that the bravery and honor with which so many of my people faced death and suffering is not slighted because of them.

In the Detention Camps

At Special Branch Headquarters in Nairobi I was led into a room used for court exhibits and confronted by three Special Branch officers. It was 9 p.m. when the interrogation started. My hands were bound and a five-foot piece of heavy chain joined my handcuffs with a long iron rail on the floor. Escape was virtually impossible.

When asked who I was, I said: "My name is Mwangi Kamau. I was trapped in your battle with that Mau Mau gang while on my way to visit my brother." Driving into Nairobi I considered how I would respond to their initial questions. If I admitted being a member of Mwangi Toto's gang there was a good chance they'd just shoot me, saying I'd been killed in the battle or while trying to escape. If I showed my informer's card they might call Seedon and be told that I'd taken the card on false pretenses and had never done anything to help Special Branch. They could also just tear up the card and remove the one chance I would have if taken to court. I thought it best to keep quiet about my card and connection with Seedon and play for time. Their opportunity to silently get rid of me would diminish as more people came to know of my capture. Many a fighter had been "killed while trying to escape;" this was justified as a means of saving Government the expense of a trial and hanging. Our comrade, Dick Mwangi, met this end at Kiambu police station.

Angered by my refusal to cooperate, the three Europeans began a process of forceful persuasion. One used a Kiboko or rhino-hide whip, another a short piece of chain and the third a club. Each time I refused to alter my story or answer their questions a flurry of blows rained down on me.

After about two hours an African Home Guard entered and identified me as David Mathu. He had seen me before at Shauri Moyo in the chief's camp. They couldn't find my picture in their photograph file and after another hour they put me in a small room where I was again chained to a long rail. In addition to my bullet wound I now had a cut head and lacerations on my back and shoulders from the whip and chain.

One of the officers pulled out a mirror and asked me to see what an ugly mess I was. He said they might have to kill me if I didn't give them what they wanted.

At 8 a.m. the DO from Embakasi Mau Mau Screening Center came into the room. He had an *askari* bring me a cup of tea and two stale rolls then took me over to the dispensary. The medical aids gave me rough treatment, stitching up my forehead without cleaning the wound, giving me no anaesthetic and ignoring my lacerations.

Back at Special Branch Headquarters they finally found my file and photograph and then brought in an old friend of mine from City Council to confirm my identity. Next I was taken to the morgue and asked to identify the bodies of my dead comrades. "What is the point in withholding their names now," I thought. "They died for their people and should have their names recorded on the list of fallen heroes."

After spending three days in the cage at Embakasi I was taken to Nairobi for more interrogation. The three bullets I dropped in the car were carefully wrapped in an envelope with my name on it. They had also found and translated my record books and discovered a photograph in which some of our fighters portrayed Home Guards being attacked and shot down. It was about 8 p.m. when I was taken into an office by two Europeans; the door was locked and guarded by an *askari*.

I was confronted with my documents and asked by the Europeans to confirm what I'd written. Most of the entries were in my own hand and signed. It would be absurd, I thought, to deny having knowledge of it. Thus began a long and grueling interrogation which lasted till morning. My intention from the start was to admit what I myself had written and participated in and refuse comment on entries made either by me or others covering activities carried out in my absence. Again, I made sure not to go beyond the information contained in the books, being thankful that I'd omitted the incident about the Kipsigis night watchman.

During the next week or ten days, as I was shuffled back and forth between Special Branch Headquarters, Kileleshwa police station and Embakasi, the questioning continued and I was taken around to point out some of the places indicated in my records where our fighters had made camp. On one occasion I was asked to assist screeners in a sweep of Makongeni location. I agreed to do this but failed to identify anyone, saying that none of the people were known to me.

But Government was not convinced of my willingness to cooperate.

They got nothing they didn't already know from my documents and were sure I was withholding important information. At Kileleshwa I was told I would have to stand trial and that my chances of escaping the death sentence were slight. I refused to add anything to my confession. A few days later I was taken once more to Special Branch Headquarters. Here, to my surprise, I was met by Seedon and another officer named Hein. They took me into an office for questioning and, after going through my records in some detail, rose to leave. Though I expected the subject to be brought up, Seedon never mentioned our earlier contact or the informer card he had given me.

As Hein walked out Seedon called me to one side and said he'd do what he could to see that my case wasn't brought to court. I said "O.K." and watched as he left the building.

Back at Kileleshwa, where I was to remain for three months, I heard nothing more about Government's case against me. Apparently Seedon had gotten them to drop it. I spent many a day trying to figure out why he had done this for me. Finally I decided that Seedon was acting solely out of self-interest. It wasn't that he thought I was acting as his agent in the bush. He just feared the embarrassment he might have to suffer if I were brought to court. The way I figured it, Seedon assumed I would plead innocent claiming that I had been serving Special Branch as an informer. He would be called as a witness and if I produced the card bearing his name, he would have to admit that he'd hired a "Mau Mau gangster" as an informer – thus appearing naive or stupid – or defend me as his informer, which might expose him to the accusation of being "soft on Mau Mau."

From Kileleshwa I was sent back to Special Branch Headquarters and then to Eastleigh police station for further questioning. Finally I was taken to Embakasi and again put in a cage within the large barrack-like structure. This building held about 200 prisoners kept in groups of 10 to 30 persons inside the wire cages. This was a good name for them since at Embakasi the detainees were treated just like animals.

It was here that I finally learned the truth about Kagema. I saw him come in one day with a group of "tieties" and begin screening some new prisoners. Most likely, Kagema had been working with Special Branch all along. Being clever, he made sure not to draw suspicion upon himself by giving information which would lead to the arrest of his "comrades" in the LFA. Instead he helped Special Branch in capturing other Mau Mau members he didn't know well and who would not suspect him as the informer. Later I learned from Helena that it was Kagema who directed the police to where she was hiding and identified her as my wife. At Embakasi it seemed he was acting openly as a Government employee. He was never detained and probably was never a loyal member of the Movement.

The food we were given wasn't fit for pigs. The maize meal was bug-ridden and the gruel watery and tasteless. All of it was poorly cooked and barely edible. After about three weeks of sending complaints to the DO in charge, I decided that some action had to be taken. Through the use of notes secretly passed from prisoner to prisoner with the help of women detainees who collected our eating utensils, I was able to successfully organize a three-day boycott of all camp food. Meals continued to be served but we all left it to be removed untouched.

On the fourth day someone told the camp officials that I had organized the boycott. They moved me to the Wakamba area of the camp where they felt I could do little damage. I was put in a solitary cell and kept under the constant guard of two *askari*. I remained in solitary until 4 April 1955 when I was taken to Nairobi to be photographed. On the following day, after my Governor's Detention Order had been signed, I was driven to the Athi River detention camp.

It was about noon when we arrived at the camp and were taken to the offices of the Camp Commandant, Colonel Knight, where our beards and heads were shaved and our clothes sprinkled with a delicing powder. The camp had nine barbed-wire enclosures and I was put into Compound 9, which was for detainees who had given satisfactory confessions and were actively cooperating with Government. By putting new detainees in this compound it was hoped that they might learn the advantages of confession and cooperation.

There were about 30 detainees in the compound and we were housed in two barracks, one for proven collaborators and the other for newcomers. The early screenings involved only friendly types of persuasion and were combined with good treatment, easy work and attempts to convert us to Christianity. Elders and chiefs came regularly to preach about the merits of the Christian faith and cooperation with Government.

I resisted these conversion attempts and refused to add anything to the confession I'd already given in Nairobi and at Embakasi. Christianity was only being used to break down our resistance and, by turning us against the "evils of Mau Mauism," make us willing and docile supporters of Government. Colonel Knight was himself a follower of Moral Rearmament and he tried to rehabilitate us through this faith. Knowing the crimes which Christian loyalists had committed against our people in the reserves, I did my best to convince the others that Christianity was a white man's religion, not suited to African needs, and was being used as a tool to turn us against our own Movement.

Learning from their spies that I was undermining the rehabilitation effort, the screeners began to take a different attitude. Their methods of persuasion became more violent. The "softcores," or rehabilitated detainees in the compound, also began to treat me coldly and with suspicion. These men were given privileges and easy jobs around the camp such as collecting firewood from the carpentry workshop, getting food from the store and cleaning up the compound.

One day a "softcore" ordered me in a very sharp tone to go collect a bag of *posho* from the store. "I'd be glad to help you," I said, "if you could ask me nicely. I'm not your servant." He said I was getting too proud and arrogant and tried to kick me. A moment later we were wrestling on the ground and had to be separated by some of the elders.

Next morning the incident was reported to David Waruhiu – son of the assassinated Senior Chief Waruhiu and a member of the rehabilitation team. He called all of us into the center of the compound and asked me to step forward. "This David Mathu thinks he's a smart fellow and very tough. Well, let's see how tough he really is. He started a fight with Kamau yesterday and now we'll let him finish it."

I didn't fear Kamau and when he stepped forward we immediately began to fight. Before I knew what was happening, however, all the others jumped in and started hitting and kicking me. They were just having a little "fun" and trying to teach me a lesson. I struggled with this mob for a few minutes and finally, when they had beaten me to their satisfaction, an *askari* was called in and ordered to take me to the small cell.

It was one of many 5' by 8' rooms off the center aisle of a large barracks. There was nothing in the cell – no blankets or bedding and no sanitary facilities. Without even a single window, the room was always dark and cold. I was given no food or water. When the need arose I was led to a sanitary bucket located at either end of the long hallway.

In the morning I was taken into the office of Colonel Knight. He wanted to question Waruhiu and myself on the fight in Compound 9.

Each of us gave our version of the incident. Knight listened carefully then said the affair was not as serious as Waruhiu had indicated. However, as I had refused to cooperate with the screeners and rehabilitation team, he would put me into a "hardcore" compound.

Compounds 1-4 were for uncooperative detainees and I was led to number 2. Inside one of the three barracks I was shown where to put my thin mat and blankets. Most of the 100 or so men were working outside the camp but those remaining treated me like a hero. They had heard about my fight and resistance and gathered around to congratulate me and talk. I was given some gruel and *kiraiko*, a local tobacco the men grew right in the compound, and we sat in the sun chatting until the main body of detainees returned about 3:30 p.m.

After taking a shower I met some old friends and we went into the mess hall for a meal of *posho*, boiled beans and a small serving of vegetables. After eating we returned to the barracks. Some of the detainees were gathered in a corner having a meeting of some sort and I was asked to attend. Guards were posted at either end of the barracks to warn of approaching *askari*. I sat and listened as the men discussed different aspects of camp life. The talk drifted to the question of our attitude toward loyalists and fence-sitters after we were released. Some felt that they should pay for their crimes and expect nothing but harsh treatment from the people. Others thought the past was best forgotten, that when the Emergency was over we whould just live and let live. No conclusions were reached. The split between loyalists and revolutionaries among the Kikuyu people still runs very deep and the conflict simmers on.

Awakened the following morning at 5 a.m. we washed, dressed, lined up for a roll call and had the usual cup of thin gruel. At six we were ready for work. Hardcores got the most difficult work. We were taken about a mile from the camp where a small dam was being constructed. Divided into work groups, we were handed picks, shovels and large metal containers used for carting dirt from the excavation site to the wall being built around the dam.

I spend the first part of the day hauling dirt. It was hard, tiring work and a friend told me to put rags on my head to ease the burden. I was about to collapse when they put me on the easier job of shoveling. At 3 p.m. we were marched back to the camp for lunch. I learned that we were on half-rations, getting only a cup of gruel made from the last night's leftover *posho*.

In the weeks to follow I learned that the hard and dirty jobs were rotated between the four hardcore compounds. One day we might work around the camp cleaning up the compounds, collecting the refuse and emptying the sanitary buckets; the next we would clean the drains or wash down the offices of the camp staff, and so on. It was only about one day in four that we were forced to work on the dam.

Softcores were given light work and spent a lot of time in rehabilitation classes or sports activities. I preferred the hard manual labour rather than to cooperate with Government. It wasn't just a matter of giving an accurate statement about ones own activities. Government already had us; they were now interested in getting information about other fighters and members of the Organization. One of our best Nyeri fighters, General Kareba, was captured and killed on the basis of information given by an Athi River detainee. Again, to prove one's willingness to cooperate often meant beating and torturing other detainees to extract confessions. Most of us in the hardcore compounds strongly condemned this "softcore" activity and refused to do anything to increase the suffering of our people.

Within each compound a leader was elected to represent the detainees in dealings with the camp commander. In the hardcore compounds men were chosen because of their loyalty to the Movement and ability to speak English.

Apart from this elected leader we had a secret organization within the four hardcore compounds. It was organized by grouping the men within each compound according to their location, division and district. In each compound there were committees representing the three Kikuyu districts plus Embu and Meru. At the top was a central committee of members from each compound and district. A system was set up in which notes, written on scraps of paper, were passed between leaders of the compounds. Where a decision had to be reached by the central committee notes were wrapped around a stone and thrown from compound to compound. Each member would indicate his agreement with what had already been written or add his own ideas. This continued until a unanimous decision was reached.

The main job of this organization was to keep unity among the hardcores and prevent conflicts from arising among the men and groups. A number of rules existed: no one was to spit in the compound, dirty the sanitary buckets or leave refuse lying about; there was to be no stealing, fighting or abusive language; elders and disabled men had to be

*To this day I don't regret having fought with my people
in what was a just struggle.*

respected and given easy jobs; no one was to try to get all the easy jobs and avoid heavy ones; no one was to take more than his share of food; and the rehabilitation schemes, religious services and other unnecessary kinds of cooperation were to be avoided and any mistreatment fought with silence and passive resistance.

The official compound leader was also the leader of our organization in each compound and we pressed Colonel Knight to allow these leaders to remain in the compound to supervise the work. He agreed and it thus became possible for each compound leader to see that our rules were obeyed. He made sure the old men got the right kind of work and that the food was properly prepared and distributed, and he was always there in case of disputes.

The central committee dealt only with major issues and cases involving dangerous violations of the rules. Most cases and minor decisions were handled within the compound. When a man violated some rule the case was taken up by a committee on our return from work in the late afternoon. If a dispute arose between two men from the same division, it would be handled by that division's committee. If, on the other hand, a fight or argument broke out between a Nyeri and Kiambu man, the matter would be dealt with by a committee from both Nyeri and Kiambu.

Punishment for violating a rule was most often a sentence of so many "months imprisonment." This meant a certain number of laps across the cemented barracks floor on the knees. A one-year sentence of six laps up and down the center aisle of the building usually resulted in bruised and bleeding knees. The guilty party also suffered a certain amount of humiliation and embarrassment in addition to the pain.

The aims, however, were to maintain unity and harmony among the men and keep up the spirits and loyalty of the hardcore detainees. Punishments were rarely harsh and a committee hearing an average case did its best to educate the guilty party or bring understanding and agreement when a conflict arose.

This organization was disrupted in July 1955 when Government transferred most of the 600 hardcores to Lodwar and Manyani. Some of us who remained were shifted into Compound 5 and kept apart from those still awaiting transfer.

During this same month a Moral Rearmament team which was making a world tour to gain adherents arrived in Kenya and visited the Athi River camp. There were about 15 of them representing several countries including Ghana, Nigeria and the Union of South Africa. Their major effort was directed toward the hardcores.

The men in Compound 5 elected me to represent them and find out what the Moral Rearmament thing was all about. None of us had ever heard of it and we were very suspicious and skeptical. Particularly since Colonel Knight was a member.

When the team came to our compound, remaining outside the fence for safety, I was asked to translate into Kikuyu what they said as well as certain passages from the pamphlets they handed out. I had long been opposed to Christianity, but on hearing and reading what these people had to say I began to wonder if Moral Rearmament might not be

230

*The compound leader made sure the old men got the right kind of work
and that the food was properly prepared and distributed,
and he was always there in case of disputes.*

a good thing. What I doubted was that these people actually practiced
what they were preaching.

The following day all detainees were called into a large open area to
hear speeches by members of the Moral Rearmament team. Most spoke
of their faults and sins before joining the movement and how belief in
the new faith made them better people. A Japanese woman told of her
great bitterness and hatred toward the United States when the atomic
bomb was dropped on Hiroshima. "As a believer in Moral Rearmament," she said, "these bad feelings have been transformed into love and
understanding. This same thing could happen to you in relation to the
Europeans if you follow the four principles of Love, Purity, Honesty and
Unselfishness. Brotherhood would then drive out hatred and bitterness."

I listened and was impressed, though suspicious, and wondered
about the 500s. collected from cooperative detainees and given to the
leaders of the team. How could they take money from such poor people?

Most of the team left Athi River the next day, leaving behind Mr.
Anderson and an American to continue the work. Anderson, knowing I
had an influence on the others, was very pleasant and spent a good deal

of time talking to me about Moral Rearmament. He tried to answer all my questions and remove the doubts I had about the organization.

A few days later I was called to Colonel Knight's office. Anderson was there and they made me an offer. If I accepted Moral Rearmament I could remain at Athi River and help teach and spread the faith; if I refused, I would be sent with the others to Lodwar.

I thought about it and finally decided to stay at Athi River. I wasn't really convinced about Moral Rearmament but thought I should stay and learn more about it.

When I told the other hardcores my decision they were angry and disappointed. Hadn't I preached to them against Christianity? And argued against active cooperation with Government? Now I was, in their eyes, abandoning them for Christianity and Government. I was a traitor.

I felt bad about the general reaction of my friends and tried hard to explain the stand I had taken. Within a few days, however, all the remaining hardcores were transferred to Lodwar. Only myself and three others stayed behind with the softcores.

For the next few months I read a lot of Moral Rearmament literature and tried to persuade other detainees to join. Under the direction of Anderson and the American we gave lectures and worked on a play written to show how Moral Rearmament could bring about understanding between the races and a better way of life. I was cast as a Mau Mau fighter. The other three converted hardcores played a European settler, an Asian trader and a Jewish businessman. The first part of the story showed the African and European fighting one another while the Asian and Jew selfishly pursued their business interests. As it went on the play revealed how unity and brotherhood was achieved when these people joined the Moral Rearmament Movement and started to live according to the cardinal principles of Honesty, Purity, Love and Unselfishness. The problems in Kenya and throughout the world could easily be solved if the people would only start reforming themselves through Moral Rearmament. This was the message of the play. I'm not sure if our audiences saw it that way. We put on performances for the detainees, visiting groups of chiefs, headmen and other loyalists, and women detainees from Kamiti prison.

It wasn't long, however, before Government lost interest in Moral Rearmament as a rehabilitation device. In May 1956 Colonel Knight was replaced by a new commandant and Major Breckanridge, well-known for his brutality at the Embu Rehabilitation Center, took over as head rehabilitation officer. Before taking up their new appointments they visited the camp and saw a performance of our Moral Rearmament play. With Breckanridge was David Waruhiu and I could tell by the look on his face that he'd not forgotten our earlier encounter. He would do his best to get even with me through Breckanridge.

I could see the dangers that lay ahead. Breckanridge had no sympathy for Moral Rearmament, as it claimed to treat men of different races as equals. He undoubtedly would use the old techniques of beatings, torture, short rations and isolation to "win" cooperation.

When they arrived we were told to forget all about Moral Rearmament. The important thing was to demonstrate our loyalty to Government by giving useful confessions. I was moved to Compound 10 with the other dozen followers of Moral Rearmament. Soon, *askari* came to search our quarters and belongings. They seized all our literature and put us into small cells.

Every morning Breckanridge came and asked if we were ready to drop Moral Rearmament and give him the kind of confession he wanted. One by one the others gave in and after about a month I was alone in the small-cell barracks.

Each time Breckanridge came to see me I refused to be intimidated into rejecting Moral Rearmament. My thoughts were not clear, however, as I had slowly been losing faith in the movement. It began during the showing of our play. I still wore the tattered clothes I had when captured except that the shirtsleeves and pant-legs had been cut up for patches. Dressed in these rags I played my role beside two well-dressed Europeans who professed to believe in brotherhood and unselfishness. Though they had plenty of clothing, never did they offer to give me even an old shirt. Was this the "unselfishness" they spoke of? Or was it, as I suspected earlier, all words and no deeds?

Again, how could Colonel Knight believe in "brotherhood and love" and still order his *askari* to beat and torture detainees who failed to please him? By the time Breckanridge came I was just acting the part of a Moral Rearmament convert. I had lost any real faith in it.

Nevertheless, I resisted the idea of being forced to give up a belief and knew that Breckanridge wanted much more than a simple rejection of Moral Rearmament. He would insist on a confession which implicated other people and contained useful information for the fight against Mau Mau.

My brother-in-law was a cooperative detainee and an assistant on the rehabilitation team. He came to see me one day in the small cell and tried to convince me to cooperate and confess. "You can do more good for yourself and our people alive and free," he said, "than locked up in a detention camp cell. Government already knows everything you could tell them anyway, so what's the use of hiding it?" I told him I would think about it and make up my own mind.

Next day a friendly Mkamba guard told me he had overheard Breckanridge and the others talking about me. What they said wasn't good. "If you want to leave Athi River alive you'd better tell Breckanridge you're through with Moral Rearmament and give him a good confession – even if you have to invent it."

I decided to accept his advice. The following afternoon I told Breckanridge I was ready to cooperate. He immediately transferred me to Compound 6 and the next morning I was interrogated for several hours, particularly about the Lukenya Prison raid. I told him a few details that went beyond what was in my documents but he was still unsatisfied. Several times, probably on the advice of Waruhiu, he accused me of trying to subvert Government's rehabilitation efforts. When they were finished I was taken to the open area and asked to confess publicly everything I had told them. About 1,500 detainees and the entire camp staff were there to hear me and when I was through they asked a number of questions. This was part of the rehabilitation or brainwashing program and all detainees had to go through it.

Breckanridge was still not convinced of my good intentions. He had me put back into a small cell. A week later I was taken with my few belongings to the Athi River railway station. This was on 27 July 1956. With some detainees from Manda Island, I was put on a train for Nairobi. Here we were joined by other prisoners and started a long journey to Lake Victoria.

The train pulled into Kisumu at night on the 29th and we were taken to a nearby prison. The following morning I went with five others to the lake shore where a launch was waiting to take us to Sayusi. Before getting on board I was questioned by a rehabilitation officer named Robertson. He said he'd looked through my file and couldn't figure out why I was being sent to Sayusi. Walking toward the launch he asked if I was willing to work on the island. Not knowing that most of the detainees had refused, I said I was willing to do the required work.

With me on the launch were two men from my division in Nyeri, Kihara Gatandi and Kahinga Wachanga. The latter was an ex-Mau Mau general and a man from my own sub-location. Both had been at Sayusi for two months already and we talked as the boat pulled out and headed for the island. This was my first time on the water and I enjoyed it immensely.

After landing we were led toward the cooperative detainees' camp on the shore of the island a short distance from the small harbor. A hardcore camp, they said, was located on the other side of the island.

I was directed into the office of a senior Special Branch officer named Parkinson. He and his assistant, Kellaway, asked me some questions and then wanted to know if I'd be willing to go to Mageta, another island detention camp in Lake Victoria, to help uncover some troublemakers who were turning the men against their rehabilitation program. Parkinson said that since my friends, Kahinga and Kihara, were assisting them he thought I might like to join them.

I knew they were asking me to act as an informer but thought it best not to anger them with an outright refusal. "I'll think about it," I said, "and let you know later." They accepted this and luckily the question never came up again. It was one thing to cooperate, but I would never agree to acting as an informer.

Parkinson soon left for Mageta with Kahinga and Kihara. Kellaway called me in and asked if I wanted to work in the tool store. I accepted this offer and for the next several weeks my job consisted of issuing construction tools to detainees in the morning and checking them back in in the afternoon when they returned from work. Some living quarters were being constructed in the open softcore camp and it wasn't long before Kellaway offered me the job of supervising the work. He learned from my file that I had been employed by Nairobi City Council and was familiar with building plans and layouts. There was only one large barracks in the camp to house the 30 detainees and our job was to build three smaller structures designed to house four to six persons each. There were about 600 hardcores in the barbed wire enclosed camp on the other side of the island and our number was expected to increase as some of these men decided to work and cooperate with the rehabilitation team.

Except for the oppressive heat and mosquitoes, and the fact that we were locked inside the barracks each night (two men had earlier attempted to escape at night on a log), life on the island for those in the open camp was quite good. Food was plentiful and we drew fresh water for drinking from the lake. Sometimes cattle were brought from the mainland but our diet consisted mainly of fish – which were easily caught on the lakeshore – and crops such as tomatoes, papaya, sugar cane and green vegetables which we grew on the fertile soil of the island. Though the heat was terrible, we were surrounded by water and allowed to cool off pretty often with a swim in the lake.

When the new buildings were completed I was transferred into Kellaway's office as a clerk. I had to keep all the detainee files in order, checking in new arrivals, entering reports and doing the general office work. I had access to all the information about the detainees on the island. Kahinga and Kihara spent most of their time in the open camp but continued to operate as informers on Mageta and in the hardcore camp. I tried to maintain friendly relations with them even though rumors circulated about their beating and generally mistreating suspect hardcores. I had the feeling they resented my good relations with the camp staff and other detainees and knew that I disapproved of their spying activities.

Soon after I'd started work for Kellaway the Presbyterian rehabilitation officer asked my help in translating sermons and religious literature from Kikuyu into Swahili for the benefit of the non-Kikuyu detainees. Before long I found myself giving Sunday services as a lay preacher. Strangely enough, I didn't consider myself a strong believer in Christianity. My main concern was with the peace and unity of the camp and this was the theme of all my sermons. The rehab officer told me to try to impart the real meaning of the Bible to the detainees and I exercised a great deal of freedom in my interpretations.

In January 1957 I came down with a serious case of malaria. I was given quinine and eventually sent to Kisumu prison dispensary for treatment. Here I was put in a large ward with patients having all sorts of diseases. I received no treatment but my condition improved a little and after 18 days I asked to be sent back to Sayusi.

Back on the island neither the quinine nor traditional Kikuyu herbs seemed to do much good. I stayed in the barracks for almost a month, too weak to do any work. Kahinga and Kihara seized this opportunity to take some revenge. They didn't visit me themselves and tried to keep other friends away by telling them I had a contagious disease. They also told Kellaway I had been trying to undermine the rehabilitation program and the spirit of cooperation in the camp. Kellaway called us into his office and told Kahinga and Kihara not to bother him with their petty jealousies and that any further lies would be dealt with harshly.

I finally recovered my health and was given the job of running the camp canteen and keeping accounts. In addition to the camp staff and *askari*, cooperative detainees could come to the canteen and purchase anything but beer. I liked the work and was in a good position to get a little extra money. By over-pricing some items I sold to *askari* I was able to buy an occasional bottle of beer, cigarettes, sugar and cooking fat for myself.

Like the other working detainees I earned one shilling per day. With the extra money I even managed to save a little. Helena, arrested shortly after my capture and taken to Embakasi, was now at Kamiti Women's Prison and I wanted to send her some money. My opportunity came when a priest named Father Joseph visited the camp. I learned he would be going to Kamiti and he agreed to take 10s. and a photograph taken of me at Athi River to my wife. It was my activities that had caused Helena's detention and I felt good finally being able to help her a little.

This was the time when a man we called "Njoroge the DO" started causing a lot of trouble and dissension in the camp. Njoroge earned his nickname by fooling the Government for over two years while posing as a district officer in Kiambu. He was extremely clever and unscrupulous, helping both Government and Mau Mau in any way he could to make money. Though likeable, this love of money made him a dangerous man not to be trusted.

Njoroge was capable of playing many games at one time. None of us was sure he hadn't been placed in the camp as an informer. Though he talked against the Government and rehabilitation program, and gained a few followers, he wasn't a man one had confidence in. His presence in the camp was slowly generating an atmosphere of conflict and dissension.

Learning the address of a detainee's parents, he wrote asking them for money and signing the man's name. He was a clerk in the office and pocketed the money when it arrived, destroying the letter. When this was discovered, we held a meeting to see if there was any way of dealing with Njoroge. There was a lot of talk but no good ideas. A short time later, and by accident, an opportunity came to get rid of him. One evening while at work in the canteen I watched Njoroge chatting with an *askari*. He always tried to befriend the right people and when he came to buy a tin of *posho* for the *askari* an idea hit me. There was a camp rule that no detainee could give gifts of money to an *askari* or staff member. Njoroge was violating that rule and it gave us a chance to get him off the island.

Next morning I went with a fellow worker in the canteen to see Kellaway. We told him what Njoroge had done and subtly indicated that we thought he might be trying to bribe the *askari*. Kellaway listened, then called in Njoroge. I don't know what went on between them but soon Njoroge was sent back to Lodwar. Kellaway said he was causing too much trouble, but we suspected that Njoroge had merely outlived his usefulness at Sayusi as an informer.

Failing to win any sympathy in a faked attempt to hang himself, Njoroge was taken to Kisumu prison and then on to Lodwar. We were to meet again several months later at Hola.

One day in early April fifteen of us were called in and told we were being transferred to camps in our home areas. We were to enter the "pipeline" which would result in our eventual release. We had all been screened every two or three months since coming to Sayusi and were now to undergo a final interrogation. We were allowed to write our statements and as I entered the office Parkinson was reading my confession. Kellaway and Father Joseph were there and the latter, after glancing through my file, exclaimed that I had been a very active terrorist and shouldn't be allowed to go home. Parkinson came to my defence saying I had been very cooperative in the camp and that he believed me fully rehabilitated. Father Joseph nodded but still argued that I wasn't fit to be set free.

After the questioning I was advised by Parkinson and Kellaway on how to act when released from detention. They stressed that I should never discuss my life or experiences in the detention camps or criticize the Government. This would be viewed as anti-Government activity and might result in my return to the camps. As I listened I couldn't help feeling this was an admission that Government wasn't very proud of its detention camp record. The rest of our discussion was the usual propaganda about the high motives of Government and the evils of Mau Mau.

Two days later we took the launch for Kisumu where we spent the night in the prison. The following morning we began our journey to Prison Headquarters, Nairobi. Here, opposite the Pepsi-Cola factory, we were put into a compound previously used for women. It was an open area surrounded by barbed wire and containing a few small barracks. We were supposed to leave in a few days but the rainy season had begun and it wasn't until June, a month and a half later, that I was taken by train to Karatina and then to the Nyeri Showgrounds Works Camp.

There were four others from the North Tetu division, including Kahinga and Kihara. As we got off the lorry we were met by a group of *askari* and rehab men who started beating us wildly as if they'd gone mad. Our few possessions – including my books, photographs and magazines – were torn to pieces and scattered over the ground and I was ordered at gun point to pull out my mustache one hair at a time. I actually tried to do this while an *askari* was beating me with his night stick. Before I managed to pull out more than a few hairs, we were ordered to pick up our belongings and run around the parking area singing in Kikuyu "May God help me if I have to spend a night at Showgrounds Works Camp."

After 20 minutes of this we were led into the camp, still being beaten with rifle butts and batons. Reaching a small dark building we were pushed inside and the door was bolted. An hour later an *askari* brought us a little food, the first we'd had in over 12 hours.

Next morning after a meal of thin gruel we were led to a field a short distance from the camp. Kahinga and another man were ordered to carry two filthy sanitary buckets for carting dirt. The *askari* stood over us like hawks and abused us continuously. We were allowed no rest and if a man slowed down a bit while digging, shoveling or hauling away soil he got a rain of blows from the *askari*. At 3 p.m. we returned to the camp. I was exhausted and fell asleep right after the evening meal.

In the field the next morning a lorry drove up and three of us were ordered to get in. We were taken to Mukurwe-ini Works Camp, situated in my location. The beatings were fewer but we were allowed almost no freedom. Smoking *kiraiko* was forbidden and we couldn't talk while at work.

Under the close supervision of *askari* we did various types of work: digging roads, building bridges, helping construct a nearby hospital, cleaning up the divisional camp and assisting *askari* dig bench terraces on their shambas. No matter how bad the weather, and it was usually pouring rain, we were taken out to work from morning till late afternoon, returning to poor meals and unlit earth-floor barracks where we slept on thin mats under dirty blankets.

One day the camp commandant saw a group of us talking in the compound. We dispersed knowing we should have been working. Most escaped punishment but two of us were caught and put in the small cell. The European commandant was given the nickname "Famine" because he always punished detainees by withholding food and water for long periods of time. In this case we remained in the small cell without food, water or bedding for almost two days. During the night I thought I would freeze to death. The temperature dropped very low in the early hours of the morning and I slept on the bare earth wrapped only in my torn and scanty clothing. "Famine" gave us a strong warning before we were taken back to the barracks.

Despite these bad conditions I was glad to be in Nyeri near my home and people. Standing by the fence I could watch villagers walking along the road a short distance from the camp. The climate I'd been raised in, cold and brisk at an altitude of 6,000 feet, seemed to restore my health and for the first time in many months I wasn't troubled by malaria.

Each day a few men were screened and some of them taken back to their homes by the chief. When I was called in the chief said I was not ready to live in his location as a free man. He seemed to have a grudge against my parents, bad-mouthing them to the Special Branch man. He took his revenge against them through me.

Soon after this screening, when I'd been at Mukurwe-ini for a month and a half, I was transferred to another camp in my location named Mweru. We were greeted by a camp commandant called Powell and searched. Powell was one of the more vicious European settlers. He always kept a huge dog by his side. When *kiraiko* was found on a detainee Powell would set this animal upon the man. This was one of his favorite games.

Despite the harsh treatment we received at Mweru, we were allowed visitors on Sundays and I was also lucky to get work in the carpentry shop. On the first Sunday I was visited by Helena. She had recently been released from Kamiti Prison and was living with her parents in a nearby village. When we met I hardly recognized her. It had been over three years and I couldn't help thinking that her movements, once so familiar, seemed strange. These feelings passed after a few minutes, however, and I realized how happy I was to see her safe and in good health.

During the following weeks I looked forward with great pleasure to these Sunday visits. Many relatives came to see me and we would share

*Many relatives came to see me and we would share the food they brought
with them. Two of my brothers had been killed in the revolution and they
were all happy just to see me alive and healthy.*

the food they brought with them. Two of my brothers had been killed in
the revolution and they were all happy just to see me alive and healthy.
These visits brought me once more into contact with life outside the
detention camps and made me aware of my isolation.

Screenings continued at Mweru and I was again asked to detail my
Mau Mau activities. The chief made weekly visits to the camp and each
time a few men were released under restriction orders. When Kahinga
and I were finally called for an interview the chief said we weren't ready
to be released and told the Special Branch officer he wouldn't accept us
in his location. At this time detainees were being released only with their
chief's approval. It seemed I had reached the end of the "pipeline" only
to be rejected and returned to a feeder camp in one of the remote areas.
This time it would be Hola.

Helena came to see me two days later and I told her the bad news.
She was very upset and disappointed, expecting me to be released any
day. She found it difficult to believe I was being sent away and feared I

might never return. Her tears did no good. We were taken from Mweru in a lorry to begin our long safari to the coast. The journey was in stages. The first night was spent at Othaya Works Camp and from there I was moved for three months to Prison Headquarters, Nairobi. Finally, after a long lorry ride I arrived at Hola on 14 January 1958.

It was about 8 p.m. when we arrived and even at this hour the heat was oppressive. As I glanced around I could see the flat barren countryside and the low, corrugated iron barracks of the camp. We passed a number of unenclosed barracks, officially known as the Open Camp, and drove on to the Closed Camp surrounded by watch towers and a high barbed wire fence. Stopping in front of the gate we were met by the DO and his *askari*. His real name was Krapf but he'd acquired the nickname "Goat-eater" because he had seized a large number of goats from South Tetu (Nyeri) peasants. He was short and always wore a blue scarf to hide a deep red scar on his throat.

After greeting us in Swahili Krapf ordered an *askari* to take us to the Open Camp. We spent the night in a single barracks. Once the door was bolted I noticed that the building had beds instead of the usual mats. "Probably because of the bugs and insects," I thought, as I lay back to consider what life might be like at Hola with the infamous Goat-eater as DO.

Next morning Krapf arrived. He asked if we were willing to work and we all said yes. Then he gave us a rundown on the rules governing detainee life in the Open Camp. Though I've probably forgotten a few, these regulations were that:

- Detainees in the Open Camp could move freely within a two mile radius of the camp, including Laza township, from the time their day's work was completed until 6 p.m.
- No one was to go beyond the two mile limit of the camp.
- No one was to be outside the barracks area after 6 p.m. without special permission.
- No one was to go outside the barracks after 9 p.m. without a light.
- All noise had to stop and lights be turned off after the 9 p.m. bugle sounded.
- No one was to mix or have anything to do with the local people of the area.
- No one was to engage in any trade or commercial dealings within the camp.

242

- No mail was to be sent out of the camp except through official channels.
- No letters could be sent to the press or to politicians.
- No one was to brew or drink beer of any kind.

Krapf handed each of us a copy of these rules and told us to go clean up the camp until the other men returned from work. When the detainees came in from the fields I was surprised to discover an old friend of mine, James Njogu. We went off to talk and he offered me some beer he made from baking soda, sugar and a few other ingredients. We were in a secluded area and I accepted his offer. Though I didn't know it at the time this would be my very last drink of beer or any other alcohol.

After our drink and talk James took me for a walk to Laza. It was a small Arab trading center and I found it interesting to observe the local people and Arab traders. The township is on the Tana River and it was my first time to see from close up this wide, dirty river which empties much of Kenya's precious water into the Indian Ocean.

It was getting late and we had to hurry to get back to the camp by 6 p.m. My thoughts were taken up by the local people I'd seen. I felt a sympathy toward these extremely backward peasants who seemed to be living as people lived thousands of years ago. They would need a great deal of help, I thought, if they were to raise themselves out of their condition of extreme physical and mental poverty.

The sergeant broke this train of thought, coming over to tell me I could sleep anywhere in the camp but would have to arrange with friends for a place in one of the barracks. James had told me there was a space next to his and now he came up with an old homemade bed he bought for me. As we carried it into the barracks I noticed a couple of men playing guitars while a number of others were gathered around singing old songs.

Someone then brought in a borrowed wind-up phonograph and they began to play records. James talked to me about religion. He pulled out an old copy of the Holy Koran which, he said, was the only one in the camp and had been given him by a Muslim teacher from Lamu. He read me a few passages, trying to explain that while he had not yet become a Muslim, Islam seemed to him a much wider and richer religion than Christianity. We talked and argued for a time. My curiosity had been aroused, however, and I took the book and started reading.

From that night on I spent one or two hours reading the Koran before going to sleep. Islam seemed more rational to me than Christianity and while it was critical of other religions it didn't preach hatred toward non-believers. James and I spent many hours discussing the Koran and Islam – sometimes agreeing, sometimes arguing. We were both trying to convince ourselves of its merits and faults, strengths and weaknesses, while at the same time debating the idea of actually becoming Muslims.

After my first three days working in the fields I got a job as an accounts clerk for the Ministry of Works. The pay was good for Hola, 66s. a month, and I moved into the MOW staff quarters. My work consisted mainly of taking the morning roll of men working on MOW projects and keeping a log book on the use of Government vehicles.

I soon learned there was a strong undercurrent of conflict in the Open Camp between Kiambu detainees and the other Kikuyu, Embu and Meru. The Kiambu people were considered both clever and cowardly. They were generally more advanced in education and had contributed many important leaders to KAU and the underground movement. Nevertheless, it was believed by Fort Hall and Nyeri Kikuyu that while Kiambu people started the Movement they didn't contribute much to the fighting once the revolution began. We also resented Kiambu people thinking they were better than other Kikuyu and acting superior.

At Hola this conflict came to the surface. The Kiambu detainees managed to get almost all the good jobs. They filled most of the clerical and labour supervisory posts and were usually appointed headmen in the Open Camp compounds by the DO.

My own feeling was that these people, by acting superior to the rest of us, were destroying the unity of the Kikuyu people for which tens of thousands had died and suffered. It was senseless to brag about Kenyatta and the Koinange's being Kiambu people. Didn't these men represent and draw their support from the whole Kikuyu people?

At my work with the MOW I tried to change this situation. When men from Kiambu loafed or did poor work I reported them to the senior officer, and when posts were vacant I recommended capable Embu, Meru or non-Kiambu Kikuyus. I also tried to stress the importance of Kikuyu unity in conversations with other detainees and pointed out that none of us were any better than the rest. But the conflict continued to simmer and, for that matter, continues to this day.

The general conditions of life at Hola were made terrible by a number of factors. First, the oppressive heat – so bad that on the advice of medical officers, and after many detainees suffered heat strokes, we

244

"Krapf!"

weren't forced to work in the afternoon. To escape the worst of it James and I often spent our afternoons in Laza. Close to the river it was a bit cooler. Second, the insects, particularly the mosquitoes and scorpions. It was impossible to escape them and we were continually bitten-up and suffering from skin diseases which itched horribly. Treatment, what little there was, seemed to do almost no good.

The third factor making life miserable at Hola was Krapf, our Goat-eater DO. He was usually drunk from liquor or *bhangi* and often mistreated us. Sometimes he would restrict a man to the camp for no reason, or forbid us to correspond with relatives. If a man didn't stand up and salute when Krapf drove by in his Land-Rover he was often beaten and kicked, the Goat-eater, in a fit of rage, not realizing that the man hadn't seen him in the car.

Nights were the worst, as Krapf was always very drunk then. One time around midnight he came and woke us by firing his pistol in the air and ordering everyone out of the barracks. He was full of *bhangi* and started abusing and beating people at random. Only when he had satisfied

245

his mad lust did he move shakily off to his own quarters. A few days later I sent a letter through a friendly guard to Tom Mboya, telling him about the bad conditions at Hola and about Krapf's behavior. I asked that he make this information known to the press and the Governor.

By this time I had already become a Muslim. It was in late February when James and I made up our minds. We approached a Somali sergeant and asked him what we had to do to become Muslims. He told us that it was very simple. All we had to do was to shave our heads and beards, wash all our clothing and bathe in the river. After doing this the sergeant gave us each a Muslim cup and name. I was to be called Mohamed Mathu and James became Omari Njogu. He then proclaimed us Muslims and that was that.

I remain a Muslim today. It has made me a more honest and less prejudiced person and has given me a cleaner way of life free of alcohol.

At Hola, however, most of the detainees resented my becoming a Muslim. They said it was an Asian faith not suited to Africans and tended to regard me as something of a traitor. Though bothered, I felt I had made a good choice and besides, it was my choice and no one else's.

After a time I made several good friends among the Arabs and other Muslims in the area. They offered help in many ways and I used to trade the *posho* served in the camp for maize and bananas at Laza. I thought about escaping from Hola toward the end of 1958 and a Somali driver helped me devise a plan. It seemed I might have to spend the rest of my life at Hola. Arrangements were being made for detainees to bring their wives and families to live with them in the camp. But I couldn't imagine bringing Helena into the miseries of this hell-like region.

My Somali friend, who worked for the medical staff, gave me a sword and compass and arranged for my escape with a group of Somali traders who made the long trip from Somalia to Laza once a year to sell cattle. It was my plan to go to Somalia with them and then send for Helena.

Before I could carry out this plan, in September 1958, I was notified that I would soon be released. I then dropped the escape plans I had so carefully made.

Months passed, however, and it wasn't until January 1959 that a group of chiefs were brought to Hola and I was called in for screening. My location chief wasn't present and the others from South Tetu, after asking the usual questions, decided I was properly rehabilitated and recommended that I be sent home. This meant entering the Government pipeline again and on 14 January I was driven with some other detainees to Agothi Works Camp near Kagumu College.

After working the first day on the Kagumu River bridge I was called in for another screening. One of the screeners was a man I knew at Mweru. He told the others I was a good man and completely rehabilitated. This helped. After giving a brief account of my activities they said they would recommend my release.

Ten days later the chiefs arrived from the various locations to do a final screening and take those they thought 'fit' back to their homes. I waited with the others outside the office but my name wasn't called. When the chief finished with the others he stepped outside and saw me standing there. He asked me my name and when I replied he said sharply: "I don't think you'll be going home."

One of the other screeners, however, called me into the office. Together with the DO he began asking the same old questions: How and when did I take the oath? Did I enter the forest? Etc., etc. My location chief returned and interrupted saying: "This Mathu is a very bad man. His entire family fought against the Government. His mother abuses me and his father always argues with me and never cooperates with the headman. He should not be allowed to go home! I'm sure he'll cause trouble!"

The DO rejected the old man's advice this time, asking him sarcastically if the trouble he was having with my parents had anything to do with my record in the camps or progress in rehabilitation. He then signed my file and told me to go prepare myself for leaving the camp.

The following day, on 4 February 1959, I was given my release and a Restriction Order confining me to the location and requiring that I report to the DO once a week. But I was out at last. I hurried to the village to see my parents, relatives and Helena.

It is now three years since my release. After marrying Helena in the traditional Kikuyu way I spent several months with my family in the reserve, finally getting back my old job with Nairobi City Council as a draftsman. We now have two young children, a girl and a boy, and I am attending school part-time to advance my technical skills. Life is still a struggle, nonetheless. I'm the only wage earner in my large family and I have heavy responsibilities toward my parents, my younger brother and the wives and children of my two dead brothers. At present I am trying to save money so that I can buy them a shamba big enough to satisfy their subsistence needs and provide some security for the future.

Looking back on "Mau Mau" today, I still consider it to have been a just and courageous struggle for freedom. Though mistakes were made, and some people entered the revolt for narrow or selfish interests, the Kikuyu people as a whole fought and suffered bravely and I am proud of them. Our fight against British colonialism, by throwing fear into the hearts of the imperialists and settlers, quickened the pace of political development and independence in Kenya. I should like to remind those African leaders who now condemn Mau Mau and tell us to forget our past struggles and suffering, that their present positions of power in the Legislative Council and elsewhere would not have been realized except for our sacrifices. I would also warn them that we did not make these sacrifices just to have Africans step into the shoes of our former European masters.

I have closely watched the activities of our political leaders and am not happy with much of what I see. Much of the money collected overseas or from our poor peasants and workers at political rallies goes into the pockets of politicians for their personal use instead of for the development of the country and the welfare of our people. Some leaders are becoming rich Africans, driving around in fancy cars, building new houses in the city and using our money for women, drink and foreign travel. They rarely talk with the poor peasants and workers whose interests they say they represent.

Remembering how many of these leaders abandoned us during the revolution, I am suspicious of those who now claim to speak in our name. Are they not abandoning us again in their quest for personal power and wealth? The vast majority of Africans remain very poor. Are the masses of people simply to become the slaves of a handful of wealthy Black men?

From the *East Africa Standard*

East African Standard, Tuesday, July 18, 1961. **7**

COURT TOLD OF 20 OATHS

Land Freedom Army documents read

TRANSLATIONS of Land Freedom Army documents, written in Kikuyu, which were stated to have been found in the possession of two brothers, alleged to have been members of Mau Mau, were read in a Nairobi court yesterday.

Because of their public interest, the 20 oaths named are reproduced here in full, together with a set of rules attributed to the so-called Kenya Parliament. The 20 oaths were alleged to bear the stamp of "the Land Freedom Army, general headquarters, Nairobi. Kenya Parliament" They read as follows: —

1 — I sincerely declare before God and before all the people, and before this organisation that from today I have become a servant of blackmen's race from Ngong to Karimatura and Kenya as a whole and I will be going wherever they shall be sending me by day or by night to fight for them or to press their case.

As I have taken the war-oath, if I will refuse to go, may this oath kill me, may this Thenge kill me, and may this meat kill me.

2 — I sincerely declare before God and before all the people, and before this organisation that if my race ever elect me to be a leader I shall never refuse.

If ever I will be given money I will never expend it in the work unknown to them but I will expend it in the work detailed by them. I will never bank it as my money and I will never trade with it.

If ever I do this with it may this oath kill me, may this Thenge kill me, and may this meat kill me

Sodam apples

3 — I sincerely declare sitting on soil from where I get my food and swear with it, sleeping with

meat as I do with a woman and continually piercing seven sodam apples with seven Mugere tree twigs and nape of the neck which are used in "Thenge" vows and oath administration and I solemnly declare that I will abide with all the things I see here all the time whether by night or by day because they are the laws of the blackmen

If ever I forget them may this oath kill me, may this Thenge kill me and may this meat kill me.

4 — I also solemnly declare that if I will ever be sent to the battle I will take courage and if we disagree with the General or anybody else I will not kill him due to our enmity, and if we ever raid a certain place I will never run away and leave others behind but will wait for orders from the General or the leader who will be in charge of us.

If I run away leaving them behind may this oath kill me, may this Thenge kill me and may this meat kill me

Musical Society

5 — Furthermore, if I will ever be made a judge by our race, I will not judge someone

250

basing the judgement on enmity or judge him friendly, but I shall decide the case according to how it is, and if ever I shall judge partially, may this oath kill me, may this Thenge kill me, and may this meat kill me.

6. — I too, solemnly declare before God and before all people and before this organisation that I shall never join Muthiko (Musical Society) or a bad organisation aimed at destroying our race, if I will be forced to join I will inform the leaders and the soldiers so that the organisation be done away with. If I fail to report anything bad may this oath kill me, may this Thenge kill me and may this meat kill me.

7. — Furthermore, if ever I tell lies while discussing with leaders or soldiers or with people who are not members of "CENTRAL," who perform duties with me.

And if ever I cheat members of the African Government, may this oath kill me, may this Thenge kill me and may this meat kill me.

Sent to spy

8. — Again, if my child, mother, father, my wife, or my brother, my sister, my friend or anybody else, does something wrong I will never withhold to the members but I will not put false allegation against him except say what he has done, and if ever I will be told to kill him I will kill him because I have taken the battle-oath.

If ever I fail to kill him, may this oath kill me, may this Thenge kill me, and may this meat kill me.

9. — If ever I will be sent by our race to spy I shall never come back and tell lies but should tell exactly what I saw, and if I shall find something to hinder my reaching there I shall come back at once and report what made me fail to reach there and I shall not tell lies but say what I saw.

It I tell lies, may this oath kill me, may this Thenge kill me and may this meat kill me.

10. — If ever I mislead my race and this be detected I shall never deny because I have sworn before the God and before all the people and before this organisation and declare that not anytime shall I ever tell lies, or falsely accuse anybody.

If I deny my errors while they are there may this oath kill me, may this Thenge kill me, and may this meat kill me.

25s. to pay

11. — Furthermore, I will be contributing money to this party and all the donations and if I don't have it I will be reporting so, and explain why I have failed to contribute.

Again, the shillings twenty-five I am asked to pay for the battle-oath here, I have to pay, and if I do not have it now I shall have to pay when I will get it.

If I fail to pay this being for battle-oath, may this oath kill me, may this Thenge kill me and may this meat kill me.

12. — I also solemnly declare before God and before all the people and before this organisation that I shall never give money to a prostitute so as to sleep with her and I shall never sleep with a European or Asian woman. I will never marry a European or an Asian because that is a bad blood.

If I do one of these things, may this oath kill me, may this Thenge kill me and may this meat kill me.

13. — I shall never be employed by a European as a soldier, and I will never perform C.I.D. work or become a Home Guard.

If ever I do one of these jobs may this oath kill me, may this Thenge kill me, may this meat kill me.

14. — I shall be adhering to all laws of the blackmen and all things they might forbid. I shall never sell land to a European or an Asian or betray anybody.

If I transgress one of them, may this oath kill me, may this Thenge kill me and may this meat kill me.

15. — Again, I shall never divulge the secrets of the blackmen to a European or to a Government servant or to a person who has not taken the battle-oath because that is revealing secrets of the blackmen.

If I divulge, may this oath kill me, may this Thenge kill me and may this meat kill me.

16. — Furthermore, I solemnly declare before God and before all the people and before this organisation that if ever I will find a gun or ammunitions I shall never leave them but I will take them to the young men of the Army, and if I have hidden it somewhere I should go for it and take it to the young men of the Army to be used in fights.

If I refuse to take it to them may this oath kill me, may this Thenge kill me and may this meat kill me

will not change the clothes I am now wearing and if I change, they shall not be washed before seven days elapse.

Again, I shall not take bath besides face and hands and feet but the remaining part of the body will be washed after seven days elapse.

If I do any of the things before seven days elapse may this oath kill me, may this Thenge kill me and may this meat kill me.

Never scorn

17 — Furthermore, I solemnly declare that I shall never tell a European or a Government Servant who administered battle-oath to me, or the one who took me to the ceremony or from where I took the oath, because that is revealing secrets of the blackmen.

If ever I reveal may this oath kill me, may this Thenge kill me, and may this meat kill me.

18 — Again, if ever I shall lead an Army or people I shall never mislead them, and I shall never scorn those who do not belong to our area, I shall treat them equally because I will be their leader.

If I hate some may this oath kill me, may this Thenge kill me and may this meat kill me.

19 — I further solemnly declare before God, before all the people and before this organisation that I shall adhere to all the things I have seen here of the battle-oath all the night and day time, because they are the laws of the blackmen. If ever I refuse to adhere to them may this oath kill me, may this Thenge kill me and may this meat kill me

20 — I also solemnly declare sitting on the soil from where I get my food and swear with it that before seven days elapse. I shall never sleep with a woman, and before seven days elapse I

Smear blood

After you have taken off the meat and the soil the first word is this.

Get hold of his finger and count one, two, three, four, five, six, seven, pierce the finger and smear the blood thereof on the meat, roll the meat round his head seven times, he should then bite the meat in the portion the blood was smeared and swallow it telling him, — may that blood kill him if he ever surrenders, make someone arrested or if ever he becomes the enemy of this country, betrays somebody or sell land to a European or an Asian or if he ever sees a soldier (terrorist) and fail to hide him, may the blood kill him.

Then take a stick and dip it into a calabash containing blood, after the blood sticks to it tell him to stick out his tongue and smear the blood on it, he should swallow the blood, make him swear the above vows.

Then take the stick and dip it into the calabash containing blood, when blood stick to it, smear it on his forehead, joints and the navel, making him swear the above vows. When you come to hand joints and the palm tell him that if ever he holds a pen and endorse a signature for selling this country may those fingers of yours fail to stretch out.

Crack-down to avoid second Emergency

A S the few remaining former Mau Mau detainees are being released from restriction, fresh threats of subversion have necessitated more restrictions in order to avoid a second Emergency in Kenya.

The Minister for Internal Security and Defence, Mr. Swann, announced yesterday that for the last three months operations had been in progress to curb the activities of the Kenya Land Freedom Army.

Yesterday the organisation was officially proscribed under its five different aliases — the Kenya Land Freedom Army, Kenya Land Freedom Party, the Kenya Parliament, the Rift Valley Government and the Rift Valley Province Parliament.

Previously it had always been possible to prosecute members of these bodies under the name of Mau Mau but it had now been thought advisable to proscribe them all separately, Mr. Swann said. The purpose of the Land Freedom Army was to take over power in Kenya. "An Emergency would be inevitable if we had not taken any action this year."

Kariuki Chotara (above) who started a Land Freedom Army in 1953-5, later admitted 18 murders. While in detention at Lokitaung he attacked Jomo Kenyatta.

Kanu and Kadu worried

Mr. Swann said he did not hope to stamp out the type of activity typified by Mau Mau and the Land Freedom Army. "In a certain section of the Kikuyu this will never stop. It has been going on from time immemorial. All you can hope to do is watch it, control it, harass and embarrass it. It is a recurring danger."

It was very encouraging, however, that African leaders had expressed a desire to help in the fight against these organisations. They realised it had to be brought under control. Both Kanu and Kadu were worried about the situation.

It was hoped to secure the help of Jomo Kenyatta after his release. "We have discussed the Land Freedom Army with Kenyatta and he is certainly not in favour of it," Mr. Swann said. "I hope to enlist him as well as other Kikuyu leaders".

But the Land Freedom Army was prepared to smash anyone who stood in its way. One man had said: "If Kenyatta gets in our way, we cut him down just the same as any Kanu or Kadu leader."

Mr. Swann explained: "The whole object of the exercise is that those who fought should have the sweets of power now." They were not terribly interested in Kenyatta's release, and had shown no great excitement. "They go their own way."

Their idea was to choose the right moment to take over the Government. "It is an anarchist organisation — you could even

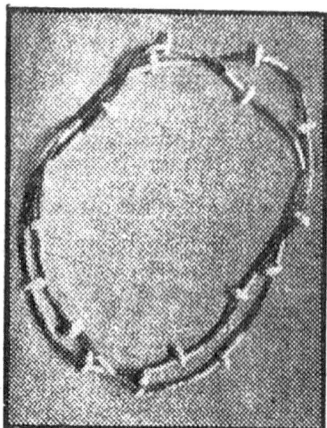

The insignia of the Mutingiri secret society — a necklace of multi-coloured beads and cowrie shells. The shells and beads were sometimes woven into the underclothing.

call it a Bolshevik organisation — though there is absolutely no Communist connection that we can see.'

Nairobi gang

Tracing the history of the organisation, Mr. Swann said it started with a man named Kariuki Chotara who had a gang called the Land Freedom Army in Nairobi in 1953-55. Chotara pleaded "Guilty" to 18 murders and was sentenced to death.

As there was some doubt, however, as to whether he was old enough to hang, he was detained instead during the Governor's pleasure. After the amnesty at the end of the Emergency he was restricted and is still in restriction.

At Lokitaung, Chotara attacked Jomo Kenyatta and tried to beat him up. He was pulled away by the self-styled "General" China.

The gang consisted of a committee representing various parts of Kenya, and it tried to make itself into the supreme command of Mau Mau. Actually its influence only covered Nairobi and Kiambu.

It revived among Mau Mau convicts in Mbagathi prison in 1957. They started work on the organisation after the amnesty calling themselves "Mutingiri." They wandered about Nairobi dressed in black shirts and trousers until the "uniform" was recognised and they started to be picked up.

"It is the same old stiffs every time under a different name," Mr. Swann commented. Last year Operation "Milltown" cracked down on the organisation and 24 of the 75 arrested are still detained. None of those released had turned up again in the Land Freedom Army, as far as was known.

Of the men known to be in the organisation, nine per cent were ex-forest terrorists, 79 per cent had Mau Mau records, 52 per cent were ex-detainees and 52 per cent had previous criminal records.

'Not killed'

Many members had a dual role, sometimes working for subversion and sometimes at ordinary crime.

For the last three months another "Milltown" had been going on. "We are not keen on it in 1961, but we can't get out of it," Mr Swann said. About 40 or 50 men were in restriction as a result.

"We have not killed it," Mr. Swann went on. "As long as it goes on we shall have to pick chaps up if we are to have any conscience for the future."

The Land Freedom Army was still organising, and had launched a recruiting campaign. Its cry was not for action now but in the future. It could be planned for the end of the year, for internal self-government or for independence. The idea was to acquire more members and more weapons now.

Mostly Kikuyu

Last year "Milltown" had disrupted the organisation for three months. This year's measures had considerably reduced oath-taking. There had been 26 successful prosecutions so far and nine more cases were pending

Unfortunately the Land Freedom Army had realised "the heat is on" Documents were being burnt all over the country, and witnesses were being intimidated. The only answer was to go back to restriction, "or else we let it grow until we declare a State of Emergency and another £3,000,000 goes out of Kenya".

The pattern of oathing was the same — to preserve secrecy, maintain unity, never co-operate with the Government or Europeans, steal arms, ammunition and money and, in certain Nairobi and Rift Valley oaths, commit murder when ordered, and to obtain land, particularly that of Europeans or Kikuyu loyalists.

The strength of the army was between 500 and 2,000, Mr. Swann said. Large lists of names were being sifted. It was believed that ex-detainees like Fred Kubai and Paul Ngei had been approached and had administered a rebuff. Kanu and Kadu were also believed to have spurned approaches. No well-known Africans were suspected of being members.

The majority of members of the army were Kikuyu with some other tribes, as in Mau Mau. A new tribe involved was the Maragoli, of whom five or six were members.

The distribution was similar to Mau Mau — Nairobi, Rift Valley, the Dumbiri Location of Kiambu, southern locations of Fort Hall and the South Tetu location of Nyeri. The Land Freedom Army had no connection with the Imente Forest terrorists.

Organisation was still on a cell basis, with little apparent mixing between cells. It was, however, better organised than Mau Mau in 1952. There was even a cyclostyled proforma for the oaths, showing how confident the organisation was. But the "army" lacked the public support that Mau Mau had, and it lacked the weapons.

Mr. Swann pointed out that no firearms had been stolen since the third week of May. This was probably due to the "Guard your gun" publicity campaign.

To help combat the threat of subversion both Kanu and Kadu had asked for lists of any of their members who might be suspect.

The Land Freedom Army collected money under a number of guises. A favourite trick was to pose as an education society collecting money to send students overseas. Many sums of 5s. had been collected from people who thought they were subscribing to a good cause.

Many of the people who had attended oathing had not the faintest idea what it was all about. A campaign by the African leaders could stop the organisation spreading among people like these, though it was doubtful if the hard core would listen to anybody but themselves.

May do good

So far there was no connection between crimes of violence and the Land Freedom Army. But it was using intimidation to get extra funds. Mr. Swann did not think intimidation had had any effect on public policy as yet.

He did not think that the release of Jomo Kenyatta would have any harmful effect on the situation and it could do good.

Mr. Swann recalled that in his days at Nyeri, where he was a District Commissioner, he had met the problem of subversion as long ago as 1938, and forecast that his successors in the Ministry would continue to meet it for many years to come.

GLOSSARY

askari – soldier, policeman or guard

batuni – warrior

bhangi – cannabis

D.C. – District Commissioner

D.O. – District Officer

duka (Swahili, from Arabic) – a store or shop

Gikuyu na Mumbi – Mythical founders of the Kikuyu tribe; a term also used for the liberation movement by its members

Kiama Kia Muingi – Council of the Community

kihei – uncastrated goat (also used to refer to a man who had taken the Batuni Oath (plural: ihei)

kindu – "thing", a code word for guns

kiraiko – locally grown tobacco

komerera – an outlaw

Kufa na Kupona – Death and Survival

mbembe – maize kernels, a code word for ammunition

muhoi – tenant farmer

Muiguithania – The Unifier, one name for the movement to unify the Kikuyu

muingi – "the community" – a word used by insiders for the liberation movement

mugaa – an acacia tree

mugere – an hibiscus shrub

mukengeria – a vine

Muma wa Uiguano – Oath of Unity

muthuthi – a tamarind tree

ndongu – a wild fruit

Ngai – The Kikuyu term for God

ngata – the bone which connects the head and the spinal column of the goat and contains seven holes. It played an important part in the seven-part 'oath of unity' ritual.

panga – a long, curved knife, sharpened on one side; a machete

pombe – homemade beer

posho – cornmeal

shamba – small farm

simi – the double-edged traditional Kikuyu sword.

thenge – a he-goat

tietie – A collaborator, someone who wore a tie like the British

uhuru – freedom, independence

uiguano – unity

Uiguano wa Gikuyu na Mumbi – Unity of Gikuyu and Mumbi (q.v.) – this and the next phrase were used as code names for the liberation movement

Uiguano wa Muingi – Unity of the Community, a code name for the liberation movement

Recent titles of interest from Daraja Press

www.ingramcontent.com/pod-product-compliance
Lightning Source LLC
Chambersburg PA
CBHW050646270326
41927CB00012B/2898